D1001566

KENT STATE

ALSO BY DERF BACKDERF

My Friend Dahmer
Trashed
Punk Rock and Trailer Parks
True Stories

DERF BACKDERF

KENT STATE

FOUR DEAD IN OHIO

ABRAMS COMICARTS, NEW YORK

Editor: Charles Kochman
Editorial Assistant: Jessica Gotz
Art Director: Pamela Notarantonio
Design assistance: Theresa Venezia and Max Temescu
Managing Editor: Mike Richards
Production Manager: Alison Gervais

Library of Congress Control Number: 2019949791

ISBN: 978-1-4197-3484-7
eISBN: 978-1-68335-861-9

Published in 2020 by Abrams ComicArts®, an imprint of ABRAMS.

Printed and bound in China
10 9 8 7 6 5 4 3 2 1

This book is a dramatic re-creation,
but all of it is based on eyewitness accounts,
detailed research, and investigation.
The notes in the back of the book list the
source material for every scene.

Dedicated to Doug Buckner, my best friend in junior high school. In that short time, he was as close a comrade as I've had in this life. Together we discovered the film, music, and (especially) the comics that inspire me to this day. He was looking forward to this book. Safe travels, my friend.

ACKNOWLEDGMENTS

A few special thanks:

Chris Butler gave me my first in-depth interview for this project. His account, full of details and color, formed the foundation from which I built the rest of this narrative.

I highly recommend Butler's own work on the shootings, and his concept album *Easy Life*, available in all the usual places. His song/monologue "Beggar's Bullets" is as moving an account of May 4 as you will find.

Jason Prufer, senior library associate at the Kent State Libraries, is the top photo archivist of all things Kent State, and was an invaluable source of the images I needed to re-create 1970 Kent State, which was a tricky task. No matter what obscure visual problem I threw at Jason, he found the photos I needed.

The staff of the May 4 Collection at Kent State University, whom I pestered regularly.

Scribbles Coffee Co. and Last Exit Books, both in Kent, for giving me a place to unwind and recover after emotionally draining research trips to the university.

My patient wife, Sheryl, who has been a self-proclaimed "comics widow" as I finished this project.

And to all the survivors of May 4 who graciously talked to me, no matter how briefly or reticently. The tears that were frequently shed during these discussions demonstrate that time does not lessen pain.

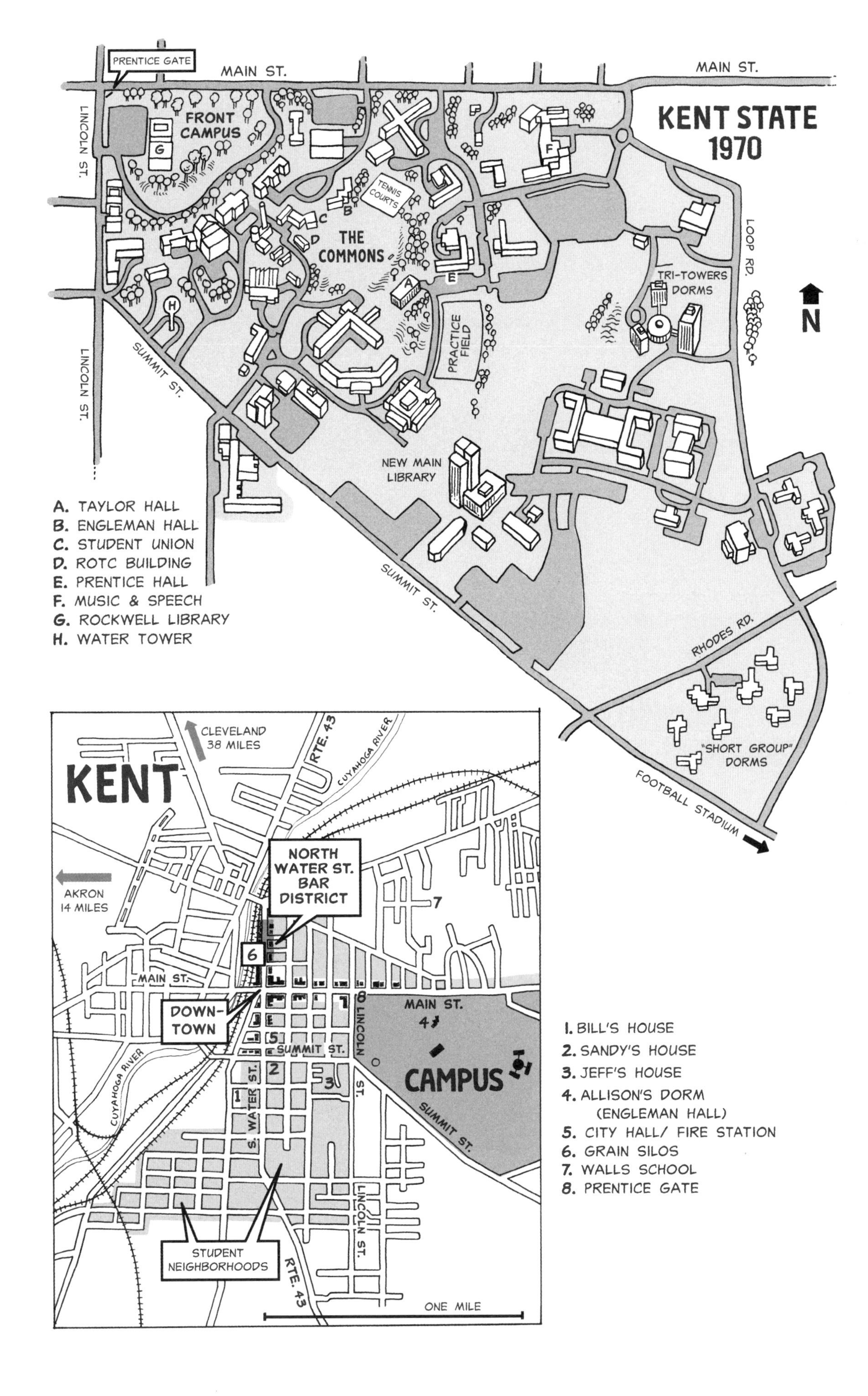
KENT STATE 1970
PRENTICE GATE
MAIN ST.
MAIN ST.
LINCOLN ST.
LINCOLN ST.
FRONT CAMPUS
G
TENNIS COURTS
B
C
D
THE COMMONS
E
F
A
H
PRACTICE FIELD
LOOP RD.
TRI-TOWERS DORMS
N
SUMMIT ST.
SUMMIT ST.
NEW MAIN LIBRARY
RHODES RD.
"SHORT GROUP" DORMS
FOOTBALL STADIUM
A. TAYLOR HALL
B. ENGLEMAN HALL
C. STUDENT UNION
D. ROTC BUILDING
E. PRENTICE HALL
F. MUSIC & SPEECH
G. ROCKWELL LIBRARY
H. WATER TOWER
KENT
CLEVELAND 38 MILES
RTE. 43
CUYAHOGA RIVER
NORTH WATER ST. BAR DISTRICT
AKRON 14 MILES
7
6
MAIN ST.
8
MAIN ST.
4
DOWN-TOWN
5
SUMMIT ST.
LINCOLN
2
3
1
CAMPUS
S. WATER ST.
CUYAHOGA RIVER
SUMMIT ST.
LINCOLN ST.
STUDENT NEIGHBORHOODS
RTE. 43
ONE MILE
1. BILL'S HOUSE
2. SANDY'S HOUSE
3. JEFF'S HOUSE
4. ALLISON'S DORM (ENGLEMAN HALL)
5. CITY HALL/ FIRE STATION
6. GRAIN SILOS
7. WALLS SCHOOL
8. PRENTICE GATE

RICHFIELD, OHIO
THURSDAY,
APRIL 30, 1970

TEAMSTERS
ON STRIKE
TEAMSTERS LOCAL 24
ON STRIKE
STRIKE
UNFAIR
UNFAIR
ON STRIKE
LOCAL
UNFAIR
ON STRIKE
TEAMSTERS LOCAL 24
ON STRIKE

P·I·E
PIE
P·I·E
PACIFIC INTERNATIONAL EXPRESS

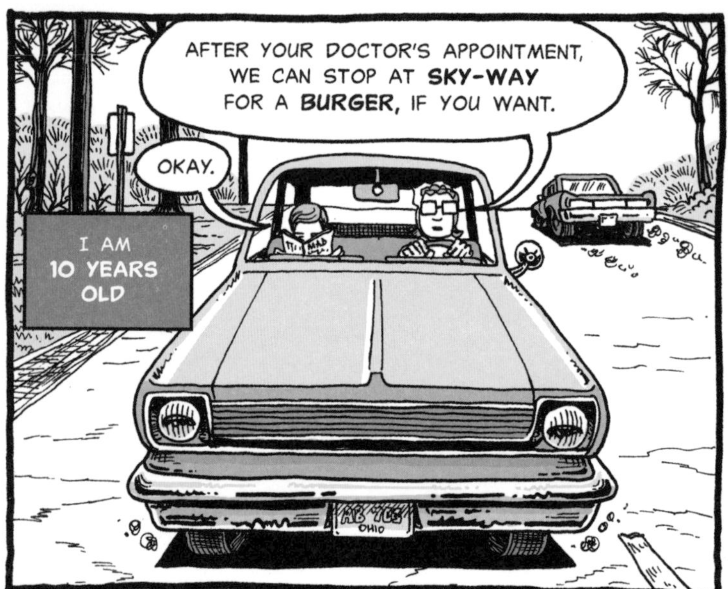
AFTER YOUR DOCTOR'S APPOINTMENT, WE CAN STOP AT SKY-WAY FOR A BURGER, IF YOU WANT.
OKAY.
I AM 10 YEARS OLD

!!
OOOOOH, CRAP! I FORGOT ABOUT THIS NONSENSE!

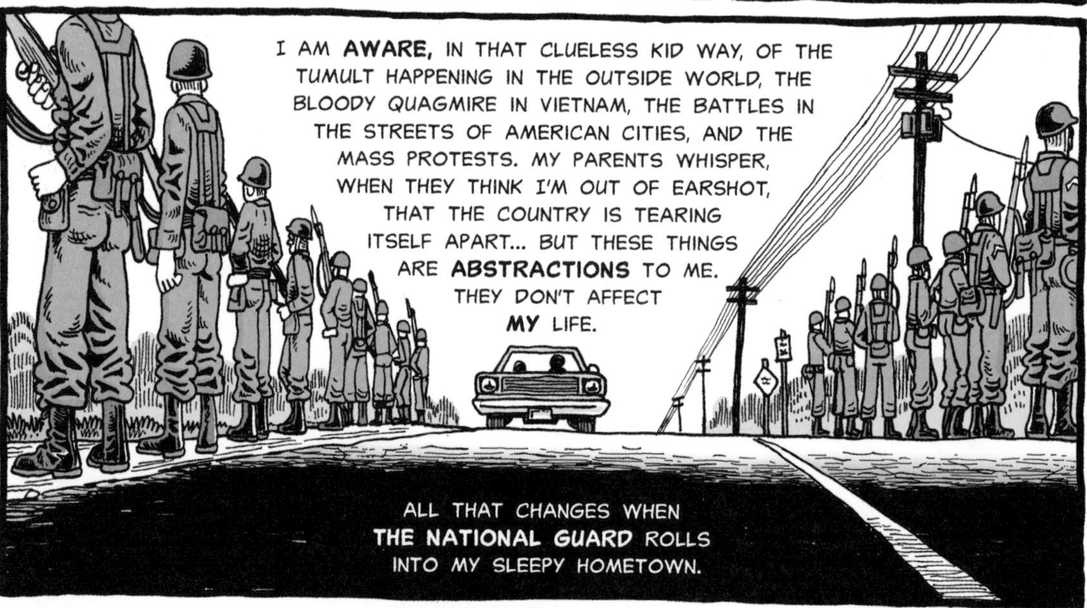
I AM AWARE, IN THAT CLUELESS KID WAY, OF THE TUMULT HAPPENING IN THE OUTSIDE WORLD, THE BLOODY QUAGMIRE IN VIETNAM, THE BATTLES IN THE STREETS OF AMERICAN CITIES, AND THE MASS PROTESTS. MY PARENTS WHISPER, WHEN THEY THINK I'M OUT OF EARSHOT, THAT THE COUNTRY IS TEARING ITSELF APART... BUT THESE THINGS ARE ABSTRACTIONS TO ME. THEY DON'T AFFECT MY LIFE.
ALL THAT CHANGES WHEN THE NATIONAL GUARD ROLLS INTO MY SLEEPY HOMETOWN.

W-W-WOW! SOLDIERS!

IT'S THE NATIONAL GUARD. THEY'RE THE ARMY OF OHIO.
RRRRRRRRRRRRRRR

THE TEAMSTERS AT THE TRUCK DEPOTS ARE ON STRIKE AND ARE CAUSING TROUBLE.
I MEANT TO GO THROUGH THE VALLEY.

AS I STARE AT BAYONETS GLEAMING IN THE SUN, FOR THE FIRST TIME THE CLASHES OF 1970 ARE ALL TOO REAL.
SOLDIERS LINE THE STREETS OF MY TOWN, AND POINT THEIR GUNS AT THE FATHERS OF MY SCHOOLMATES, DADS I KNOW, MEN I SEE AT THE TOWN DINER, OR WHO WATCH MY LITTLE LEAGUE GAMES.

IT LEAVES ME SHAKEN AND DISTURBED.
TERRY POINT INN
MAD

RRRRRRR

OKAY!
BAYONETS UP!
TERRY POINT INN -Liquor-

TH' TRUCK CONVOY IS LEAVING TH' DEPOT! ON YER TOES!
U.S. ARMY
CF FREIGHT

TERRY POINT INN

LET'S GIT 'EM!
SCABS!
BANG!
AMVETS

SHUT 'EM DOWN!!

USARMY

PRIVATE FRANK KARLOVIC, AGE 22
CRASH!
ARR!
YOU OKAY, FRANK?

TERRY POINT INN
~Liquor~
RRRRRR

KRAK!
Ford

I CAIN'T BELIEVE YOU BOYS IS PERTECTIN' THEM SCAB DRIVERS!
BACK!

YER JUST DOIN' GUVNER RHODES'S UNION BUSTIN' FOR HIM!
WHY AIN'T YOU GIRLS OVER IN VIETNAM FIGHTIN' COMMIES?
HA!

HOLD THE LINE!

THAT EVENING
AT 9 P.M.

WE INTERRUPT THIS REGULARLY SCHEDULED BROADCAST...
WHAT? AWWW.

...TO BRING YOU A LIVE ADDRESS FROM PRESIDENT NIXON.
OH GREAT. WHAT IS HE GOING TO PRATTLE ABOUT NOW?
LOOKS LIKE THE TOM JONES SHOW WILL GET PREEMPTED, HUH?

YOUR MOTHER IS QUITE TAKEN WITH TOM'S TIGHT PANTS!
GRUNT.

GOOD EVENING, MY FELLOW AMERICANS.
ZENITH
abc

I'LL BE **BACK** WHEN TOM IS ON.
SERVES YOU RIGHT FOR VOTING FOR NIXON! HEH-HEH.
YAWN!

TONIGHT... **AMERICAN** AND **SOUTH VIETNAMESE FORCES** WILL ATTACK THE HEADQUARTERS OF THE **ENTIRE** COMMUNIST OPERATION IN SOUTH VIETNAM.
abc

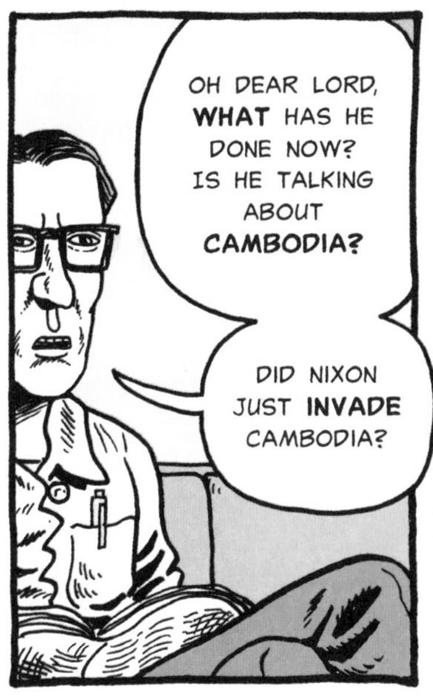
OH DEAR LORD, **WHAT** HAS HE DONE NOW? IS HE TALKING ABOUT **CAMBODIA?**
DID NIXON JUST **INVADE** CAMBODIA?

...FOR THE PURPOSE OF **ENDING** THE WAR IN VIETNAM AND WINNING THE **JUST PEACE** WE ALL DESIRE.

TWO WEEKS AGO, HE ANNOUNCED HE WAS BRINGING THE TROOPS **HOME**...
...AND **NOW** HE'S **SPREADING** THE WAR TO A **SECOND** COUNTRY?

...MY FELLOW AMERICANS, WE LIVE IN AN **AGE OF ANARCHY**, BOTH ABROAD AND AT HOME...

SIGH.
THE COLLEGE CAMPUSES ARE GOING TO **EXPLODE** TOMORROW.
AKRON BEACON JOURNAL

FRIDAY, MAY 1, 1970
KENT STATE UNIVERSITY,
20 MILES FROM MY HOMETOWN
DING! DING! DING! DING! DING! DING! DING! DING! DING!
IT'S THE FIRST WARM DAY OF SPRING, AFTER A LONG, COLD WINTER. THE LEAVES ON THE TREES HAVEN'T EVEN EMERGED YET.

CLICK!
SCREEEEEE!
SORRY 'BOUT THAT. UH... SOME ANNOUNCEMENTS BEFORE WE GET STARTED...
THE KENT FILM FESTIVAL CONTINUES TONIGHT... AND NEXT WEEK IS THE PROJECT EARTH ECOLOGY SYMPOSIUM.
THERE'S ALSO A BLACK UNITED STUDENTS RALLY ON FRONT CAMPUS LATER TODAY.
AHEM! AND NOW...

BROTHERS AND SISTERS! I AM PLEASED TO ANNOUNCE THE FORMATION OF W.H.O.R.E., WORLD HISTORIANS OPPOSED TO RACISM AND EXPLOITATION!

WE, THE MEMBERS OF WHORE, CHARGE THE NIXON ADMINISTRATION WITH LAWLESSNESS REGARDING CAMBODIA!

I WILL NOW PERFORM THE DEEPLY SORROWFUL TASK OF... BURYING THE U.S. CONSTITUTION!

WE NOW DECLARE THE CONSTITUTION IS DEAD!

NO! WE CAN'T DO THIS!
THE RUSSIANS PROMISED THEY WOULD "BURY" US! AND WE'RE DOING THE JOB FOR THEM HERE!
SHADDUP!
SIDDOWN!
BOO!
BOO!
Pocket Constitution
The Constitution of the United States
CLAP!
CLAP!
CLAP!
CLAP!
CLAP!
CLAP!
CLAP!
Pocket Constitution
THANK YOU, WHORE!
THE PROTEST MOVEMENT HERE AT KENT STATE HAS FRACTURED.
WE NEED TO COME TOGETHER!
THIS MONDAY, MAY 4, AT NOON, THERE WILL BE AN ANTIWAR RALLY HERE ON THE COMMONS!
SPREAD TH' WORD! TELL YOUR FRIENDS!
TELL EVERYONE!
CLAP!
CLAP!
CLAP!

WELL, THAT WAS ENTERTAINING.
A GROUP OF HISTORY GRAD STUDENTS, I OVERHEARD SOMEONE SAY.
BILL SCHROEDER, AGE 19

SIGH. CAMBODIA HAS ME QUESTIONING EVERYTHING WE'RE DOING IN SOUTHEAST ASIA.
YEAH.

NIXON PROMISED TO WIND DOWN THE WAR...
...INSTEAD...
...HE'S INVADING ANOTHER COUNTRY?

I DON'T BLAME PEOPLE FOR BEING ANGRY ...OR SCARED!
YEAH, WELL, YOU'LL BE HEADIN' THERE IN A COUPLA YEARS, SINCE YOU'RE ROTC!
LOO-TENANT!

NAW, THIS ISN'T A JOKE, MAN. IT'S DEADLY SERIOUS!

I'M STUDYING TO BE AN ARMY PSYCHOLOGIST...
I MIGHT NOT HAVE THAT OPTION NOW.

ALL US ROTC GRADS WILL BE HEADING STRAIGHT FOR 'NAM... OR CAMBODIA!
I DON'T WANNA BE JUST ANOTHER COMBAT OFFICER.
I HOPE TO MAKE A BETTER CONTRIBUTION.

SORRY, BILL.
YOU'RE RIGHT. IT'S **NO** JOKE.
WHY IS ROTC STILL STANDING?

CLIK!

CLIK! CLIK! CLIK!

WHY ARE YOU TAKING **PHOTOS** OF THE PROTEST?

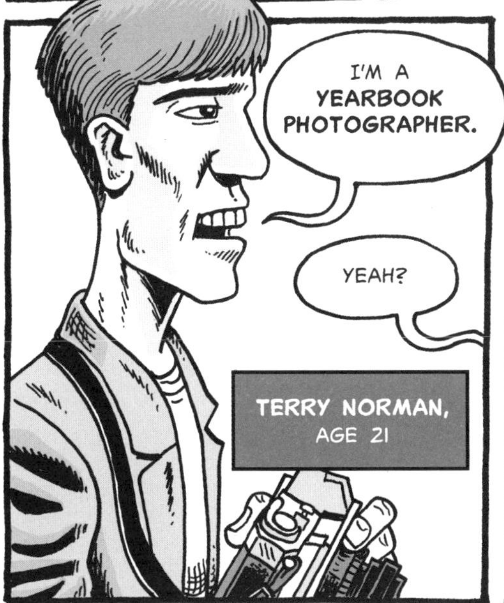

I'M A **YEARBOOK PHOTOGRAPHER.**
YEAH?
TERRY NORMAN, AGE 21

STRANGE... BECAUSE **I** WORK FOR THE YEARBOOK AND I'VE **NEVER** SEEN YOU BEFORE!
SO I'LL ASK **AGAIN.** WHO ARE **THE PHOTOS** FOR?

I... UH... MUTTER...

NARC!

LISTEN TO THIS, BARRY...

"SCREAMING STUDENTS AND NATIONAL GUARDSMEN, BAYONETS AT THE READY, CLASHED REPEATEDLY ON THE OHIO STATE CAMPUS THURSDAY, IN A SECOND DAY OF VIOLENCE."
ALLISON KRAUSE, AGE 19
BARRY LEVINE, HER BOYFRIEND, ALSO 19

WOW. SOUNDS BAD.
300 STUDENTS ARRESTED... OVER 100 INJURED...
...THREE KIDS SHOT BY... WELL, NO ONE KNOWS.
IT'S TOTAL CHAOS IN THE STATE CAPITAL!

YES, THE WORLD IS GOING TO HELL!
AH, BUT IT'S A GORGEOUS DAY IN KENT, OHIO!

KENT STATE UNIVERSITY
WAS FOUNDED IN THE ROLLING OHIO COUNTRYSIDE IN 1910 AS A TEACHER TRAINING COLLEGE. BY 1970, IT IS THE 24TH-LARGEST PUBLIC UNIVERSITY IN AMERICA. KENT STATE'S ENROLLMENT WAS A MERE 6,000 IN 1955. IN THE ENSUING 15 YEARS, THE STUDENT BODY BALLOONS TO 21,000. ROLLING STONE IN 1970 DESCRIBES KENT STATE AS "THE COUNTRY'S LARGEST UNKNOWN UNIVERSITY."
KENT IS JUST 38 MILES SOUTH OF SPRAWLING CLEVELAND AND 14 MILES EAST OF AKRON, THE GRITTY RUBBER CITY, MAKING THE UNIVERSITY A POPULAR CHOICE FOR KIDS FROM BOTH RUST BELT CITIES. EIGHTY-FIVE PERCENT OF THE STUDENTS ARE FROM OHIO, THE SONS AND DAUGHTERS OF BLUE-COLLAR FACTORY WORKERS.
WITH THE EXPLOSION IN ENROLLMENT COMES A BUILDING BOOM. KENT STATE HAD JUST 29 BUILDINGS IN 1963. SEVEN YEARS LATER, IT HAS 97. THE CAMPUS ERUPTS FROM ITS ORIGINAL CLUSTER OF STATELY BUILDINGS AND SPREADS ACROSS FARMLANDS TO THE EAST AND SOUTH. NEW BUILDINGS ARE ERECTED AT BREAKNECK SPEED, ESPECIALLY NEW DORMS FOR BURGEONING INCOMING CLASSES.
THIS FRANTIC EXPANSION MAKES KENT STATE FEEL A BIT SLAPPED TOGETHER, BUT WITH ITS GRASSY HILLS, TALL TREES, AND IMPORTED BLACK SQUIRRELS, IT'S AN ATTRACTIVE CAMPUS.
ACADEMICALLY, KENT ENJOYS A GOOD REPUTATION. IT REMAINS A RESPECTED EDUCATION SCHOOL, TRUE TO ITS ROOTS, AND OFFERS EXCELLENT PROGRAMS IN BUSINESS, JOURNALISM, PSYCHOLOGY, AND BOTH FINE AND COMMERCIAL ART. A GROWING ROSTER OF ENERGETIC, YOUNG FACULTY IS APPEALING TO A GENERATION SKEPTICAL OF THE OLD WAYS.

THE STUDENTS ARE A MIX OF SMALL-TOWN AND URBAN KIDS. IT IS OVERWHEMINGLY WHITE, ALTHOUGH THERE IS A RECENT INFLUX OF BLACK KIDS, MOSTLY FROM INNER-CITY CLEVELAND. IT'S A TYPICAL QUIET MIDWESTERN UNIVERSITY.
IT'S **HARDLY** A HOTBED OF RADICAL POLITICS, BUT THERE IS A SMALL BUT COMMITTED CONTINGENT OF **STUDENT ACTIVISTS.** MORE ON THAT LATER.
HOWEVER THE POLITICS OF AVERAGE KENT STUDENTS ARE CHANGING RAPIDLY. BY 1968, **71 PERCENT** OF THEM OPPOSE THE WAR IN VIETNAM, ACCORDING TO A STUDENT POLL.
AS KENT STATE GROWS, THE LOCAL **COUNTERCULTURE** BLOSSOMS.
ARTISTS AND MUSICIANS FLOCK TO TOWN, TURNING KENT INTO **A CREATIVE HAVEN.** FILM, THEATER, AND LECTURES ARE IN ABUNDANCE ON CAMPUS AND OFF. **THE MUSIC SCENE** IS ESPECIALLY VIBRANT, WITH FANS DRIVING IN FROM ALL OVER THE AREA TO PACK INTO FUNKY CLUBS LIKE JB'S AND THE KOVE TO HEAR LOCAL POWER-BLUES HEROES **JOE WALSH AND THE JAMES GANG.**
THE YOUNG AKRON KIDS WHO WOULD FORM THE GROUNDBREAKING ART-PUNK BAND **DEVO** ARE AT THE UNIVERSITY, ALREADY COMBINING ART AND STRANGE SOUNDS, AS IS FRESHMAN **CHRISSIE HYNDE,** FUTURE FRONT WOMAN OF **THE PRETENDERS.**
THIS RAPID METAMORPHOSIS PRODUCES A **TOWN VS. GOWN** DYNAMIC THAT REACHES CRITICAL MASS IN 1970.
KENT TOWNSFOLK ARE TRADITIONAL MIDDLE AMERICANS, CONSERVATIVE IN POLITICS AND ATTITUDES. THEY REGARD THE GROWING STUDENT HORDE WITH SUSPICION.
NOW THAT THE UNIVERSITY HAS COMPLETELY TAKEN OVER THE TOWN, PHYSICALLY, ECONOMICALLY, AND CULTURALLY, SUSPICION TURNS INTO **PARANOIA** AND **OPEN HOSTILITY.**

HEY, HOW WAS THAT **HERMANN HESSE** YOU WERE READING?
DID YOU **FINISH** IT?
I DID. IT'S **GOOD.**
I DUNNO... I USED TO **LOVE** HESSE... BUT I'M JUST LOSING INTEREST IN **FICTION.**
LATELY, IT SEEMS SO **FRIVOLOUS.**

BUT... YOU'RE RIGHT... IT'S A **BEAUTIFUL** DAY.

SANDY SCHEUER,
AGE 20
SPEECH PATHOLOGY
BASICS OF MATH

OOF!
GAWD, I'M SO **CLUMSY!**
TRIP!

HI, BARB!
"SANDY BEACH"! JUST GETTIN' BACK FROM **SPEECH LAB?**

YEP. I WAS WORKING WITH **MY STUDENT.**
HE'S **REALLY** COMING ALONG.
THERE'S SOME **MAIL** FOR YOU ON TH' TABLE.

GROAN. OH, NOT **AGAIN.**
WHAT IS IT?

ANOTHER GIRL I WENT TO HIGH SCHOOL WITH IS GETTING **MARRIED.** MOM SENT ME THE ANNOUNCEMENT FROM THE PAPER.
HA! NOT EXACTLY **SUBTLE,** IS SHE?

ALL MAMA WANTS IS FOR YOU TO FIND A **NICE JEWISH BOY** AND GIVE HER A DOZEN **GRANDCHILDREN,** SANDY, DEAR.

HEY, I DATE **PLENTY.** I'M GOING OUT **TONIGHT,** IN FACT.
I JUST HAVEN'T FOUND **THE** GUY... THAT'S ALL. THESE KENT BOYS ARE **SO** SERIOUS. MAYBE **THAT'S** THE PROBLEM.

THEY THINK JUST BECAUSE I'M **NOT** OUT MARCHING TO END THE WAR AND THROWING BRICKS AT COPS THAT I'M SOME **BUBBLEBRAIN.**
NO ONE THINKS THAT.

I **HATE** THE WAR AS MUCH AS ANYONE. POLITICS JUST **ISN'T** MY THING.
GUYS ARE POLITICAL THESE DAYS, MISS BEACH.

THEY'RE ALL IN DANGER OF BEING **DRAGGED OFF** TO **VIETNAM!** HELL **YEAH,** THEY'RE POLITICAL!
I KNOW, I KNOW.

SANDY! DID YOU GIVE BLOOD **AGAIN?**
YEP.

GOT $11 AT THE BLOOD BANK! IF YOU GO **BEFORE** 10 A.M., THEY GIVE YOU AN **EXTRA BUCK.**
HA. YOU KNOW **ALL** TH' ANGLES!

I WENT WITH SHARON, BUT THEY **WOULDN'T** TAKE **HER** BLOOD. THEY SAID SHE WAS **ANEMIC!**
BUT WE BOARDMAN, OHIO, GIRLS ARE **TOUGHER!** GRRR.

A FEW BLOCKS AWAY, IN A HOUSE AT THE END OF AN UNNAMED ALLEY.

CRASH!

JEFF MILLER,
AGE 20
BOOM!
BA-DA-BOOM!
CRASH!
KRASH!
KRASH!
KRASH!
BA-DA-BANG!
THUMP!
BA-DA-BOOM!
LIVE DEAD
LIVE
HIS FRIEND,
CHRIS BUTLER,
ALSO 20
YEAH!
HI, GUYS!
STEVE!

ANOTHER SESSION OF THE BUTLER-MILLER EXPERIENCE, EH?
YOU GUYS ARE GONNA WEAR OUT THAT "LIVE DEAD" ALBUM!
LEARNIN' FROM THE BEST!

IT'S LIKE JIDDU KRISHNAMURTI'S "AT THE FEET OF THE MASTER."
BUT WE'RE SOUNDING BETTER, RIGHT?
YOU ARE!
THAT CONSTANT PRACTICE IS PAYING OFF.

HEY, IT'S LIKE A SUMMER DAY OUT THERE. I'M MEETING SOMEONE OVER AT ORVILLE'S... YOU GUYS WANNA WALK OVER?
SURE!

YOU'VE BEEN HERE, WHAT?... FIVE MONTHS, JEFF? WHADDAYA THINK OF KENT?
AW, MAN, I LOVE IT HERE! I HATED MICHIGAN STATE. THIS IS TH' COLLEGE EXPERIENCE I WAS LOOKING FOR.
YEP. TOLD YA!

TH' OFF-CAMPUS NEIGHBORHOODS ARE GREAT. THE PEOPLE HERE ARE INTERESTING AND FUN. IT'S A REAL OASIS!
OASIS IS RIGHT! CUZ A MILE IN ANY DIRECTION AND IT'S CRACKER LAND!
Mets

THERE'S ALWAYS SOMETHING GOING ON. KENT IS JUST BIG ENOUGH TO BE COOL, BUT SMALL ENOUGH TO WALK EVERYWHERE.
I FELT AT HOME TH' DAY I MOVED HERE.
JONES
OPTICAL
KENT
MAN CALLED HORSE
7:30 9:30
KEEP KENT KLEAN

NO MORE WAR
AND WHAT OTHER COLLEGE TOWN HAS GIANT GRAIN SILOS SMACK IN THE MIDDLE OF IT... SURROUNDED BY BARS AND HEAD SHOPS?
THAT'S SO INEXPLICABLY RANDOM!
THE WILLIAMS BROTHERS MILL, IN BUSINESS SINCE 1879

STEVE LURED ME TO KENT, HIM AND NEAL, ANOTHER PAL FROM BACK HOME IN LONG ISLAND.
Mets
SO THAT'S HOW ALL YOU ISLANDERS WOUND UP HERE!

ORVILLE'S IS THE GATHERING SPOT FOR CAMPUS BOHEMIANS.
WRITERS, POETS, RADICALS, AND POSERS, THEY ALL COME TO ORVILLE'S.
Orville's
Orville's
BIG DAD PIZZA

WOW. IT'S ALREADY PACKED.
THERE'S A TABLE. I'LL SNAG IT. YOU GET TH' BEER.
DRINKING AGE FOR 3.2% "LOW" BEER IS 18.

WE GOTTA LIGHT IT UP, MAN!

TONIGHT... HERE ON TH' STRIP... SHIT IS GONNA HAPPEN!
WE NEED TO KNOCK THESE BASTARDS RIGHT ON THEIR ASS!

BRING TH' WAR HOME!
OH CRAP.
BAM!

S-SORRY, GUYS.
BAR TOWEL!
HEH. THESE HARD-CORE SDS TYPES SURE DO GET WORKED UP, HUH, BUTLER?
Mets
SDS: STUDENTS FOR A DEMOCRATIC SOCIETY

TH' ONES THAT ARE LEFT AT KENT! SDS GOT KICKED OFF CAMPUS LAST YEAR, AND THEIR LEADERS GOT EXPELLED... AND JAILED!

AND JUST WHEN WE NEED ORGANIZED PROTEST MORE THAN EVER!
DAMN RIGHT.

OVER 11,000 KILLED LAST YEAR IN VIETNAM. WE ALL KNEW NIXON WAS A LIAR, BUT THIS INVASION OF CAMBODIA IS OFF THE CHARTS!
Mets

THESE SDS CATS ARE KIND OF A CARICATURE... BUT THEY AIN'T WRONG!

STUDENTS FOR A DEMOCRATIC SOCIETY IS THE LARGEST STUDENT PROTEST ORGANIZATION IN U.S. HISTORY WITH, AT ITS PEAK IN 1968, OVER 100,000 MEMBERS. FOUNDED IN 1959, SDS ROSE TO PROMINENCE DURING THE CIVIL RIGHTS MOVEMENT, THEN GREW RAPIDLY IN THE SIXTIES AS THE MAIN OPPOSITION TO **THE VIETNAM WAR.**

AFTER 1965, WHEN THE FIRST BIG MILITARY CALL-UP TAKES PLACE, WITH 230,991 BOYS INDUCTED, SDS FOCUSES ON **THE WAR.** THE PRESIDENT OF SDS AT THIS TIME IS **CARL OGELSBY**, A FORMER KENT STATE STUDENT.

CAMPUSES ERUPT IN PROTESTS. ANTIWAR MARCHES BRING HUNDREDS OF THOUSANDS TO WASHINGTON, D.C. SDS, WHICH PROCLAIMS ITSELF **THE NEW LEFT**, QUICKLY GROWS INTO A FEARSOME POLITICAL FORCE, STOKING TERROR IN OLDER AMERICANS THAT A MASS YOUTH REVOLUTION IS NIGH. THE GROUP IS INFILTRATED BY THE **FBI**. THE FEDS' MISSION IS TO **DESTROY SDS** FROM WITHIN. IT SUCCEEDS.

AFTER 1968, THE MILITANT RADICAL WING OF SDS, WHO WILL COME TO BE KNOWN AS **THE WEATHERMEN,** GAINS MORE AND MORE POWER IN THE ORGANIZATION. MORE ON THEM LATER.

SDS COMES LATE TO **KENT.** ESTABLISHED IN FALL 1968, THE KENT CHAPTER IS SMALL, WITH ONLY ABOUT 300 MEMBERS, BUT ITS LEADERS, LED BY PRESIDENT **RICK ERICKSON,** HIS WIFE, **CANDY,** AND THE TOP LIEUTENANT, **HOWIE EMMER**, ARE PASSIONATE AND CHARISMATIC. SDS PUTS A CHARGE INTO THE RATHER SEDATE KENT ANTIWAR MOVEMENT.

KENT STATE, AS THE LARGEST AREA UNIVERSITY, QUICKLY BECOMES **THE CENTER** OF SDS ACTIVITIES IN THE POPULOUS NORTHERN PART OF THE STATE. KENT SDS ACTIVISTS MAKE A NAME WHEN THEY DISRUPT A **NIXON CAMPAIGN SPEECH** IN 1968 IN NEARBY AKRON, DROWNING OUT NIXON WITH CHANTS AND CATCALLS. NIXON DOES **NOT** FORGET KENT SDS.

THE UNIVERSITY ADMINISTRATION DECIDES THAT KENT SDS IS **A THREAT.** THE CHAPTER IS CLOSELY WATCHED AND AGGRESSIVELY OPPOSED.

IN APRIL 1969, AN SDS ANTIWAR RALLY DEVOLVES INTO A SCUFFLE WITH RIGHT-WING STUDENTS AND CAMPUS POLICE. SIX SDS LEADERS ARE ARRESTED.

A WEEK LATER, AN EXPULSION HEARING FOR THE ACCUSED TURNS INTO A MELEE WHEN HUNDREDS OF SUPPORTERS STORM THE BUILDING. THERE ARE 60 ARRESTS. UNIVERSITY PRESIDENT ROBERT WHITE IMMEDIATELY **BANISHES** SDS FROM CAMPUS, AND SUSPENDS ALL ITS MEMBERS. SDS IS FINISHED, AFTER BARELY EIGHT MONTHS ON CAMPUS.

ERICKSON, EMMER, AND TWO OTHER SDS LEADERS BEGIN SERVING **SIX-MONTH JAIL SENTENCES** IN OCTOBER 1969. A DOZEN OTHER SDS MEMBERS RECEIVE SHORTER SENTENCES.

DIDJA WATCH NIXON'S SPEECH LAST NIGHT, WHEN HE ANNOUNCED THE INVASION? IT WAS NUTS!

"I WAS IN 'THE PIT' AT TRI-TOWERS. PEOPLE WERE SCREAMING AND CRYING! THAT ROOM WAS FULL OF FEAR AND RAGE."
PING!

WHAT'S YOUR DRAFT NUMBER AGAIN?
223.

HIGH ENOUGH THAT I PROBABLY DON'T HAFTA WORRY... BUT WHO KNOWS?
WHAT WITH TH' WAY THINGS ARE GOING, RIGHT?
MMM.

YOU GOT 223? YER LUCKY, MAN! MINE IS 34!

I GRADUATE IN A COUPLE WEEKS, SO THERE GOES MY STUDENT DEFERMENT.
I'LL BE IN BOOT CAMP BY AUGUST!

CHEERS! GOOD LUCK, MAN.
THANKS.

HEY, BUTLER... HOW LONG DO YOU THINK IT WOULD TAKE TO CANOE ACROSS LAKE ERIE TO CANADA?
HA.

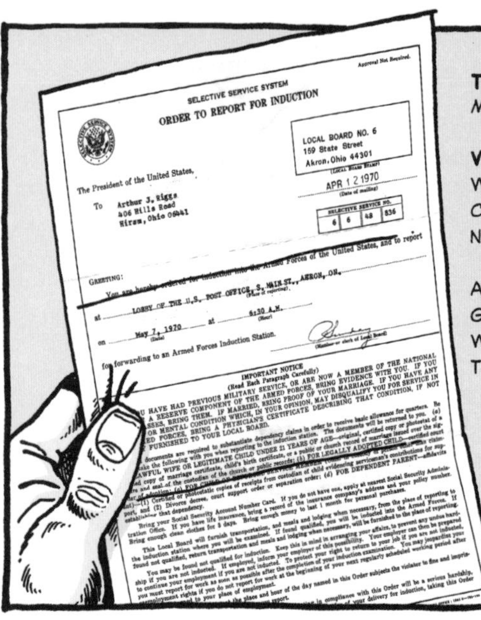
Approval Not Required.

SELECTIVE SERVICE SYSTEM

ORDER TO REPORT FOR INDUCTION

LOCAL BOARD NO. 6
159 State Street
Akron, Ohio 44301
(Local Board Stamp)

The President of the United States,

To Arthur J. Riggs
406 Hills Road
Hiram, Ohio 06441

APR 1 2 1970
(Date of mailing)

SELECTIVE SERVICE NO.

6	6	48	836

GREETING:

You are hereby ordered for induction into the Armed Forces of the United States, and to report

at LOBBY OF THE U.S. POST OFFICE, S. MAIN ST., AKRON, OH.
(Place of reporting)

at 6:30 A.M. (Hour)

on May 7, 1970 (Date)

for forwarding to an Armed Forces Induction Station.

(Member or clerk of Local Board)

IMPORTANT NOTICE
(Read Each Paragraph Carefully)

THE MILITARY DRAFT IS THE FUSE THAT LIGHTS THE MASS ANTIWAR REVOLT OF 1970.

VIETNAM IS NOT A WAR FOUGHT BY **VOLUNTEERS**, AS WARS HAVE BEEN EVER SINCE. NEARLY A THIRD OF COMBAT TROOPS ARE **FORCIBLY CONSCRIPTED**. NEARLY 17,000 DRAFTEES DIE IN THE JUNGLES.

AFTER **PRESIDENT LYNDON JOHNSON** MOBILIZES GROUND TROOPS IN 1965, DRAFT CALL-UPS **DOUBLE**. WITH EACH PASSING YEAR, A BLOODY JUNGLE WAR TURNS INTO AN **UNWINNABLE QUAGMIRE.**

TWENTY-SEVEN MILLION YOUNG MEN LIVE IN FEAR OF BEING SENT TO VIETNAM. IT IS THE **BANE OF THEIR GENERATION.** AS THE BODY BAGS STREAM HOME, THE PANIC GROWS AND FEEDS **THE ANTIWAR MOVEMENT.**

THERE ARE A FEW WAYS TO **AVOID** BEING DRAFTED. THE MOST COMMON IS THE **STUDENT DEFERMENT**. A MAN WHO IS A FULL-TIME COLLEGE STUDENT CAN AVOID SERVICE. MANY PURSUE GRADUATE DEGREES UNTIL THEY ARE TOO OLD TO BE DRAFTED.

MEN FROM POLITICALLY CONNECTED FAMILIES ARE OFTEN GRANTED SPECIOUS DEFERMENTS. **DONALD TRUMP** RECEIVES FOUR CONSECUTIVE STUDENT DEFERMENTS, THEN LANDS HIS FAMOUS MEDICAL DEFERMENT, FOR BONE SPURS IN HIS HEELS. **BILL CLINTON** HAS STUDENT DEFERMENTS, THEN USES HIS STATUS AS A RHODES SCHOLAR STUDYING ABROAD AT OXFORD TO AVOID THE DRAFT.

A YOUNG MAN CAN **REFUSE** INDUCTION AND EITHER GO **ON THE RUN** OR BE **JAILED.** THE MOST FAMOUS TO REFUSE IS **MUHAMMAD ALI.** AN ESTIMATED **500,000 MEN** BECOME DRAFT DODGERS, EITHER LIVING IN HIDING IN THE STATES OR FLEEING ACROSS THE OPEN BORDER INTO CANADA.

IN DECEMBER 1969, IN RESPONSE TO CRITICISM OF THE DRAFT'S INEQUITIES, THE SELECTIVE SERVICE CREATES **A DRAFT LOTTERY.** DAYS OF THE YEAR ARE WRITTEN ON PIECES OF PAPER AND PULLED FROM A DEEP GLASS JAR, ONE BY ONE. THE FIRST BIRTH DATE PICKED IS ASSIGNED "001." THE LOWER THE NUMBER ASSIGNED TO YOUR BIRTH DATE, THE GREATER THE LIKELIHOOD YOU WILL BE HEADING TO VIETNAM. THE LOTTERY IS HELD ON NETWORK TV AND IS WATCHED BY MILLIONS OF TENSE YOUNG MEN. **STUDENT DEFERMENTS** ARE ALSO ENDED FOR GRADUATE STUDENTS AND ARE DRASTICALLY PARED FOR UNDERGRADUATES.

AS A RESULT, WHEN NIXON ANNOUNCES THE EXPANSION OF THE WAR JUST A FEW MONTHS LATER, COLLEGE CAMPUSES ACROSS THE NATION **EXPLODE IN PROTEST.**

OLD ENOUGH TO **DIE** IN VIETNAM BUT **NOT** OLD ENOUGH TO **VOTE** AGAINST THE CREEPS WHO SEND US THERE.
LAND OF TH' FREE, BABY.
THE VOTING AGE IN 1970 IS 21.

I GOT IN **A FIGHT** WITH MY BROTHER OVER BREAK ABOUT THE WAR.
HE **FLIPPED OUT** WHEN I SAID I'D GO TO **CANADA** IF I WAS DRAFTED. HE'S PRETTY **PATRIOTIC.**
Orville's
BIG DADDY

WELL, HEY, MAN... HAFTA **RUN.** I GOT **A DATE.** NEED TO CLEAN UP.
Mets

FINISHED UP **YOUR FLING** WITH MY NEIGHBOR'S GIRLFRIEND? ***GOOD!*** YOU WERE PLAYIN' WITH FIRE THERE. THAT DUDE IS **NOT** A NICE PERSON.

JUST LOOKIN' FOR A LITTLE **LOVE**, BUTLER. I HAVEN'T HAD MUCH LUCK WITH TH' **GIRLS** HERE.
Mets

MUST BE YOUR **LONG ISLAND ACCENT.**
HA. I'LL WORK ON MY **OHIO TWANG.**

HEY! DON'T FORGET YOU PROMISED TO COME TO MY **PLAY** TOMORROW NIGHT*!*
YEP. I'LL BE THERE*!*
Mets

AAAAAAAW.
CLOSED?
TELEGRAPH here
WESTERN UNION

WESTERN UNION
SIGH.
LOOKS LIKE NIXON WILL HAVE TO WAIT FOR YOUR TELEGRAM OF REPRIMAND UNTIL TOMORROW, ALLISON!

DARN IT.
C'MON. LET'S GO TO ORVILLE'S.

YOU SURE I'M NOT A THIRD WHEEL HERE?
BONNIE! DON'T BE SILLY.
YOU'RE MY BEST FRIEND!

SAY, ISN'T THAT JEFF MILLER?
JEFF!
HI!

HAVEN'T SEEN YOU GUYS IN A WHILE. HEADIN' TO TH' BARS?
YEAH.

BE WARNED, THEY'RE ALREADY PACKED. EVERYONE IS OUT TONIGHT AND IT LOOKS LIKE KIDS ARE DRIVING IN FROM ALL OVER.
GOTTA RUN. SEE YA.

POLICE
CAMPUS POLICE
KENT STATE UNIVERSITY

THEY'RE WAITING FOR YOU IN ROOM 203, TERRY.
THANKS.
YEAH?
RAP! RAP!
AFTERNOON, AGENTS.
MR. NORMAN. RIGHT ON TIME.
THESE ARE THE ROLLS I SHOT TODAY.
GOOD, GOOD.
HERE'S SOME MORE FILM...
...AND A LIST OF STUDENTS WE NEED PHOTOS OF.
Kodak
Kodak Film
KEEP UP THE GOOD WORK, TERRY.
NOT A GOOD IDEA USING THAT KID. HE'S WORKED FOR US BEFORE. HE'S TRIGGER-HAPPY.
OH, HE'LL BE FINE.
I'M TELLIN' YA, HE THINKS HE'S JAMES BOND.
LOOK, CHIEF SCHWARTZMILLER, THE FBI NEEDS INFORMERS ON CAMPUS WHO CAN BLEND IN WITH THE PROTESTERS.

LAW ENFORCEMENT IS TERRIFIED OF A LARGE ANTIWAR UPRISING AT KENT STATE, THE SECOND-LARGEST UNIVERSITY IN OHIO,

AS A RESULT, THERE ARE, INCREDIBLY, **FIVE** LAW ENFORCEMENT AGENCIES WORKING ON OR AROUND CAMPUS IN 1970, ALL OPERATING INDEPENDENTLY AND OFTEN BLUNDERING INTO ONE ANOTHER.

THE UNIVERSITY'S **CAMPUS POLICE**, WITH A FORCE OF 23 MEN, OPERATES ONLY ON CAMPUS. WITH A LARGE NETWORK OF PLANTS AND INFORMANTS, IT'S A VIRTUAL SECRET POLICE FORCE.

THE **COUNTY SHERIFF'S DEPARTMENT,** WITH 29 FULL-TIME DEPUTIES, AND THE **STATE HIGHWAY PATROL,** WITH 1,075 OFFICERS STATEWIDE, HAVE JURISDICTION ON CAMPUS. BOTH WERE USED TO CRUSH EARLIER PROTESTS.

THE **KENT CITY POLICE,** WITH 22 OFFICERS, PATROLS THE OFF-CAMPUS AREAS AND ONLY COMES ON CAMPUS WHEN ASKED TO ASSIST.

THE FBI HAS A LARGE FIELD OFFICE IN CLEVELAND AND A SMALLER ONE IN AKRON. UNDER ORDERS FROM **THE NIXON ADMINISTRATION** AND FBI DIRECTOR **J. EDGAR HOOVER**, THE BUREAU IS SPYING ON, AND DISRUPTING, OFTEN BY ILLEGAL MEANS, ALL ORGANIZATIONS DEEMED A "THREAT." THE FBI IS NOW A CONSTANT PRESENCE AT KENT STATE.

IN ADDITION, **MILITARY INTELLIGENCE** IS ORDERED BY THE NIXON WHITE HOUSE TO SPY ON **ANY** CAMPUS WHERE ANTIWAR ACTIVITY TAKES PLACE. THE WELL-PUBLICIZED **KENT SDS** ACTIVITIES OF 1968-69 ATTRACTED THE PENTAGON'S ATTENTION. IT'S ALSO LIKELY THE CIA IS WATCHING THE CAMPUS.

THE ***AKRON BEACON JOURNAL*** IDENTIFIED A MILITARY INTELLIGENCE AGENT WHO WAS WORKING UNDERCOVER AT KENT STATE, AND A "SQUAD" OF COVERT FBI AGENTS. THEIR ACTIVITIES THIS WEEKEND? UNKNOWN.

10:45 P.M.
SCREW NIXON!
YAY!
WOO!!
RC
KENT KOVE

NIXON END THE WAR

WHEW! MAN, BILL, IT WAS A REAL SAUNA IN THERE.
YEAH.

BUT WHAT A GAME, HUH? JERRY WEST WAS UNSTOPPABLE! I STILL LIKE THE KNICKS TO TAKE THE FINALS, THOUGH.
WISH I HAD A TV SO WE DIDN'T HAFTA WATCH IN A BAR.

MAN! IT'S LIKE 70 DEGREES! SPRING IS HERE AT LONG LAST!
I'M STARVING.

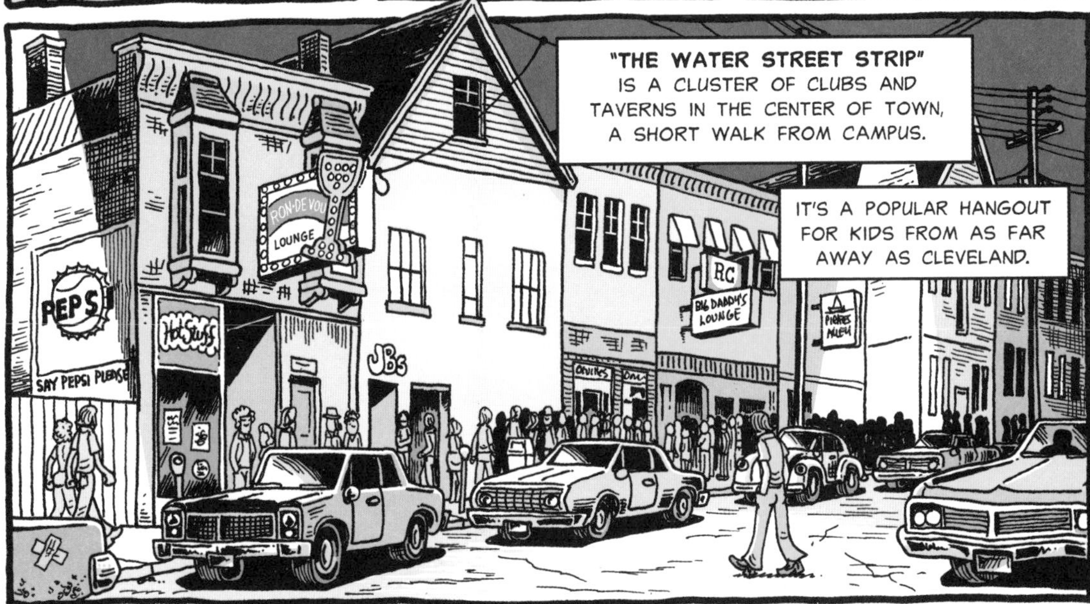
"THE WATER STREET STRIP" IS A CLUSTER OF CLUBS AND TAVERNS IN THE CENTER OF TOWN, A SHORT WALK FROM CAMPUS.
IT'S A POPULAR HANGOUT FOR KIDS FROM AS FAR AWAY AS CLEVELAND.
PEPSI
SAY PEPSI PLEASE
RON-DE-VOU LOUNGE
Hot Stuff
JB's
RC
BIG DADDY'S LOUNGE
PIRATES ALLEY

DOWN WITH NIX-ON! DOWN WITH NIX-ON!
SMASH THE BANKS, END THE WAR!
YEAH, MAN!
YOW!
PEPSI

FOLKS ARE A LOT ANGRIER THAN THEY WERE AT THE RALLY TODAY ON CAMPUS, HUH?
SCREW YOU, TRICKY DICK!
HAW!
WOO!

THIS ROCK SURE WOULD LOOK GOOD GOING THROUGH A BANK WINDOW!
HAHA!

I'M GETTING A HEADACHE.

YEAH, THERE'S A BAD VIBE HERE TONIGHT. WHY DON'T WE HEAD BACK TO CAMPUS?

EVERY COLLEGE TOWN HAS THAT ONE COP THAT ALL STUDENTS DETEST.
OINK! OINK!
BOOOOOO!
SOOEY!
HEADS UP! IT'S RON CRAIG!
PUTT PUTT
KENT
POLICE
RRRRR
IN KENT, THAT COP WAS OFFICER RON CRAIG.
WHAT AN ASSHOLE!

PISS OFF, CRAIG!
RESIST THE DRAFT

AND JUST LIKE **THAT**, THE MOOD TURNED...

...WITH ONE EMPTY **STROH'S BOTTLE!**

KRA'SH!!
KENT POLICE
RRRRRR

HA HA!
YEAH!
LOOKIT HIM RUN!
REEEEEEEEEEEEE
SCREEEEE
HAW!
HA HA HA!

WHOOP!
WOO!
YOW!
THE STREET IS OURS!
YEE-HA!
PIRATE ALLEY
USED TIRES

BEEEEEEEEEP!

LOOK OUT!
HEY!
THUD!
BUMP!

YEAH! GIT HIM!
JERK!
PANG!

TRASH IT!
SMASH!
PING!
KRASH!
THUD!

BRAAAAAAAA

KENT POLICE CHIEF ROY THOMPSON, AGE 59
MILLER JONES -SHOES-
POLICE

I TOLD YA THERE'D BE TROUBLE TONIGHT. THE RADICALS HAVE BEEN SPRAY-PAINTIN' BUILDINGS ALL WEEK.

I **KNEW** THIS WOULD HAPPEN WHEN THE UNIVERSITY ALLOWED THAT COMMIE **JERRY RUBIN** TO SPEAK ON CAMPUS!
YEP. YOU **CALLED IT,** ALL RIGHT, CHIEF.

ANTIWAR ACTIVIST **JERRY RUBIN** IS ONE OF **THE CHICAGO SEVEN**, THOSE TRIED FOR LEADING THE MASSIVE STREET DEMONSTRATIONS AT THE **1968 DEMOCRATIC CONVENTION.**
HE SPOKE TO A LARGE CROWD ON APRIL 10, URGING STUDENTS TO "KILL THEIR PARENTS."
STUDENTS GOT THE JOKE, OF COURSE. TERRIFIED OLDER KENT TOWNSFOLK DID **NOT**.

CAN'T BELIEVE THEY LET ONE OF THEM **WEATHERMEN** RILE UP TH' STUDENTS.
I THOUGHT RUBIN WAS A... WHADDAYA CALL... A **YIPPIE?**
TH' WEATHERMEN ARE DIFFERENT. TH' **WORST** OF THOSE SDS RADICALS, ACCORDING TO TH' **FBI ALERT.**

THE YIPPIES, THE YOUTH INTERNATIONAL PARTY, ARE A RADICAL ACTIVIST GROUP THAT FAVORS **STREET THEATER** AND **MEDIA STUNTS.** LEADERS RUBIN AND ABBIE HOFFMAN ARE NATIONAL CELEBRITIES.
THE YIPPIES ARE ALLIES OF, BUT **NOT** PART OF, SDS.

WHAT **DIFFERENCE** DOES IT MAKE? THEY'RE **ALL** COMMUNISTS!

HEY, CHIEF! JUST HEARD FROM **TH' CAMPUS POLICE.** SCHWARTZMILLER SAYS WE'RE **ON OUR OWN.** HIS MEN HAFTA PROTECT CAMPUS BUILDINGS.
DAMMIT!

CALL TH' **COUNTY SHERIFF**... AND ALL TH' **NEIGHBORING TOWNS.** HAVE 'EM SEND **EVERY** MAN THAT CAN BE SPARED!
ROGER.

THE STREET NOW BELONGS TO THE PEOPLE!
LET'S HAVE A FESTIVAL!

KEEP KENT KLEAN

BURN, BABY, BURN!
Chosen
Few

HA HA HA!
Chosen
Few
SSSSSS

SEEM TO BE MORE BIKERS THAN USUAL ON WATER STREET TONIGHT.
DIDN'T YOU HEAR?

THOSE **CLOWNS** AT THE **CAMPUS PRANK CLUB** INVITED SOME BIKER GANGS FOR A **CHOPPER PARADE** EARLIER TODAY.
IT WAS A **CAMPAIGN STUNT** FOR A JOKE CANDIDATE THEY'RE RUNNING FOR **CLASS PRESIDENT.**

GUESS THEY **STUCK AROUND** FOR A NIGHT AT THE BARS.
LET'S HOPE THEY **STAY COOL** AND DON'T START **BUSTIN' HEADS.**
YEAH, NO **KIDDING.**

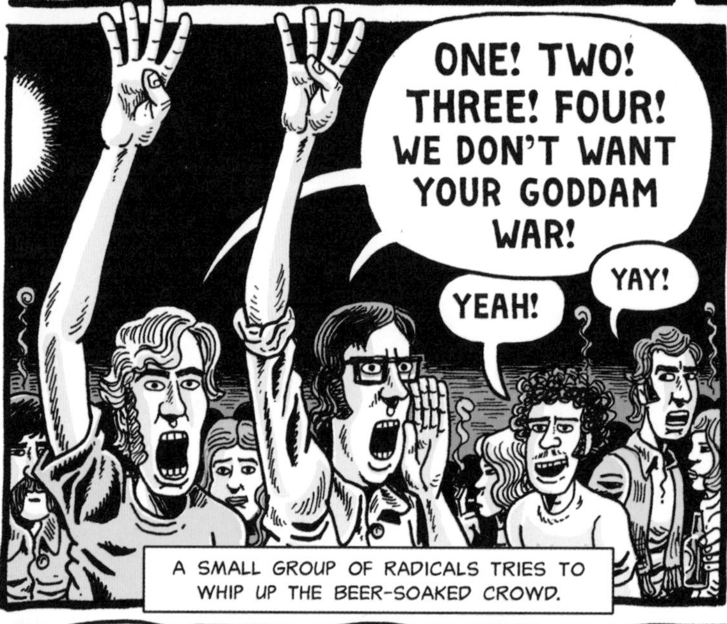
ONE! TWO! THREE! FOUR! WE DON'T WANT YOUR GODDAM WAR!
YEAH!
YAY!
A SMALL GROUP OF RADICALS TRIES TO WHIP UP THE BEER-SOAKED CROWD.

WE GOTTA TAKE THESE BASTARDS!
WOO!
CHEW CHEW.

BILL! HEY, BILL!
YEAH!
SCREW NIXON!

THIS IS **ELISSA...** AND **SALLY!** THEY CAME HERE FROM AKRON FOR THE **THE MEASLES** GIG AT JB'S AND NOW THEY'RE **STRANDED.**
HI.
GIGGLE. HELLO.

THIS IS **BILL**, LADIES. I **KNOW** HE LOOKS LIKE A **NORDIC STEREOTYPE**, BUT HE'S ACTUALLY A PRETTY **INTERESTING DUDE.**

OH GEE, **THANKS, AL!**

WHOA. THIS IS TURNING INTO A **BAD SCENE** HERE. I CAN'T TELL IF IT'S **POLITICS OR BEER**, BUT THIS IS **NOT** WHERE WE WANNA BE.

YEAH. WE SHOULD **SPLIT**.

BACK IN RICHFIELD...

THANK GOD IT'S WARMED UP, EH KARLOVIC? I WUZ FREEZIN' MY ASS OFF IN THIS GODDAM TENT.
MMMM.

WHATCHA READIN' THERE, COLLEGE BOY?
SOCIOLOGY. GOT A FINAL PAPER DUE THIS WEEK.
ALREADY MISSED A TEST, THANKS TO THIS TEAMSTER NONSENSE.

HOW LONG DO YOU THINK WE'LL BE ON BABYSITTING DUTY HERE?
WHO KNOWS.

IT'S PRETTY INTENSE. THESE TEAMSTERS MEAN BUSINESS!
NO SHIT. I'M SO STRESSED OUT, I HAVEN'T SLEPT DECENT IN DAYS!

I KEEP THINKIN' ABOUT ONE-A THOSE HILLBILLY TRUCK DRIVERS SNIPIN' AT A SCAB DRIVER AND SHOOTIN' ME BY MISTAKE! I DON'T GIVE A CRAP WHO WINS THIS STRIKE!

THIS IS MY **FIRST** GUARD ACTION SINCE JOINING UP. I WAS **SHAKIN'** AFTER TODAY'S SKIRMISHES!

I **DIDN'T** THINK GUARD DUTY WOULD BE SO **HAIRY.**
THIS IS **NUTHIN'!**
TALK TO TH' OLDER GUYS ABOUT TH' **CLEVELAND RACE RIOTS** A COUPLE YEARS BACK.

WHOLE BLOCKS IN FLAMES, PEOPLE SHOOTIN' AT THEM OUTTA WINDOWS, BRAWLS, MOLOTOV COCKTAILS... IT SOUNDS LIKE **A NIGHTMARE!** LET'S HOPE TH' COLOREDS DON'T START UP WITH **THAT** AGIN!

OOF! MAN, I'M TIRED OF **TENTS!**
I LIVE **JUST** A HALF HOUR AWAY IN **KENT.**

A HOT SHOWER... A NICE SOFT BED... IT'S **SO NEAR**... BUT **SO FAR.**
WHAT AN **ORDEAL** THIS IS.

THERE ARE 300,000 GUYS IN **VIETNAM** WHO WOULD TRADE PLACES WITH YOU IN A **SECOND!** THE GUARD IS A **SWEET** GIG. I'M PRETTY HAPPY TO HAVE **MY** SPOT.

I JUST **WISH** I COULD GET SOME DAMN **SLEEP.**

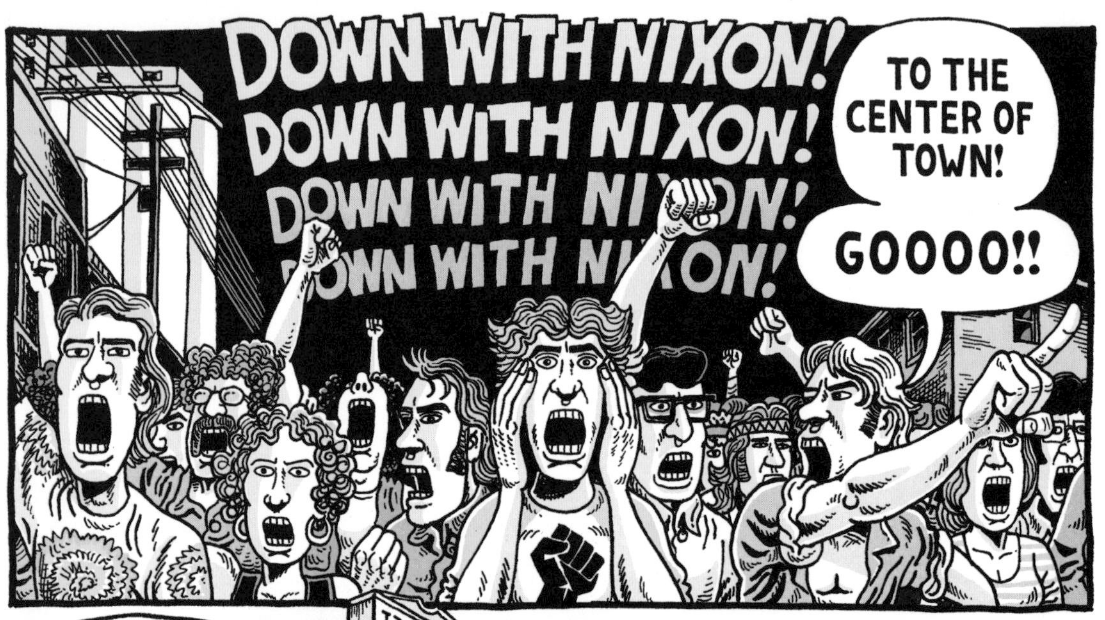
DOWN WITH NIXON!
DOWN WITH NIXON!
DOWN WITH NIXON!
DOWN WITH NIXON!
TO THE CENTER OF TOWN!
GOOOO!!

HOME
SAVINGS
SMASH TH' BANKS!
END TH' WAR!
LET 'EM HAVE IT!
YOW!
HOME SAVINGS & LOAN

HOME SAVINGS & LO
CRASH!
SMASH!
SMASH!
KRAK!
KRUSH!
THUD!
KRASH!

GETZ HARDWARE
LET'S GIVE IT TO OLD MAN GETZ, TOO!
DO IT!

FREE LAWN EQUIPMENT, EVERYONE!

LOOKIT ME! I'M ONE-A TH' BOURGEOISIE!
RATTLE! RATTLE! RATTLE!

FIRST FEDERAL BANK
FIRST FEDERAL BANK
SMASH!
SMASH!
SMASH THE BANKS, END THE WAR!
SMASH THE BANKS, END THE WAR!

OKAY, MEN, I WAS HOPIN' THEY'D SIMMER DOWN ON THEIR OWN, BUT THAT ISN'T HAPPENIN'!
POLICE

WE HAVE ENUFF MAN POWER NOW.
I WANT THOSE GODDAM BARS CLOSED!
POLICE
ICE

PIGS!!
RUN!
YAAAA!
POLICE
POLICE
OFF TH' STREET!

BRAP! BRAP!
BRRAAAAAAAAAAAAAAAA
TH' BIKERS ARE SPLITTING!
THAT'S NOT A GOOD SIGN!

WHERE ARE YOU LEADING US, BILL?
A SECRET ESCAPE ROUTE FROM WATER STREET.

TH' RAILROAD TRACKS RUN BEHIND TH' BAR STRIP. THEY'LL TAKE US RIGHT TO FRANKLIN STREET, WHERE I LIVE...
...AND GET US PAST THAT COP BARRICADE.

REEEEEEEEE
CRASH!
BOOM!
MAN! SOUNDS LIKE A FIREFIGHT UP ON TH' STREET!
OTHERS HAVE YOUR IDEA, TOO.

THE REVOLUTION IS HEEEEEERE!

I HAD FUN TONIGHT, SANDY.
ME, TOO, JEFF! I HAVEN'T BEEN ROLLER-SKATING IN AGES.

YEAH, THE MOON-GLO RINK IS A REAL TIME MACHINE.
HOW'S YOUR KEISTER? YOU TOOK SOME IMPRESSIVE FALLS.
GIGGLE. SORE!

WILL I SEE YOU AGAIN THIS WEEKEND?
GROAN. I HAVE A TON OF HOMEWORK.
SO I'LL BE GLUED TO THE BOOKS.

WHY DON'T YOU COME OVER FOR DINNER SUNDAY? I ALWAYS MAKE MORE FOOD THAN MY ROOMMATES CAN EAT.
COOL! I'M TIRED OF MY RICE AND BEANS.

ROLLING STONES LET IT BLEED

YEEEEAH.

HAHA. **ALWAYS** THE STONES! BILL WANTS TO **BE** MICK JAGGER!
DAMN STRAIGHT!
MICK LIVES ON HIS **OWN TERMS!** HE TAKES NO **SHIT!**

THESE ARE MAGAZINES **MY DAD** READS.
TIME
BILL IS A **SERIOUS** GUY.

WHAT'S THIS **POSTER** ABOUT?
IS THAT **SUPPOSED** TO BE **YOU,** BILL?
Cadet Schroeder
SIR, YES, SIR!
TRIP!

YEAH, ONE OF MY **SMART-ASS ROOMMATES** DREW THAT.

THEY LIKE TO RAZZ ME ABOUT BEIN' IN **ROT-SEE.**
SIR, YES, SIR!
TRIP!
HA HA!

NOT JUST **IN!** BILL **IS** ROTC! THEY GAVE HIM A **SCHOLARSHIP,** HE'S SUCH STELLAR **OFFICER MATERIAL!**

WOW. ARE YOU GOING TO **VIETNAM?**
WE'LL SEE.

I'M KINDA **DOWN** ON ROT-SEE AT THE MOMENT. I'M HAVING **SERIOUS DOUBTS** ABOUT THE WHOLE THING.
ALL THE OTHER CADETS ARE **REAL GUNG HO.** I DON'T HAVE ANY **FRIENDS** IN THE UNIT.

MY ADVISER IS THE ONLY GUY I CAN TALK TO. HE'S STILL IN HIS TWENTIES BUT HAS DONE A TOUR IN **'NAM.** HE KNOWS **THE SCORE.**

IT'S A LITTLE UNSETTLING THAT HE TAKES **NOTES** DURING OUR RAP SESSIONS THOUGH.

AND THE THINGS THEY **TEACH US** IN ROT-SEE! LAST WEEK, WE LEARNED HOW TO **KILL A MAN** WITH **TWO STICKS** AND A **PIECE OF WIRE!**

REALLY? HOW DO YOU DO THAT?
WITH A GARROTE. IT'S A FAVORITE ASSASSINATION DEVICE... OF THE MAFIA!

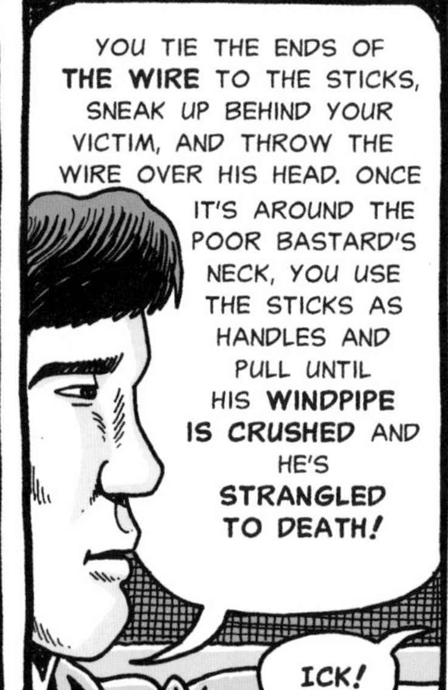
YOU TIE THE ENDS OF THE WIRE TO THE STICKS, SNEAK UP BEHIND YOUR VICTIM, AND THROW THE WIRE OVER HIS HEAD. ONCE IT'S AROUND THE POOR BASTARD'S NECK, YOU USE THE STICKS AS HANDLES AND PULL UNTIL HIS WINDPIPE IS CRUSHED AND HE'S STRANGLED TO DEATH!
ICK!

YEAH. IT'S INCREDIBLE, Y'KNOW? AND THEN RIGHT AFTER ROT-SEE CLASS, I HAD PSYCH AND WE HAD A LECTURE ON DR. SCHWEITZER!
SNIK SNIK SNIK
NOBEL LAUREATE PHILOSOPHER

YEAH... IT WAS A SURREAL DAY.

JUST ONE OF MANY.

PURRRRRRR

I CAN'T BELIEVE YOU HAVEN'T GOTTEN BUSTED FOR HAVING A CAT IN YOUR DORM ROOM!
HE'S ONLY A KITTEN.

NO ONE CARES ANYMORE. THE YEAR IS ALMOST OVER AND THE DORM OFFICIALS HAVE KINDA GIVEN UP.

SO MY BOYFRIEND SNEAKS IN AFTER CURFEW AND I HAVE A CAT.
I THINK MY REP WORKS IN MY FAVOR, TOO. THEY'RE ALL SCARED OF ME!
MMM.

BESIDES, UNIVERSITY OFFICIALS ARE TOO BUSY FREAKING OUT ABOUT WEATHERMEN SNEAKING ONTO CAMPUS AND TURNING US ALL INTO BOMB-THROWING REVOLUTIONARIES!
HAHA. TRUE. I OVERHEARD SOME TOWNIES TALKING ABOUT ALL THE OUT-OF-STATE PLATES THEY'VE SEEN IN KENT.

THIS WAS PROOF TO THEM THAT MILITANTS HAD INFILTRATED THE TOWN!
DIDN'T SEE THE POINT IN EXPLAINING TO THEM THAT KENT STATE HAS SHITLOADS OF OUT-OF-STATE STUDENTS...

MARCH ON WASHINGTON NOV 14-15
...DRIVING CARS WITH OUT-OF-STATE PLATES!
THERE'S NO POINT IN DEBATING PEOPLE THAT PARANOID.
THAT'S REFLECTIVE OF THE TIMES WE LIVE IN.
YEP.

YOSSARIAN, FROM "CATCH-22." GOOD NAME, BUT HE'S NOT AS CYNICAL AS HIS NAMESAKE.
THAT'S WHY "YO-YO" SUITS HIM BETTER.

BANG!
THERE'S A RIOT ON WATER STREET!
Peace

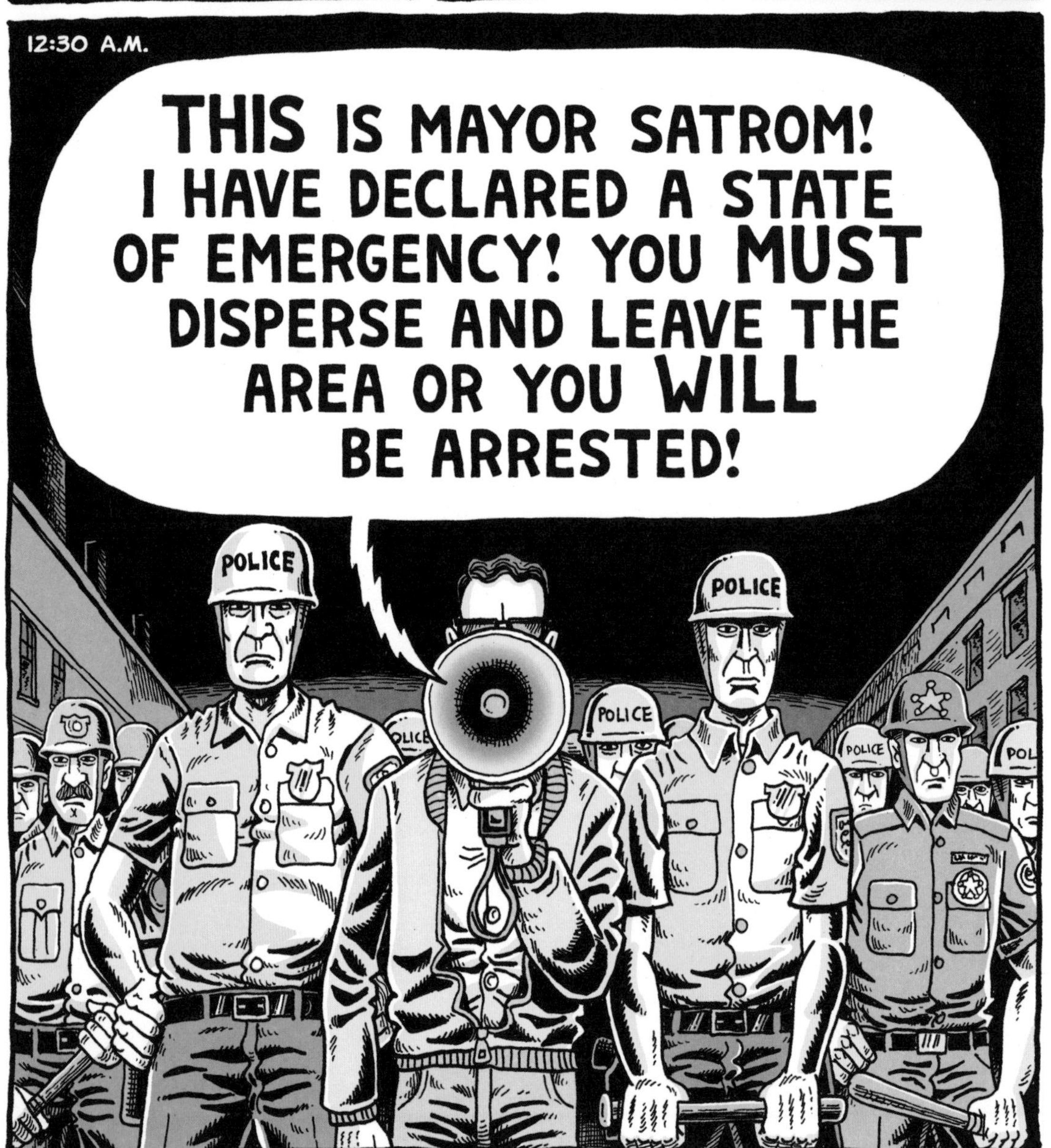
12:30 A.M.
THIS IS MAYOR SATROM! I HAVE DECLARED A STATE OF EMERGENCY! YOU MUST DISPERSE AND LEAVE THE AREA OR YOU WILL BE ARRESTED!
POLICE
POLICE
POLICE
POLICE

DOWN WITH NIXON! DOWN WITH NIXON!
HELL NO, WE WON'T GO! HELL NO, WE WON'T GO!
HO-HO-HO CHI MINH! HO-HO-HO CHI MINH!
HOME
SMASH!
CRASH!
SMASH! BASH!
KRASH!
CRASH!

DAMMIT! THERE'S TWICE AS MANY OF THEM ON TH' STREET NOW! LOOKS LIKE 500 AT LEAST.
GUESS I SHOULDA THOUGHT OF THAT BEFORE EMPTYING TH' BARS!
OK, MEN! FORM UP!
POLICE
POLICE

CLEAR 'EM OUT!
POLIC

TOK!

DEPUTY

LET'S SPLIT!
ONE MORE!

BINGO!
CRASH!

GODDAMMIT! THAT'S MY OFFICE WINDOW!
THE MAYOR, A CONSULTING ENGINEER BY TRADE, HAD HIS BUSINESS OFFICE IN ROOM #207 OF THE FIRST FEDERAL BUILDING, OVERLOOKING WATER STREET.

BACK! BACK!

SOB!
AUGH!
SHIT!

THAT'S IT! HERD THEM UP TH' ALLEYS!
CHASE 'EM BACK TO CAMPUS!
POLICE
NATIONAL
BANK

MR. MAYOR, TH' CHIEF ASKS THAT YOU DRIVE SOME OF THESE CLOWNS TO TH' CITY JAIL IN YOUR CAR.
TH' PADDY WAGON IS ALREADY FULL AND ALL OUR MEN ARE NEEDED HERE.
O-OKAY.
UUUUUH.

1:10 A.M.
WH-WH-WHAT
THE HELL
IS HAPPENING HERE?
POLICE
POLIC
CE

SATURDAY, MAY 2
10 A.M.
WESTERN UNION
OR
OP
FORD

WOW. WOTTA MESS.
FIFTY-SIX BROKEN WINDOWS

YOU STUDENTS SHOULD ALL BE LOCKED UP FOR WHAT YOU DID TO OUR DOWNTOWN! EVERY LAST ONE-A YA!
LADY, I SPENT THE WHOLE NIGHT STUDYING IN MY DORM ROOM.
EVERY ONE-A YA!

REMEMBER, STAN, IF YOU BOYS SEE ANY STUDENTS WHO EVEN LOOK LIKE TROUBLE TODAY...
...DON'T ASK QUESTIONS...
VFW
...JUST LET 'EM HAVE IT!

NOTICE
ALCOHOL PROHIBITED ON RANGE
DANGER
SAFETY FIRST
BLAM! BLAM! BLAM!
BLAM! BLAM! BLAM!

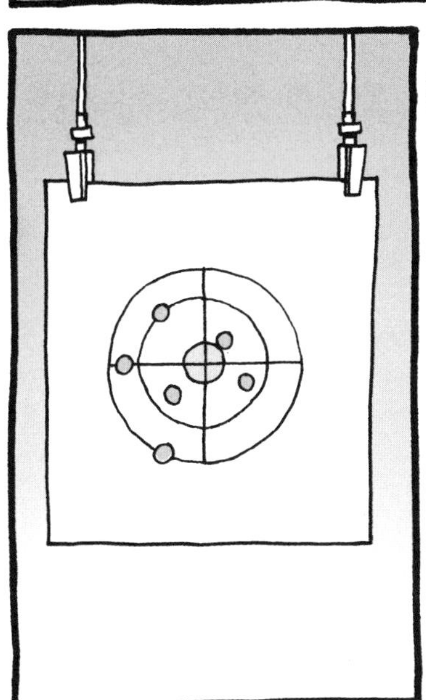

NICE BIT A SHOOTIN', SON.
THANKS.

JUST TRYIN' TO GET COMFORTABLE WITH IT. I'M WORKIN' FOR TH' FBI!
YEAH?

AT KENT STATE. I'M HELPING THEM OUT WITH THE RADICALS.
WOW. AREN'T YEW KINDA YOUNG?

YEAH, BUT I'M A LAW ENFORCEMENT MAJOR...
...SO I'VE BEEN TRAINED FOR THIS.

I PICKED UP THIS .38... FOR PROTECTION.
SNAP!

I **ALWAYS** CARRY IT NOW.

WORKIN' UNDERCOVER IS **DANGEROUS WORK**, WITH ALL TH' **WEATHERMEN INFILTRATORS** IN TOWN.
IT'S AWFUL HOW THEM **STUDENTS** WRECKED TH' TOWN.

PROFESSIONAL REVOLUTIONARIES WERE BEHIND THAT. THEY HAVE A SECRET HQ IN **CLEVELAND.**
GEEZ.
THE BUREAU SEZ THEY WERE TRAINED IN **CUBA!**

WH-WHY DON'T TH' FBI **TAKE OUT** TH' BASTARDS?
WE'RE **WORKING ON IT.**
SOMETHING **BIG** IS BREWING AT KENT STATE.
BUT WE'LL BE **READY** FOR 'EM.

SPRING
SPEECH LAB
HOURS
M-F 8AM-9PM
SA 9AM-5PM
THAT WAS **GREAT**, MATT!

LET'S TRY NUMBER THREE.
OKAY, SSSAAANDY.

NOW **DRAW OUT** THOSE SOUNDS.

REMEMBER TO ALWAYS PRESET YOUR **DEPTH OF FIELD**, BILL...
KLIK!

...SO YOU DON'T HAVE TO CHECK YOUR **LENS FOCUS** ALL THE TIME.
GOTCHA.
NOW, **I** PREFER CARRYING A SMALL **RANGE FINDER**, LIKE MY LEICA ONE HERE. MAKES IT A LOT EASIER.
KLIK!
I **REALLY** APPRECIATE THE **PHOTO LESSONS**, BRUCE... AND YOU LOANING ME THE NICE CAMERA...
...**AND** FOR SCROUNGING UP TH' FREE FILM!

HEY, NO PROBLEM. WE HAVE MORE CAMERAS THAN WE NEED IN THE CINEMATOGRAPHY OFFICE. YOUR TUITION PAYS FOR THEM, TOO!

THE FILM I GET FREE FROM THE UNIVERSITY. I'M HAPPY TO SHARE.

NICE THAT YOU HAVE FREE TIME THIS QUARTER.
YOU WERE SUCH A WORKHORSE WITH SCHOOL, JOBS, AND ROTC, WE HARDLY HUNG OUT AT ALL.
I KNOW, I KNOW.

I DON'T WANT MY FOLKS PAYING MY WAY. SO I'VE ALWAYS HAD PART-TIME JOBS DURING TH' YEAR.

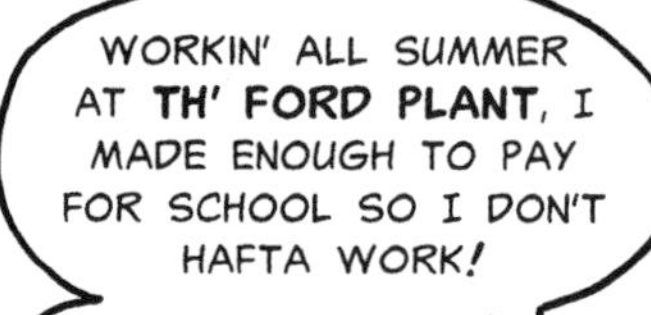
WORKIN' ALL SUMMER AT TH' FORD PLANT, I MADE ENOUGH TO PAY FOR SCHOOL SO I DON'T HAFTA WORK!
NOW I HAVE TIME TO TAKE ADVANTAGE OF ALL KENT HAS TO OFFER.

I FINALLY FEEL LIKE I'M GETTING A PROPER COLLEGE EDUCATION.
KLIK!
CRAP. WRONG F-STOP.
WHAT WAS THAT CRAZY SCHOOL YOU USED TO ATTEND?

HAHA. THE COLORADO SCHOOL OF MINES! I WENT THERE TO STUDY GEOLOGY... AND HALFWAY THROUGH MY FRESHMAN YEAR THEY ELIMINATED THE ENTIRE PROGRAM!
I LIKE KENT BETTER. CLOSER TO HOME, TOO.

ΣΧ

NICE JOB TEARIN' UP TH' TOWN, FREAKS!
YOU DICKS!

I WASN'T THERE! YELL AT SOMEONE ELSE!
MAN! FRAT BOYS!
I USED TO BE ONE, TOO, YA KNOW.
WHAT? YER KIDDING!
YEAH, AT MICHIGAN STATE. RUSHED MY BROTHER'S FRAT. I THOUGHT THAT'S WHAT YOU DID IN COLLEGE.
IT WAS A REAL DRAG.
AS WAS MICHIGAN STATE.
SO WHAT HAPPENED?

OH, NOTHIN' DRAMATIC. I JUST LOST INTEREST.
I GOT HIPPER AND TH' FRAT WAS REAL SQUARE.
THEY WERE PRETTY RELIEVED WHEN I QUIT COMING AROUND.
HA.
HEY, GUYS! WANT SOME FRESH MUSHROOMS?
DO OR DIE!
RAVENNA ARSENAL
7.62-43

GOT 'EM AT THE FARMER'S MARKET. JUST **ROAST 'EM** OVER THE BURNER...
...AND **DIP 'EM** IN THE BUTTER.

MMM. WHO'S **TH' CHICK?**
OH, **SOME KID** WHO WAS HANGING OUT ON WATER STREET LAST NIGHT. SHE **FREAKED OUT** WHEN IT GOT NASTY, SO I TOLD HER SHE COULD **CRASH** HERE.
SHE'S OUT LIKE A LIGHT!
FOR THE
Z

SAID SHE **HITCHED** UP FROM FLORIDA AND GOT **STRANDED.**
HER NAME IS **MARY ANN.**
ANOTHER?
SURE!

DAAAAAAMN, YOU GUYS! WHEN'S TH' LAST TIME YOU **CLEANED UP** THIS DUMP...
...**FALL QUARTER?**
BAH! PETTY MIDDLE-CLASS CONCERNS!
WANNA GET **HIGH?**

YAAAAAAAAAAAAA

SPLASH!

DAMN!! THIS WATER IS COLD!
NICE ONE!
HAHA!

A STUDENT HOVEL WITH A POOL! I CAN'T BELIEVE SUCH A THING EXISTS!

YEAH, IT'S SWEET. THE GUYS NEXT DOOR FILLED IT YESTERDAY, BUT IT'S NOT QUITE WARM ENOUGH YET FOR A DIP. MAYBE IN A FEW DAYS.

STEVE FOUND THIS PLACE. LUCKY FOR ME HE HAD A SPARE ROOM WHEN I TRANSFERRED HERE IN JANUARY.

GLAD YOU DIDN'T GET BUSTED LAST NIGHT, BUTLER.
YEAH, THAT WAS PRETTY HAIRY.

WE PLAY RIGHT INTO NIXON'S HANDS WITH SHIT LIKE THAT. RANDOM VIOLENCE GIVES HIM ALL THE REASON HE NEEDS TO BRING TH' BOOT DOWN.
I HEAR YA.

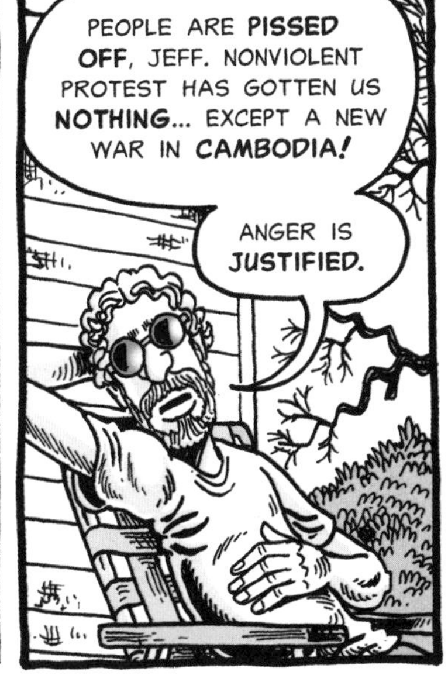
PEOPLE ARE PISSED OFF, JEFF. NONVIOLENT PROTEST HAS GOTTEN US NOTHING... EXCEPT A NEW WAR IN CAMBODIA!
ANGER IS JUSTIFIED.

I JUST THINK THESE MILITANT SDS-ERS, THE WEATHERMEN TYPES, ARE GONNA SCREW UP THE WHOLE ANTIWAR MOVEMENT.
I AGREE!
SIGH. THE COUNTRY IS A TOTAL MESS RIGHT NOW... THE WORST IT'S EVER BEEN!
I FEEL GUILTY THAT MY LIFE IS GOING SO WELL. LAST SUMMER, I WAS IN THE DUMPS, TOO. MY FOLKS SPLIT UP, MY GIRLFRIEND BROKE UP WITH ME...
...THEN THAT MICHIGAN STATE BULLSHIT...

BUT I MOVED TO KENT, AND JUST LIKE THAT...
SNAP!

SPLASH!
...IT ALL CHANGED.

WHAT'S YER MAJOR NOW? I FERGIT.
PSYCH!
WASN'T IT ARCHITECTURE BEFORE?

YEP! WAIT... THERE'S LOGIC TO IT!
I JUST FIGURED, WHAT'S THE POINT OF MAKING FANCY BUILDINGS IF THEY'RE ALL FULL OF MISERABLE, MESSED-UP PEOPLE?

I DECIDED IT'D BE BETTER TO WORK ON THE PEOPLE.
AW, BUT WHO KNOWS IF I'LL STICK WITH PSYCH.
I MAY NOT EVEN BOTHER WITH A DEGREE.

DID YOU SEE THE MESS ON WATER STREET, BONNIE?
NO, I HAVEN'T GONE INTO TOWN. HEARD ABOUT IT THOUGH.
HOW ARE SMALL BUSINESSMEN IN KENT TO BLAME FOR CAMBODIA?
IT'S SO STUPID.
I'M GOING TO MISS YOU WHEN YOU TRANSFER, ALLISON.
I WISH YOU WOULDN'T LEAVE.
I'LL MISS YOU, TOO! BUT KENT IS JUST NOT WORKING OUT. CLASSES ARE TOO REGIMENTED. I'VE HAD A COUPLE OF GOOD PROFS, BUT MOST OF THEM HAVE BEEN JADED AND DULL.
I'M IN HONORS COLLEGE AND IT'S A REAL DISAPPOINTMENT.
I EXPECTED MORE ACTIVISM HERE, TOO. I WENT TO A FEW SDS MEETINGS... OFF CAMPUS, SINCE THEY GOT BOOTED OUT!
WHAT A BUNCH OF FINKS.
KENT STATE JUST ISN'T WHAT I'D THOUGHT IT WOULD BE. I'M NOT CHALLENGED HERE.
I WANT MORE.
MAYBE IT'S TOO SMALL-TOWN MIDWEST.
MY FOLKS USED TO DRIVE US DOWN HERE FOR WEEKEND LUNCHES WHEN WE LIVED IN CLEVELAND HEIGHTS. I WAS ENCHANTED. THE BLACK SQUIRRELS, THE TREES...
...I THOUGHT IT WAS SO LOVELY.

I DECIDED THEN AND THERE THAT THIS WOULD BE MY UNIVERSITY.
FUNNY HOW THINGS WORK OUT.
AND YOU THINK BUFFALO WILL BE BETTER?
I DO!
IT'S A LIBERAL ARTS SCHOOL, FOR ONE. AND BARRY HAS FRIENDS THERE. THEY LOVE IT.
WE'LL HAVE TO START IN NIGHT SCHOOL SINCE WE MISSED THE REGULAR TRANSFER DEADLINE.
BUT THAT'S ONLY A TEMPORARY BUMMER.
WHAT DO YOUR PARENTS THINK ABOUT ALL THIS?
HEH. THEY'RE NOT THRILLED... BUT IT'S MY LIFE.
HEY, AT LEAST KENT GAVE YOU BARRY!
TRUE! I MET HIM RIGHT AWAY ...AT A DONOVAN CONCERT!
IT WAS LOVE AT FIRST SIGHT! IT'S HOKEY, I KNOW.
YOU'RE A PERFECT COUPLE.
HAHA. WELL, WE'LL ALWAYS BE TOGETHER.
AFTER WE GRADUATE MAYBE WE'LL MOVE TO CANADA. WE CAN'T STAY IN THE U.S. THE WAY IT'S GOING.
I'D LIKE TO OPEN A GALLERY.
BUFFALO IS RIGHT THERE ON THE BORDER, JUST A BRIDGE AWAY.
SO... IN A FEW WEEKS, IT'S GOOD-BYE KENT STATE!
ATTENTION! PEOPLE OF THE CAFETERIA!

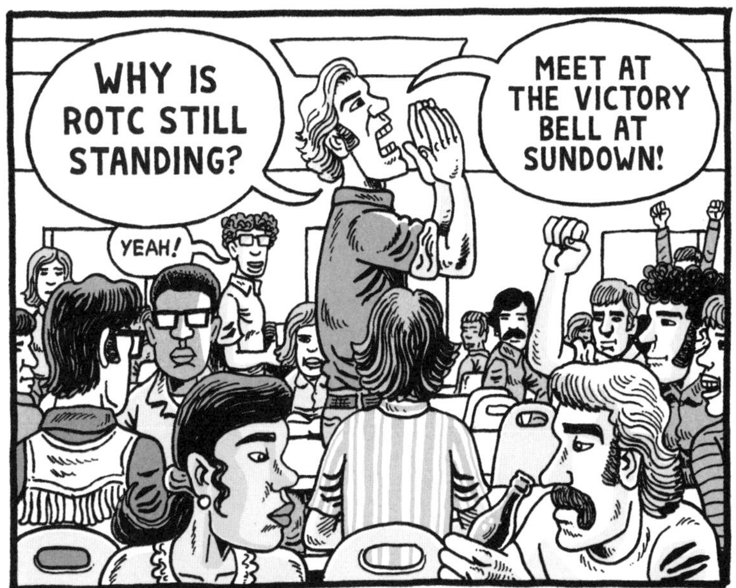

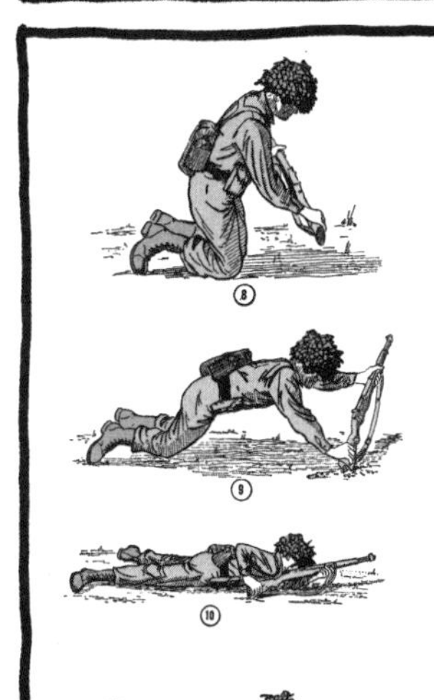

Positions 8, 9, 10, and 11
Figure 29—Continued.

IN ADDITION TO THEIR REGULAR CLASSWORK IN WHATEVER MAJOR THEY CHOOSE, CADETS ALSO TAKE **ROTC CLASSES** IN TACTICS, BASIC MILITARY SKILLS, LEADERSHIP FUNDAMENTALS, AND MILITARY HISTORY.

THEY HAVE **WEEKLY DRILLS** IN MARCHING, PHYS ED, COMBAT FIRST AID, HAND-TO-HAND FIGHTING, AND ALL MANNER OF ARMS.

ILLUSTRATIONS FROM *"THE ROTC MANUAL,"* 1968

Figure 35. Flash and sound distance estimation.

THE ROTC BUILDING, OFFICIALLY NAMED **EAST HALL**, IS ON THE EDGE OF **THE COMMONS**, IN THE HEART OF CAMPUS.

IT IS A RICKETY, REASSEMBLED **ARMY FIELD HOSPITAL** THAT SERVED AS THE FIRST STUDENT UNION. WHEN A NEW UNION WAS CONSTRUCTED RIGHT NEXT DOOR, THE OUTDATED BUILDING BECAME HOME TO ROTC. REGARDED AS AN EYESORE, IT HAS OFFICES FOR ROTC FACULTY, LOCKERS FOR CADETS, AND, UNBEKNOWNST TO MOST OUTSIDE ROTC, A SHOOTING RANGE IN THE BASEMENT AND A LARGE CACHE OF **WEAPONS AND AMMUNITION.**

OF THE 6,600 COMMISSIONED OFFICERS WHO DIED IN VIETNAM, OVER 5,000 ARE **ROTC GRADUATES.**

IN 1968, THE DEADLIEST YEAR IN THE WAR, MORE THAN 150,000 U.S. STUDENTS ARE ENROLLED IN ROTC.

AS **THE WAR** DRAGS ON AND **ANTIWAR PROTESTS** REACH A FEVER PITCH, ROTC FACILITIES AND ACTIVITIES BECOME **A MAIN TARGET** OF STUDENT PROTESTERS, FOR BEING A COG IN THE MILITARY MACHINE AND ANATHEMA TO A UNIVERSITY'S ACADEMIC MISSION. IN 1969 AND 1970, **DOZENS OF ROTC BUILDINGS** ARE ATTACKED BY PROTESTERS.

MANY ARE TORCHED.

ROTC OFF CAMPUS

KENT CITY HALL, 3 P.M.
I AGREE, CHIEF.

POLICE
WE'RE FACING THE **GREATEST THREAT** IN THE CITY'S HISTORY! WHAT'S THE STATUS OUT THERE TODAY?

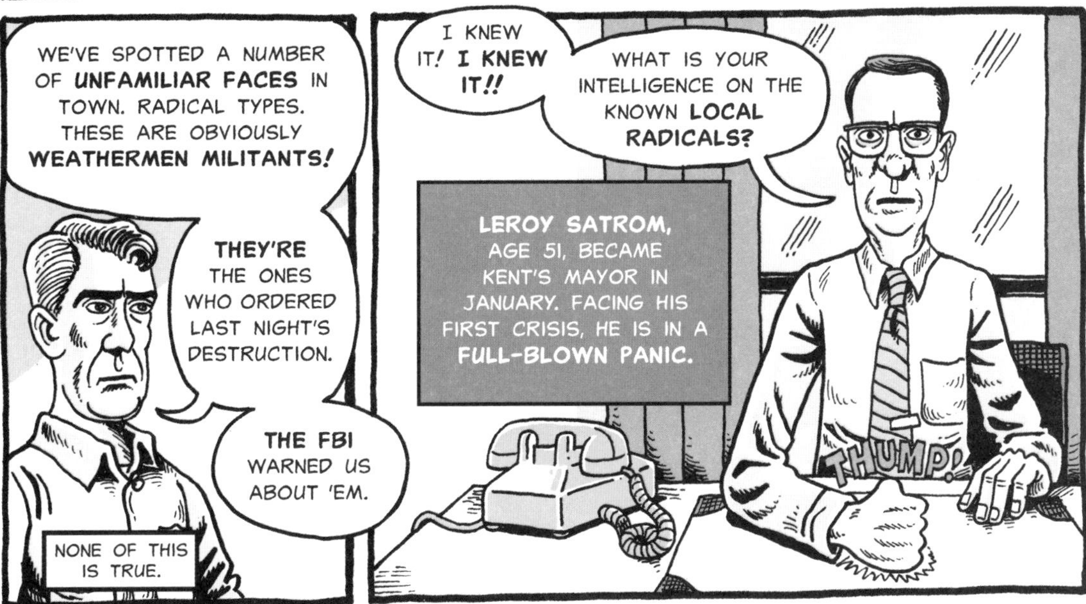
WE'VE SPOTTED A NUMBER OF **UNFAMILIAR FACES** IN TOWN. RADICAL TYPES. THESE ARE OBVIOUSLY **WEATHERMEN MILITANTS!**
THEY'RE THE ONES WHO ORDERED LAST NIGHT'S DESTRUCTION.
THE FBI WARNED US ABOUT 'EM.
NONE OF THIS IS TRUE.
I KNEW IT! **I KNEW IT!!**
WHAT IS YOUR INTELLIGENCE ON THE KNOWN **LOCAL RADICALS?**
LEROY SATROM, AGE 51, BECAME KENT'S MAYOR IN JANUARY. FACING HIS FIRST CRISIS, HE IS IN A **FULL-BLOWN PANIC.**
THUMP!

TWO OF THE WORST... ...UH, LESSEE... **ERICKSON AND EMMER...** WERE **JUST** RELEASED FROM JAIL ON WEDNESDAY.
IT'S **NO** COINCIDENCE TROUBLE FLARED UP SOON AFTER!
NONE OF THE FORMER SDS LEADERS TOOK PART IN THE WATER STREET RIOT, OR IN ANY OF THE PROTESTS THIS WEEKEND. MOST, IN FACT, FLED KENT AND NEVER RETURNED.

"THOSE TWO GOT **SIX MONTHS** FOR STORMING A CAMPUS BUILDING OVER, I DUNNO, SOME COMMIE DEMAND. THE HIGHWAY PATROL **ARRESTED** A WHOLE BUNCH OF THEM RADICALS!"
APRIL 1969

THAT LITTLE STUNT GOT SDS BOOTED OFF-A CAMPUS AND A BUNCH OF 'EM BANNED FROM SETTIN' FOOT ON UNIVERSITY GROUNDS.
THEM SDS-ERS HAVE BEEN LAYIN' LOW, BUT I GUESS NOT ANYMORE!

LOOK AT WHAT'S HAPPENIN' DOWN AT OHIO STATE! THOUSANDS RIOTING FOR DAYS, TH' NATIONAL GUARD CALLED IN, WIDESPREAD DAMAGE. WE'RE IN THE MIDDLE OF A COMMIE REVOLUTION, MAYOR!

"ONE OF MY MEN FOUND A PILE OF EMPTY POP BOTTLES BEHIND A BUILDING NEAR CAMPUS, OBVIOUSLY FOR MAKIN' MOLOTOV COCKTAILS!"

WE ALSO HAVE CREDIBLE INFO THAT WEATHERMEN RADICALS ARE SMUGGLIN' GUNS INTO TH' DORMS!
ALSO UNTRUE.

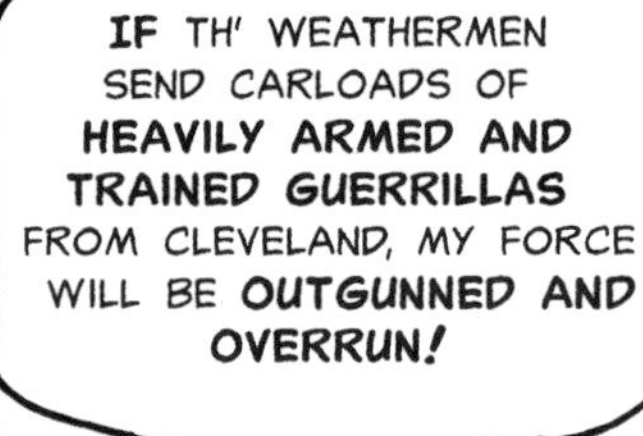
IF TH' WEATHERMEN SEND CARLOADS OF HEAVILY ARMED AND TRAINED GUERRILLAS FROM CLEVELAND, MY FORCE WILL BE OUTGUNNED AND OVERRUN!

CHIEF THOMPSON'S FEARS ARE ALL WILDLY INACCURATE.

MY GOD.

THERE ARE 21,000 STUDENTS AT THAT UNIVERSITY! IF THEY GO BERSERK, THEY'LL BURN THE TOWN TO THE GROUND!
HE ACTUALLY FEARED THAT STUDENTS WOULD RISE UP AS ONE.

I'M CALLING IN THE NATIONAL GUARD!

THE WEATHERMEN ARE AMERICA'S FORGOTTEN TERRORISTS, BUT IN 1970 THEY GENERATED THE SAME FEAR AMONG THE PUBLIC AND LAW ENFORCEMENT THAT JIHADISTS DO NOW.
THE WEATHERMEN ARE THE MILITANT RADICAL WING OF SDS. THEIR LEADERS ARE SOME OF THE BIGGEST STARS OF THE ANTIWAR LEFT.
THEY ARE KEY TO UNDERSTANDING THE CLASHING PASSIONS OF 1970.
WE ARE SDS!!
AFTER SEVERAL YEARS OF POLITICAL MANEUVERING, THE WEATHERMEN SEIZE CONTROL OF SDS AT THE DISASTROUS SDS NATIONAL CONVENTION IN CHICAGO IN JUNE 1969, WITH A CHAOTIC PARLIAMENTARY COUP THAT RIPS SDS APART.
THE WEATHERMEN THEN EXPEL THEIR RIVALS, PURGE THE MODERATES, AND MAKE THEIR REVOLUTIONARY VIOLENCE OFFICIAL SDS POLICY.

THE WEATHERMEN KICK OFF THEIR AGENDA IN OCTOBER 1969 WITH A PLANNED RAMPAGE, CALLED THE "DAYS OF RAGE," IN CHICAGO. THEY HOPE FOR 15,000 RADICALS, BUT BARELY 300 SHOW UP. IT IS A DEBACLE.

NIXON GLEEFULLY POINTS TO THE WEATHERMEN AS EMBLEMATIC OF ALL ANTIWAR PROTESTERS. WHEN HE RANTS ABOUT "BUMS" AND "THUGS," HE SPEAKS OF THE WEATHERMEN. THEIR EVER-MORE-OUTLANDISH EXTREMISM TARNISHES THE ENTIRE MOVEMENT...
POLICE
...AND PANICS THE AMERICAN PUBLIC.

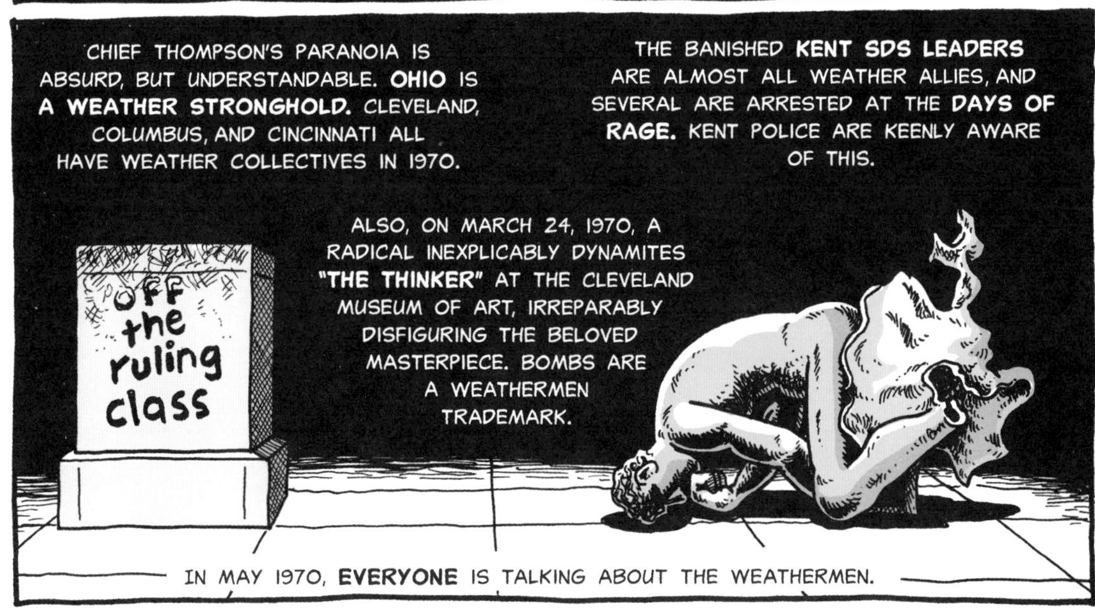
CHIEF THOMPSON'S PARANOIA IS ABSURD, BUT UNDERSTANDABLE. OHIO IS A WEATHER STRONGHOLD. CLEVELAND, COLUMBUS, AND CINCINNATI ALL HAVE WEATHER COLLECTIVES IN 1970.
THE BANISHED KENT SDS LEADERS ARE ALMOST ALL WEATHER ALLIES, AND SEVERAL ARE ARRESTED AT THE DAYS OF RAGE. KENT POLICE ARE KEENLY AWARE OF THIS.
off the ruling class
ALSO, ON MARCH 24, 1970, A RADICAL INEXPLICABLY DYNAMITES "THE THINKER" AT THE CLEVELAND MUSEUM OF ART, IRREPARABLY DISFIGURING THE BELOVED MASTERPIECE. BOMBS ARE A WEATHERMEN TRADEMARK.
IN MAY 1970, EVERYONE IS TALKING ABOUT THE WEATHERMEN.

IN REALITY, THE **VAST MAJORITY** OF SDS MEMBERS AND ANTIWAR ACTIVISTS **REJECT** THE WEATHERMEN AND THEIR CARTOONISH MILITANCY.

SDS MEMBERSHIP **PLUMMETS** THROUGHOUT FALL 1969. FOR A TIME THERE ARE **TWO** SDS, AS THE PURGED RIVALS OF THE WEATHERMEN FORM THEIR OWN VERSION.

BY DECEMBER, AN ORGANIZATION THAT JUST SIX MONTHS EARLIER BOASTED OF **100,000 ACTIVE MEMBERS** IS A SMOLDERING RUIN.

THE WEATHERMEN SHUTTER AND ABANDON THE SDS HQ.

AT THE DAWN OF 1970, SDS IS **FINISHED.**

THE REMAINING 100 OR SO CORE WEATHERMEN GO **UNDERGROUND** TO CONTINUE THEIR REVOLUTION. THE FBI COMICALLY INFLATES THEIR NUMBERS BY MANY FOLD.

WEATHER LEADER JOHN "J.J." JACOBS

WE ARE FIGHTING AGAINST EVERYTHING THAT IS **GOOD AND DECENT** IN HONKY AMERICA!

WE WILL **BURN AND LOOT AND DESTROY!**

THE WEATHERMEN ISSUE **A DECLARATION OF WAR** AGAINST THE U.S. GOVERNMENT AND UNLEASH **A BOMBING CAMPAIGN.** POLICE, GOVERNMENT BUILDINGS, AND CORPORATE INTERESTS ARE TARGETED. EACH EXPLOSION TRIGGERS **MASSIVE MEDIA COVERAGE.** WEATHERMEN FILL THE **FBI'S MOST WANTED LIST.** THEY BOMB MORE THAN 20 TARGETS DURING 1970.

ADDING TO THE PANIC OF KENT OFFICIALS IS THE REVELATION THAT ONE OF THE TOP LEADERS IS **TERRY ROBBINS**, WHO HELPED FOUND THE KENT SDS AND WAS JAILED FOR THE 1969 CAMPUS INCIDENT. HE IS RELEASED FROM THE COUNTY JAIL IN FEBRUARY 1970...

...AND VANISHES.

WHAT KENT POLICE DON'T KNOW IS THAT ROBBINS **IS DEAD!** HE DIED IN A **SECRET BOMB FACTORY** IN GREENWICH VILLAGE ON MARCH 6, 1970, WHEN A BOMB HE WAS CONSTRUCTING **WENT OFF.** TWO OTHER WEATHERMEN ARE KILLED AND THE ENTIRE BUILDING IS DESTROYED.

SUCH IS THE BLAST THAT THERE **ISN'T** ENOUGH LEFT OF ROBBINS TO IDENTIFY! IT WILL BE MONTHS BEFORE THE WEATHERMEN ADMIT IT WAS HIM.

THE TOWN HOUSE IS **SHOCKING PROOF** OF WEATHERMEN INTENTIONS. THE FBI NOW REALIZES THIS IS A SERIOUS TERRORIST ORGANIZATION.

MOM!
WHAT A SURPRISE!
HI, HONEY.
I BROUGHT YOU THOSE SUMMER CLOTHES YOU WANTED.

I... ALSO WANTED TO MAKE SURE YOU WERE STEERING WELL CLEAR OF ALL THE NONSENSE DOWN HERE.

NONSENSE? WHAT ARE YOU TALKING ABOUT?
SANDRA!

THERE WAS AN AWFUL RIOT IN DOWNTOWN KENT LAST NIGHT! IT WAS ALL OVER THE NEWS!
REALLY? I DON'T KNOW ANYTHING ABOUT IT.
I WASN'T DOWNTOWN LAST NIGHT.

GUESS I DIDN'T HAVE TO WORRY.

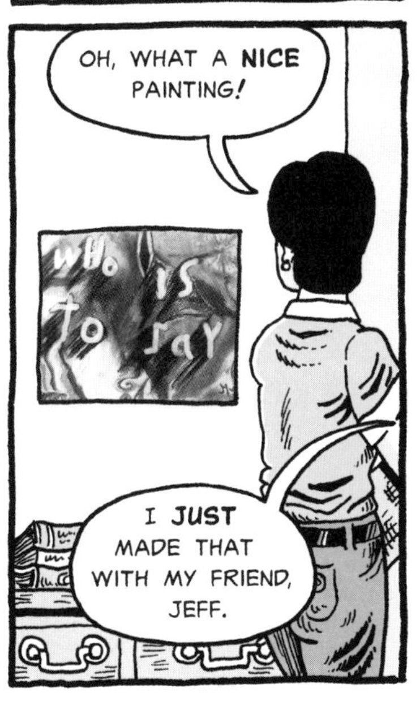
OH, WHAT A NICE PAINTING!
who is to say
I JUST MADE THAT WITH MY FRIEND, JEFF.

who is to say
FRIEND?

APRIL 12
JB's
HI, DAD. IT'S ME.

JB's
ALLISON! GLAD YOU CALLED. WHAT IS GOING ON OVER THERE? A STUDENT RIOT? EVEN THE PITTSBURGH MEDIA HERE IS REPORTING ON IT.
OH, IT WAS JUST A BUNCH OF ANGRY KIDS WHO HAD WAY TOO MUCH TO DRINK.

I DON'T UNDERSTAND WHY THEY DID IT. MAKES NO SENSE.
I UNDERSTAND THE ANGER... WITH NIXON, THE WAR, EVEN THE UNIVERSITY.
I'M ANGRY, TOO.

I ALSO READ THAT THE NATIONAL GUARD WAS SENT TO OHIO STATE TO STAMP OUT PROTESTS THERE. THIS IS NO JOKE, ALLISON!

THOSE ARE AMATEUR SOLDIERS. THEY'RE SCARED AND JUMPY. STAY CLEAR OF THEM!
THERE'S NO GUARD HERE, DAD.

YES, BUT I KNOW GOVERNOR RHODES! THAT GUY SENDS IN THE GUARD WITH THE SLIGHTEST EXCUSE!
JUST... BE CAREFUL, OKAY?
I WILL.
I PROMISE.

5 P.M., BACK IN RICHFIELD
OKAY, LISSEN UP!

WE RECEIVED NEW ORDERS! WE'RE GOING TO KENT STATE.
ARR!
GROAN!

THAT'S RIGHT, GIRLS! SEEMS TH' KIDDIES AT KENT TRASHED TH' TOWN LAST NIGHT. WE'RE TO RESUPPLY AT TH' RUBBER BOWL IN AKRON, THEN MOVE IN AND RESTORE LAW AND ORDER.

I CAN'T BELIEVE THIS SHIT! HOW LONG ARE WE GONNA BE PULLIN' DUTY?

I HEARD ON TH' RADIO THAT TH' RADICALS ARE ON A RAMPAGE AT KENT STATE!

WORD IS THEY SHOT SOME COPS AND BURNED A BUNCHA STORES. TH' STUDENTS ARE ARMED AND SHOOTIN' AT TH' COPS FROM DORM WINDOWS!
THERE'S SNIPERS IN TH' WOODS AROUND TOWN, TOO.
NONE OF THIS IS REMOTELY TRUE.

HOLY CRAP! THOSE SDS JERKS HAVE BEEN ASKIN' FOR IT FOR YEARS!
NOW WE GOTTA CLEAN IT UP!

KARLOVIC!
SIR!

I UNDERSTAND YOU'RE A KENT STATE STUDENT?
YES, SIR, I AM.
GOOD. YOU RIDE WITH ME. I NEED SOMEONE WHO KNOWS HIS WAY AROUND.

LOOKIT YOU, FRANKY! YER FIRST DUTY AND YOU'RE ALREADY INDESPENSABLE!

7:45 P.M.
ENOUGH IS ENOUGH! ROTC MUST BE DRIVEN FROM CAMPUS!
TONIGHT'S TH' NIGHT!
PREACH IT!
LET'S DO IT!

IT'S AN ABOMINATION TH' UNIVERSITY SUPPORTS TH' WAR MACHINE!
YEAH!

DOWN WITH ROT-SEE!
DOWN WITH ROT-SEE!
DOWN WITH ROT-SEE!

WE NEED MORE PEOPLE! LET'S MARCH TO TH' DORMS!

OUT OF THE DORMS AND INTO THE STREET! OUT OF THE DORMS AND INTO THE STREET!

HIIIIIIIIIIISSSSSSSSSS
IS IT TRUE?
IS IT TRUE?
THAT YOU AND ADAM?
MAY DO ANYTHING?
MAY DO ANYTHING?
IN THE GARDEN?

HIIIIIIIISS
The Serpent
JEAN-CLAUDE VAN ITALLIE

MEANWHILE, IN AKRON...
THE DRAFT HOUSE IS ON THE LEFT, BILL.
SEE IT.

THE Draft House
FINE FOOD
THE GIRLS PICKED THIS JOINT. WONDER IF THEY'RE HERE YET?

I'M HAPPY TO BE OUT OF KENT! IT'S TOO NUTS THERE!
AND TH' DUMBASS MAYOR CLOSED ALL TH' KENT BARS!

SO WE'D HAFTA COME INTO AKRON FOR A BEER ANYWAYS.

8 P.M.
RUMBLE RUUUUUUBLE RUMBLE RUUUUMBLE
RRRRRRRRROOOOOOOAARRR

ROOOAR
RRRRRRRRR

JEEZUS! WE'RE HITTIN' 'EM WITH EVERYTHING WE'VE GOT!

8:10 P.M.
YAAAEEEOOOW!!
WOO!
OW!
YEH!

DOWN WITH ROT-SEE!!
DOWN WITH ROT-SEE!!

CRASH!!
SMASH!
THUD!
THUD!
KRASH!
THUD!

WHAT'S GOING ON OUT THERE? THERE'S A BIG CROWD ON THE COMMONS.

OMIGAWD! THEY'RE ATTACKING THE ROT-SEE BUILDING!
WHAT?

STAND BACK! ROAD FLARE!
SSSSS
WHOA!

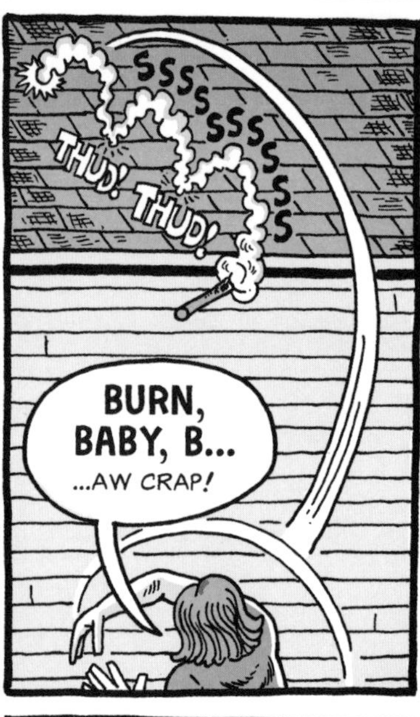
SSSSSSSSSSS
THUD! THUD!
BURN, BABY, B... ...AW CRAP!

CHIEF SCHWARTZMILLER! I'M GLENN FRANK. I'M A FACULTY MONITOR.
AREN'T YOU GOING TO STOP THIS?
POLICE

I ONLY HAVE 18 MEN HERE, PROFESSOR. THERE MUST BE A THOUSAND KIDS OUT THERE!
POLICE
THE HIGHWAY PATROL WAS SUPPOSED TO BE HERE BY NOW TO ASSIST.
I DON'T KNOW WHAT THE DELAY IS.

I JUST PUT IN AN EMERGENCY CALL TO THE SHERIFF. DEPUTIES ARE ON THEIR WAY.
POLICE
AS SOON AS THEY ARRIVE, WE'LL MAKE OUR MOVE!

8:53 P.M.
THEY'VE BEEN AT IT FOR AN HOUR! THEY FINALLY GOT A FIRE STARTED.
WHERE ARE THE COPS?

BOO!!
NO!
BOO!
NO IDEA. BUT THERE'S THE FIREMEN AT LAST!
KENT FIRE

LET IT BURN!!
BURN!!
BURN
KENT FIRE

HEY! LEGGO!
LET IT BURN!

BOO!
BOO!!
KENT FIRE
FOOSH!

GET TH' HOSES!
STAB 'EM!
STAB!

MEANWHILE, AT AN ACADEMIC SUMMIT IN MASON CITY, IOWA.
SORRY TO INTERRUPT DINNER, PRESIDENT WHITE. THE CALLER SAYS SHE'S YOUR HOUSEKEEPER.

CORA?
ROBERT WHITE, AGE 61, PRESIDENT OF KENT STATE
WHAT'S THE MATTER?

THERE'S A RIOT ON C-CAMPUS! THEY'RE ATTACKING ROTC!
WHAT!?!

IT'S A HUGE GROUP OF STUDENTS! I'M WORRIED THEY'LL ATTACK THE PRESIDENT'S HOUSE NEXT. WHAT SHOULD I DO?
MY GOD.
OK, STAY CALM. I'LL CALL VICE PRESIDENT MATSON AND FIND OUT WHAT'S GOING ON!

9:14 P.M.
RING!

MATSON.
BOB? IT'S WHITE! WHAT THE HECK IS HAPPENING THERE?
THE BASTARDS WRECKED ROT-SEE!
I WAS JUST ABOUT TO CALL YOU.

WE'RE PUTTING OUR EMERGENCY PLAN INTO ACTION. THE HIGHWAY PATROL IS ON ITS WAY. THEY'LL DEAL WITH THOSE CLOWNS.
I'LL FLY HOME AS SOON AS I CAN.
BLINK! BLINK!

HANG ON, PRESIDENT. I HAVE A CALL. COULD BE NEWS.
MATSON HERE.

WHAT THE HELL DO YOU MEAN THE NATIONAL GUARD IS MOVING IN!?!

9:17 P.M.
TO HELL WITH THIS! WE'RE LEAVING!

WE'LL COME BACK WHEN THE CAMPUS COPS DEAL WITH THIS CROWD.
I'M NOT SURE THAT FIRE IS OUT!
WE'LL HAFTA CHANCE IT.
LEAVE TH' DAMAGED HOSES! LET'S MOVE!!

TEN MINUTES LATER...
OK, TH' FIREMEN ARE CLEAR!
FOOM!!
FIRE GAS!

LOOKS LIKE THE COPS GOT REINFORCEMENTS.
IS THAT TEAR GAS?
IT'S WATER STREET ALL OVER AGAIN.
OH MAN.

YAAA!
SHIT!
KOFF!
GAG!
BOOSH!

9:45 P.M.
TURN OUT THE LIGHTS, ALLISON.
I CAN'T SEE WHAT'S HAPPENING OUT THERE!
OK.
KLIK!

THE PROTESTERS HAVE ALL BEEN DRIVEN AWAY. LET'S HOPE THAT TEAR GAS DOESN'T DRIFT OVER HERE!
HEY! SOMETHING IS GLOWING INSIDE THE BUILDING!

WHOOSH!
POP! CRAK!
BANG! CRASH!
POW!
SNAP!
BOOM!

BURN, BABY, BURN!
I THOUGHT THAT FIRE WAS OUT!
TH' FIRE DEPARTMENT IS BACK... BUT THEY CAN'T SAVE IT NOW!
WOW!

LISTEN TO ALL THOSE EXPLOSIONS! THAT PLACE MUST HAVE BEEN FULL OF AMMO!
POP! POP! POP!
BANG! BANG!
BOOM! BANG!

THIS SOLVES NOTHING.

HOLY CRAP, CAPTAIN! LOOK AT TH' SKY GLOWING! TH-THE WHOLE DAMN TOWN IS IN FLAMES!
RRRRRRRRRRRR

ROGER THAT.
THIS ROAD WILL TAKE US RIGHT DOWNTOWN, DOES IT NOT, KARLOVIC?
CORRECT, SIR.

WE'RE MOVIN' IN FROM THREE DIRECTIONS! WE'LL HIT THESE PUNKS FAST AND HARD! TH' COPS SAY THERE'S THOUSANDS OF STUDENTS MOVIN' AROUND TH' CAMPUS!
NO REPORTS OF SNIPERS... YET!

GENERAL DEL CORSO HIMSELF RUSHED UP FROM COLUMBUS HQ TO OVERSEE THIS OPERATION! SO BIG BRASS IS ON HAND!

DO YOU KNOW WHERE WALLS ELEMENTARY SCHOOL IS, KARLOVIC? WE UNLOAD THERE, THEN MOVE ONTO CAMPUS.
YES, SIR. IT'S A FEW BLOCKS NORTH OF CAMPUS.

STAY ON YER TOES!
IT'S DARK AND TH' RADICALS HAVE LOTS OF COVER. THEY KNOW THE TERRAIN AND WE DON'T.
RRRRRRRR
U.S. ARMY

WE'LL SEND OUT JEEP PATROLS IMMEDIATELY. IT'S ALREADY PAST CURFEW, SO IF YOU SPOT ANYONE OUTSIDE...
RRRRRRR RRRR

...BUST THEIR ASS!

10:10 P.M.
STUDENTS REGROUP AT PRENTICE GATE.
KOFF!
MAN! THAT WAS ROUGH! WHEEZE!
UGH.

WE STILL GOT ABOUT A HUNDRED KIDS HERE! LET'S MARCH DOWNTOWN!
SCREW THAT! I'VE HAD ENOUGH. KOFF KOFF!
WHAT'S THAT NOISE?
BRING the WAR
RUUUUMMMMMMMBLE

CLANK CLANK CLANK CLANK
RRRRRRRRRRRRRRRRRR
RUMBLE!
Esso

RRRRRUMMMMMBLE
OMIGOD.
CLANK CLANK CLANK CLANK CLANK
BRING the WAR HOME

RUUUUUUMMMMBLE
PIZZA
8GP27
U.S. ARMY SA2728
107 CAV
CLANK CLANK CLANK
RATTLE RATTLE RATTLE

THE Draft House
FINE FOOD

PING! BONG!
BING!
BONG!
BEEP!
OH YEAH! JUST TOPPED YOUR SCORE, BILL!
HAHA.
OKAY, CHAMP.
NEXT ROUND IS ON ME.

LIVE
KENT STATE
Pabst Blue Ribbon BEER

H-HOLY SHIT! THE KENT STATE ROT-SEE BUILDING IS ON FIRE!
SAY WHAT?
BONG! BING! PING!

WHAT HAVE THOSE IDIOTS DONE?

YOU ARE IN VIOLATION OF THE OHIO RIOT ACT! DISPERSE AT ONCE!
U.S. ARMY

I'M OUTTA HERE!
SCREW YOU!

ADJUTANT GENERAL SYLVESTER DEL CORSO, COMMANDER OF THE OHIO NATIONAL GUARD
BRIGADIER GENERAL ROBERT CANTERBURY, HIS TOP FIELD OFFICER

THIS HAS GONE ON LONG ENOUGH.
AGREED.

DON'T MOLLYCODDLE THESE STUDENTS, MAJOR!
I WANT THIS CAMPUS CLEARED AND SECURED!
YES, SIR, GENERAL. RIGHT AWAY!

GUARD!
LET'S CLEAR 'EM OUT!

RAAAAWR!

WHAT DIDJA THINK, JEFF?
LOVED IT, TIM! I SAW ITALLIE'S "AMERICA HURRAH" IN NEW YORK AND...

HOLY SHIT!
IS THAT ROT-SEE?

PANT! PANT! SOLDIERS ARE COMING!
HUH?

THERE'S H-HUNDREDS OF THEM!! THEY'RE MARCHING ACROSS CAMPUS FROM ALL DIRECTIONS!
BUT WE'RE NOT PROTESTERS!

THEY DON'T CARE! THEY'RE ATTACKING ALL STUDENTS! THEY'RE GOING NUTS!
GET INSIDE A DORM FAST!

CRAP! I LIVE ON THE OTHER SIDE OF CAMPUS! I'M CUT OFF!
I'M IN TRI-TOWERS.
LET'S GO THERE!

HERE THEY COME!
RUN!

THERE'S SOME MORE! GAS 'EM!
JONES

SSSSSSSSSSSSSSSSS

KOFF!
YAAA!
WE WERE AT A PLAAAAAY!
SSSSS
BONK!

KOFF! LET'S CUT ACROSS TH' GREEN TO TRI-TOWERS!
HACK!
RIGHT BEHIND YA!

WE GOTTA PROTECT TH' FIREMEN UNTIL THEY GET THIS BLAZE OUT!
KARLOVIC! BROWN! TAKE TH' LEFT FLANK!

J-JESUS CHRIST! JESUS CHRIST!
KEEP YER COOL!

HALT!
D-D-DON'T MOVE!
WHOA! HOLD ON!

I'M A FACULTY MONITOR! SEE THE BLUE ARMBAND?
I NEED TO SPEAK TO YOUR COMMANDING OFFICER.

KRAK!
GIT YER ASS OUTTA HERE!

I'M NOT FALLIN' FER THAT TRICK!

GASP!
THUD!
THUD!
THUD!

GET OFF OUR CAMPUS!
WH-WHERE ARE THEY?
SOMEWHERE IN TH' TREES!

SHIT!
THUD!
THUD!

CALM DOWN. I'LL TAKE CARE OF 'EM FOR YA.
TH-THANKS, OFFICER.

BOOF!

GASP!
KOFF! KOFF!
BAMF!

I'VE NEVER BEEN THIS SCARED IN MY LIFE, FRANK!

ON THE OTHER SIDE OF CAMPUS, GEN. DEL CORSO LEADS A SWEEP THROUGH THE DORM AREA.
TROMP!
TROMP
TROMP!

SYLVESTER "TONY" DEL CORSO, AGE 57, JOINED THE GUARD AT 15. A HIGHLY DECORATED WWII COMBAT VETERAN, HE WAS PICKED BY GOVERNOR RHODES TO LEAD THE GUARD IN 1968. THEY SHARE A ZEAL TO USE TROOPS TO CRUSH CIVIL UNREST. DEL CORSO FLAGRANTLY POLITICIZED HIS POSITION, WHICH IS UNPRECEDENTED. HE URGED HIS MEN TO VOTE FOR NIXON! THAT LED TO LOUD CALLS FOR HIM TO BE FIRED, BUT RHODES STUCK BY HIM. THE GENERAL DESPISES ANTIWAR ACTIVISTS, WHO HE BELIEVES ARE ALL COMMUNISTS.

THERE! I WANT ALL THOSE STUDENTS INSIDE A BUILDING!
NOW!

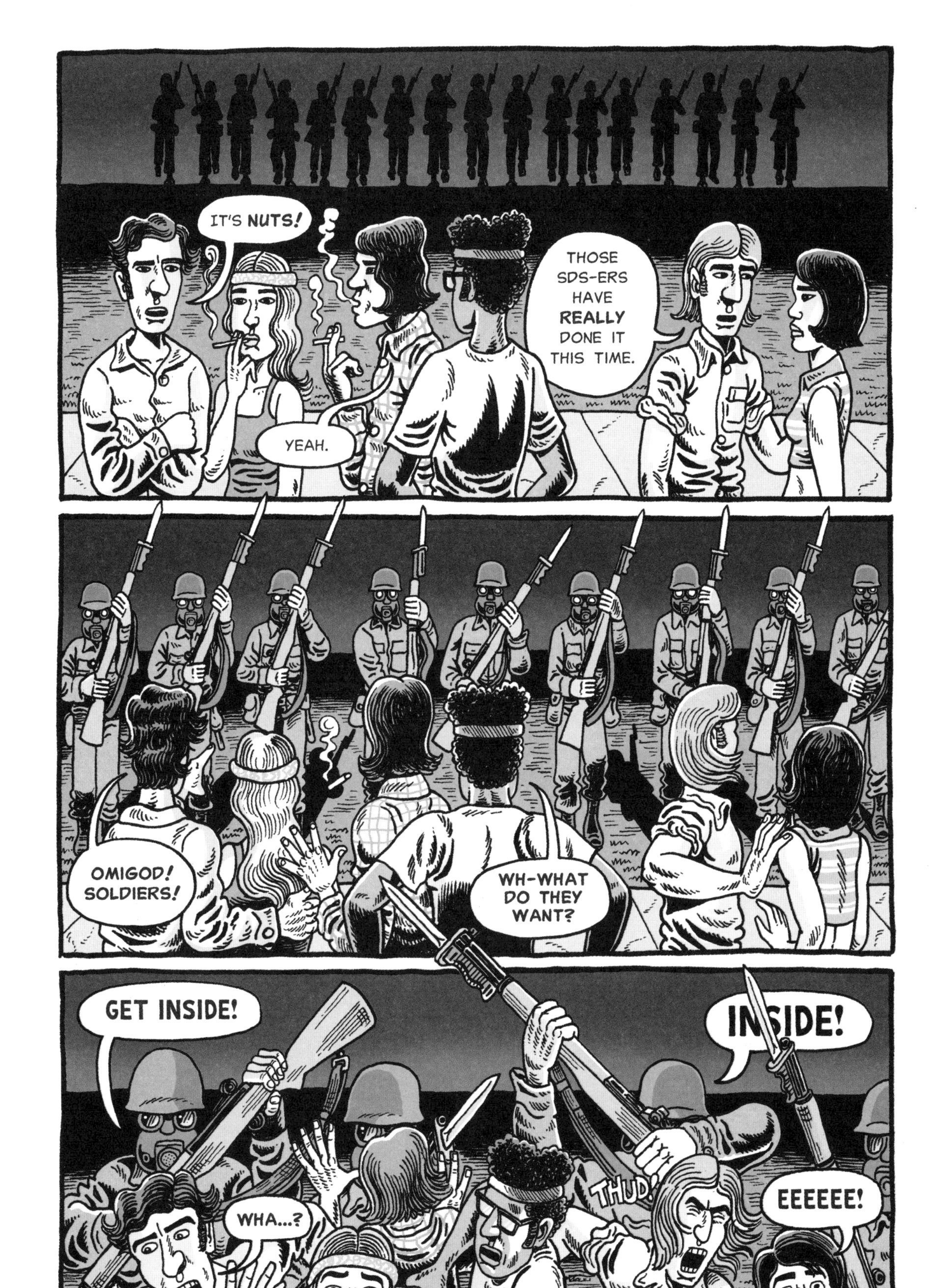

IT'S NUTS!
YEAH.
THOSE SDS-ERS HAVE REALLY DONE IT THIS TIME.
OMIGOD! SOLDIERS!
WH-WHAT DO THEY WANT?
GET INSIDE!
INSIDE!
WHA...?
THUD!
EEEEEE!
AAAA!

THOP THOP THOP THOP
ATTENTION!

THOP THOP THOP TH
GET AWAY FROM THE WINDOWS!
SSSSSS

AUGH!
WE'RE LOOKING FOR SNIPERS!
THE BASTARDS GASSED THE DORM!
KAFF!
KOFF!

SNIPERS? WHERE DO THEY THINK THEY ARE?
SAIGON?
IT'S CRAZY!
THEY'RE ATTACKING INNOCENT STUDENTS!

CLOSE ALL THE ROOM DOORS! STAY IN THE HALL! AND GET SOME TOWELS TO SEAL THE DOORS!
QUICK!
KLIK!

IT'S LIKE A **HUNDRED DEGREES** IN THIS HALL, WITH NO AIR CIRCULATING.
GROAN.
KOFF KOFF!
Z
SNIFF.
SNIFF.

GONNA BE A **LONG** NIGHT.

THOP THOP THOP TH P

ATLANTIC CITY
S

SANDY! THERE'S ARMY JEEPS ROARING UP AND DOWN TH' ROAD!

AND THERE'S SOME KIND OF FIRE ON CAMPUS!
SOMETHING BIG!

GENERAL CANTERBURY! I'VE SWEPT THE SOUTHEAST QUADRANT. ALL THE STUDENTS ARE INSIDE.
SENTRIES ARE POSTED.
EXCELLENT, GENERAL.
SQUADS HAVE CLEARED THE REST OF CAMPUS AND LOCKED DOWN THE TOWN.

NICELY DONE, BOB. I'LL BE HEADING BACK TO COLUMBUS TOMORROW SINCE YOU HAVE THE SITUATION WELL IN HAND HERE.
I'LL CALL IN THE REPORT.

11:55 P.M.
HQ, THIS IS CANTERBURY.
THE SITUATION IN KENT... IS UNDER CONTROL.

I CAN'T BELIEVE TH' CAPTAIN GAVE US STREET PATROL.
WE'VE BEEN ON DUTY SINCE 6 A.M.!
RRRRRR

DAMN! THESE SIDE STREETS ARE PITCH-BLACK! ALL THESE DARK ALLEYS AND DRIVEWAYS...

THERE COULD BE SNIPERS HIDIN' ANYWHERE AND WE'D NEVER SEE 'EM!
...UNTIL IT WUZ TOO LATE!

QUIT BEIN' SUCH A PUSSY! NO RADICAL SHITS ARE GETTIN' ME WITHOUT A FIGHT!
RRRRRR

14243
145TH
RRRR

THANKS FOR TURNING KENT INTO A PRISON, FASCISTS!
SIEG HEIL!

STOP TH' DAMN JEEP, KARLOVIC!
WHA...? JEEZUS, PERKINS!
SCREEE!
KRASH!

GRRR.
KLIK!

WHO WANTS TO BE FIRST, YOU BASTARDS!?!

THAT'S WHAT I THOUGHT!
SLAM!

BEFORE THIS IS OVER, I'M GONNA **TEACH** SOME OF THESE PUNKS A HARD LESSON!

K
RRRR

K
THOP! THOP! THOP!

GOOD THING WE CAN CRASH AT **MY BROTHER'S.** KENT IS SEALED OFF.
TAKE A LEFT.

SIGH.

SUNDAY, MAY 3
10 A.M.
EIGHT HUNDRED GUARDSMEN NOW OCCUPY CAMPUS. ANOTHER 400 PATROL THE TOWN.

KLIK!
WKYC
3
NBC

WOW. **LOOK** AT ALL **THE PRESS** HERE TODAY!
GUESS WE'RE A **BIG STORY.**

AND THERE'S A BUNCH OF **SIGHTSEERS** CHECKIN' OUT THE CRAZY COLLEGE RADICALS. **THAT** COUPLE BROUGHT **A PICNIC LUNCH!**
SURREAL.

I LIKE WATCHING OVER THESE **COLLEGE GIRLS** A LOT MORE THAN UGLY **TEAMSTERS!**
I HEAR THAT.

IS THAT A **REAL** GUN?
OF COURSE!

DON'T WORRY. IF YOU BEHAVE YOURSELF, I PROMISE **NOT** TO SHOOT YOU!
GIGGLE.

YEP. A **LOT** BETTER THAN TEAMSTERS!

YOU, TOO, SWEETS!

PAMPERED LITTLE **BITCH.**

TH' ORDERS THIS MORNING WERE TA BE **FRIENDLY** WITH STUDENTS TO "EASE TENSIONS."
HOW WE SUPPOSED TA BE FRIENDLY WITH **THAT?**
I JUST HOPE TA GET SOME **SHUT-EYE** TODAY. I DIDN'T GIT OFF DUTY UNTIL **OH-300!**
NOTE: THAT'S 3 A.M.

THE KENT WATER FACILITY
CITY of KENT WATER PLANT

I **CALLED** MY GIRLFRIEND FROM A PAY PHONE. SHE'S GONNA BRING US SOME **LUNCH.**
AWRIGHT! THANKS, FRANK. A WEEK OF **GUARD CHOW** IS ENOUGH.

I CAN'T GET OVER LAST NIGHT. **THAT** WUZ **IN-TENSE!**

YA KNOW... TH' STUDENTS **OUTNUMBER** US HERE LIKE **20 TO 1!** IF THEY ALL TURN ON US, WE DON'T HAVE **A CHANCE!**
I DON'T LIKE THIS **AT ALL!**

I HEARD SOME OF **TH' OFFICERS** TALKIN'...
...ABOUT RADICALS IN **RED HEADBANDS.**

THEY WUZ TH' ONES DIRECTIN' TH' MOB, **NOT** STUDENTS.
THESE GUYS WERE **OLDER.**
THEY'RE **PROFESSIONALS,** FROM CHICAGO OR DETROIT!

THAT'S WHY WE'RE GUARDING TH' TOWN **WATER SUPPLY.** SO TH' RADICALS DON'T **SPIKE** TH' DRINKING WATER...
...WITH LSD!
JEEZUS!

NUMEROUS **RUMORS** ROAR THROUGH THE GUARD RANKS, BECOMING PROGRESSIVELY MORE **PREPOSTEROUS.**

PROFESSIONAL COMMUNIST MASTERMINDS ARE BEHIND EVERYTHING. MACHINE GUNS WERE DISCOVERED HIDDEN NEAR BRADY LAKE. CACHES OF HEAVY ARMS ARE STASHED IN THE CORNFIELDS OUTSIDE OF KENT, WAITING FOR BUSLOADS OF WEATHERMEN GUERRILLAS, COMBAT-TRAINED IN CUBA, WHO ARE ON THE WAY TO TOWN. THE MORE **THE OUTLANDISH STORIES** SPREAD, THE **JUMPIER** THE EXHAUSTED GUARDSMEN BECOME.

ALL STUDENTS, NOT JUST THE PROTESTERS, ARE NOW SUSPECT. **TENSIONS MOUNT** BETWEEN STUDENTS AND GUARDSMEN AS THE DAY WEARS ON.

GENERAL DEL CORSO SEES A COMMIE PLOT AROUND EVERY CORNER IN KENT, WHICH ONLY **ADDS** TO THE PARANOIA. SO DOES KENT POLICE CHIEF **ROY THOMPSON,** AND THE CHIEF OF THE OHIO STATE HIGHWAY PATROL, **ROBERT CHIARAMONTE,** WHO RECKLESSLY WARNS THAT STUDENTS ARE LIKELY **ARMED AND DANGEROUS.**

THIS IS A REFLECTION, OF COURSE, OF **NIXON'S** FEAR OF THE STUDENT LEFT. HE BELIEVES **SDS** TAKES ORDERS DIRECTLY FROM MOSCOW.

THE WEATHERMEN ARE CERTAINLY COMMUNIST REVOLUTIONARIES, BUT TO DISMISS THE **ENTIRE ANTIWAR MOVEMENT** AS NOTHING MORE THAN REDS IS JUST POLITICAL GRANDSTANDING.

CIVILIANS IN TOWN CHIME IN WITH **MORE** OUTLANDISH CLAIMS.

THIS SOUNDS KINDA CRAZY TO ME... BUT I'LL TAKE A NICE, QUIET DUTY LIKE THIS OVER PLAYIN' TAG WITH RADICAL CREEPS IN TH' DARK.
U.S. ARMY

LAST NIGHT WAS NOT TYPICAL OF KENT STATE.
THAT WASN'T MY UNIVERSITY!
IT REALLY PISSES ME OFF!

OH YEAH. HERE.

ELECTRICAL TAPE?
WHAT'S THIS FOR?

ALL TH' GUYS ARE COVERING UP THEIR NAME TAGS.

SO TH' RADICALS CAN'T TRACK US DOWN AT HOME LATER.
UNLESS YOU WANT A MOLOTOV COCKTAIL SAILING THROUGH YOUR FRONT WINDOW... COVER UP!

VIC

RRRRRR
107 CAV
13
B73342

GASP! ARE YOU POINTING YOUR GUN AT US?
AT MY CHILD!?!

WHAT THE HELL IS WRONG WITH YOU?

JERKS!!
RRRRRRR
107 CAV

YAWN!

CHECKPOINT!
LET'S SEE YER **STUDENT I.D.**

AGAIN? THIS IS THE **THIRD TIME** JUST WALKIN' ACROSS CAMPUS!
TOUGH.

I'M ONLY TRYING TO GET **HOME**, MAN. I LIVE OFF SUMMIT STREET, RIGHT PAST TH...
SHUDDUP.
K
JEFF MILLER

OKAY. GO HOME.

K

IT'S A DAMN **POLICE STATE!**

THE OHIO NATIONAL GUARD, WITH 16,000 MEN, WAS FORMED IN 1802 AS A STATE MILITIA. GUARD UNITS ARE SPREAD ACROSS OHIO. **THE 145TH INFANTRY** IS BASED IN NEARBY STOW, A SUBURB OF AKRON. **THE 107TH ARMORED CAVALRY** IS BASED IN CLEVELAND.

UNLIKE TODAY'S NATIONAL GUARD, DURING THE VIETNAM WAR MOST GUARD UNITS **SERVED STATESIDE.** IT'S A WAY FOR DRAFT-AGE MEN TO AVOID JUNGLE COMBAT. IT'S A CUSHY DEAL, BUT BECOMES LESS SO AS THE COUNTRY **DISINTEGRATES** INTO NEAR CIVIL WAR.

THE OHIO GUARD IS SENT IN TO CONTROL **LABOR STRIKES**, AS IN RICHFIELD, TO CRUSH THE LARGE **AFRICAN AMERICAN UPRISINGS** IN CLEVELAND, AKRON, AND CINCINNATI, AND NOW, IN 1970, TO SMOTHER **STUDENT PROTESTS** ROILING THE COLLEGE CAMPUSES.

THE GLENVILLE RIOT, 1968

UPON ENLISTING, GUARDSMEN ARE SENT TO **U.S. ARMY BOOT CAMP** FOR BASIC TRAINING. ONCE PLACED IN A GUARD UNIT IN OHIO, THEY HAVE TO REPORT FOR SCHEDULED DRILLS EVERY MONTH, NORMALLY ON WEEKENDS. THIS GIVES BIRTH TO THEIR DERISIVE LABEL OF **"WEEKEND WARRIORS."**

GUARDSMEN EARN $12.80 A DAY WHILE ON DUTY AND ARE ALWAYS **"ON CALL."** IF NEEDED, THEY HAVE TO DROP EVERYTHING, LEAVE SCHOOL OR WORK BEHIND, AND REPORT FOR DUTY. FAIL TO DO SO, AND A MAN COULD LOSE HIS GUARD SPOT AND BE **DRAFTED** INTO THE REGULAR ARMY AND SHIPPED TO VIETNAM.

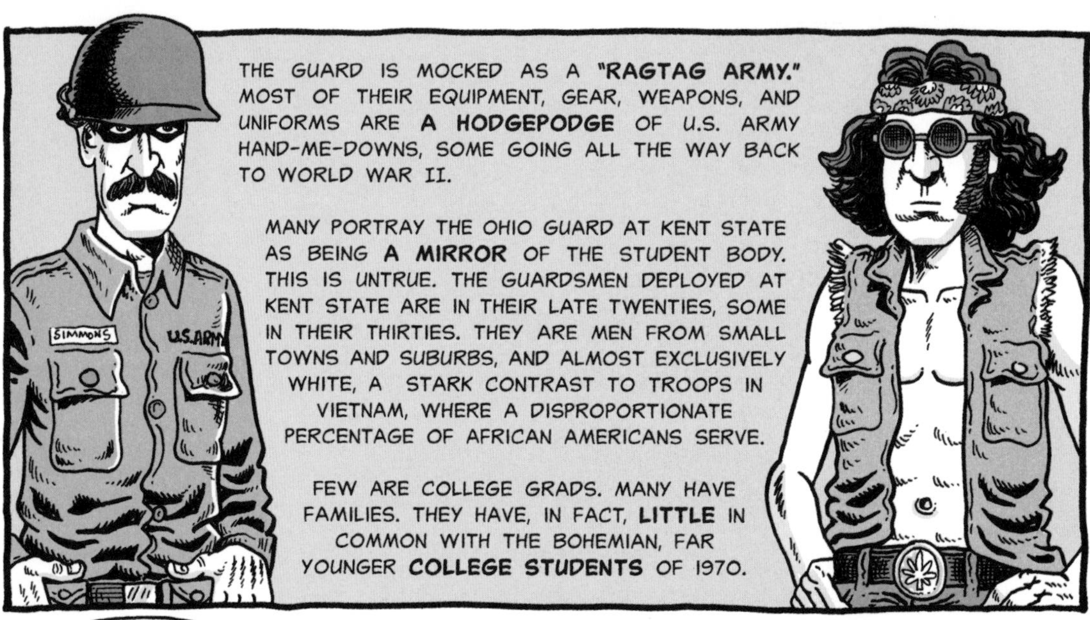
THE GUARD IS MOCKED AS A **"RAGTAG ARMY."** MOST OF THEIR EQUIPMENT, GEAR, WEAPONS, AND UNIFORMS ARE **A HODGEPODGE** OF U.S. ARMY HAND-ME-DOWNS, SOME GOING ALL THE WAY BACK TO WORLD WAR II.
MANY PORTRAY THE OHIO GUARD AT KENT STATE AS BEING **A MIRROR** OF THE STUDENT BODY. THIS IS UNTRUE. THE GUARDSMEN DEPLOYED AT KENT STATE ARE IN THEIR LATE TWENTIES, SOME IN THEIR THIRTIES. THEY ARE MEN FROM SMALL TOWNS AND SUBURBS, AND ALMOST EXCLUSIVELY WHITE, A STARK CONTRAST TO TROOPS IN VIETNAM, WHERE A DISPROPORTIONATE PERCENTAGE OF AFRICAN AMERICANS SERVE.
FEW ARE COLLEGE GRADS. MANY HAVE FAMILIES. THEY HAVE, IN FACT, **LITTLE** IN COMMON WITH THE BOHEMIAN, FAR YOUNGER **COLLEGE STUDENTS** OF 1970.
SIMMONS
U.S. ARMY

GOVERNOR JIM RHODES IS THE COMMANDER IN CHIEF OF THE GUARD. HE HAS JUST ARRIVED IN KENT AND IS HOPPING MAD.
SHAMEFUL.
ABSOLUTELY SHAMEFUL.
RHODES, AGE 60, IS OHIO'S TWO-TERM GOVERNOR. HE'S A FOLKSY, DOWN-HOME **GLAD-HANDER,** BUT IS ALSO A **LAW-AND-ORDER STRONGMAN** WHO DOESN'T HESITATE TO USE MILITARY FORCE. INDEED, RHODES DELIGHTS IN IT.
HE SENDS OUT THE GUARD MORE THAN ANY OTHER U.S. GOVERNOR, **40 TIMES** IN THE PREVIOUS TWO YEARS. OHIO IS ALSO ONE OF ONLY TWO STATES THAT ORDERS ITS GUARDSMEN TO CARRY LOADED GUNS IN CIVIL DISTURBANCES.
RHODES CAN'T SERVE ANOTHER CONSECUTIVE TERM AS GOVERNOR, SO HE'S SEEKING A SPOT ON THE NOVEMBER BALLOT AS THE **GOP CANDIDATE** FOR U.S. SENATE. HE IS LOSING BADLY IN THE PRIMARY TO **CONGRESSMAN ROBERT TAFT.** THE ELECTION IS TUESDAY, A MERE TWO DAYS AWAY.

"DID YOU LISTEN TO THE DEBATE? TAFT **REALLY** TORE INTO RHODES FOR THE WAY HE'S DEALT WITH STUDENT PROTESTS. JIMBO WAS **SEETHING!**"

THE NEXT DAY, OHIO STATE EXPLODES! A CROWD OF 4,000 ON THE OVAL, THE CAMPUS GREEN, IS GASSED AND THE BATTLE IS ON. A CLASSROOM BUILDING IS FIREBOMBED! THE RIOT SPILLS INTO SURROUNDING STUDENT NEIGHBORHOODS. EVERY COP IN THE CITY RUSHES TO CONTAIN IT.
THE NATIONAL GUARD AND POLICE EVENTUALLY SECURE THE CAMPUS. THE GOVERNOR IS PELTED WITH CRITICISM FOR ALLOWING THE SITUATION TO GET OUT OF HAND.
LONG'S
TEXTBOOKS AND CLOTHING

JIMBO WAS JUST ITCHING FOR A CHANCE TO SHOW WHAT A TOUGH GUY HE IS.
THESE DUMBASS KIDS HERE IN KENT HANDED HIM THAT OPPORTUNITY ON A SILVER PLATTER.

THE GUARD ROARING INTO KENT IS ALL ABOUT WHAT HAPPENED AT OHIO STATE.
IF THERE WAS NO RIOT THERE, THERE'D BE NO SOLDIERS HERE.
IT'S ALL A BIG ACT FOR TH' VOTERS.
PRESS

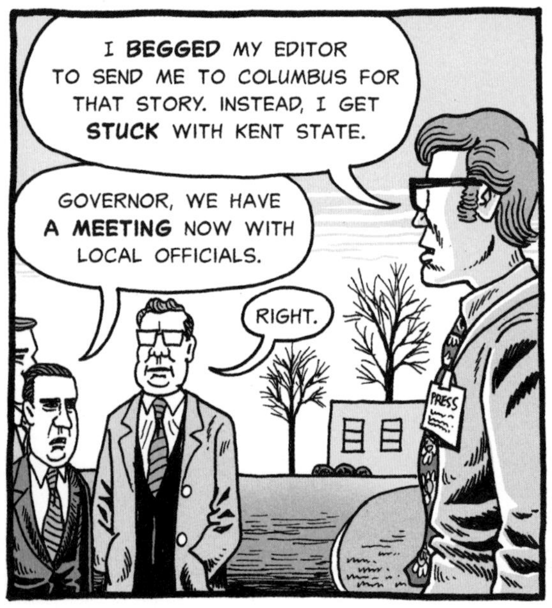
I BEGGED MY EDITOR TO SEND ME TO COLUMBUS FOR THAT STORY. INSTEAD, I GET STUCK WITH KENT STATE.
GOVERNOR, WE HAVE A MEETING NOW WITH LOCAL OFFICIALS.
RIGHT.
PRESS

WELL... WE BETTER FOLLOW HIM TO THIS MEETING. IF THERE'S PRESS THERE, YOU CAN BET RHODES WILL HAVE A PRESS CONFERENCE.

GIGGLE. NICE TOUCH WITH THE FLOWER!
THANKS.

THIS MILITARY OCCUPATION ISN'T RIGHT.
THIS IS OUR CAMPUS.
HEY, I DON'T WANT TO BE HERE.

THEN WHY DON'T YOU LEAVE?
YEAH, I CAN'T.
PRIVATE!

DOESN'T THIS COMPANY HAVE RIFLE DRILLS THIS WEEK?
YES, SIR.
AND WILL YOU BE SHOWING UP WITH THAT SILLY FLOWER IN YOUR GUN?

NO, SIR!
THEN WHY IS IT IN THERE NOW!?!
IT WAS A GIFT, SIR.
AND DO YOU ALWAYS ACCEPT GIFTS?

GOOD!

FLOWERS ARE BETTER THAN BULLETS!

U.S.A

THAT'S GAME!
FOOSH!
ARGH! LUCKY SHOT!

THAT'S SKILL, NOT LUCK, MY FRIEND!
YER TOO GOOD FOR ME, THAT'S FOR SURE.

I THOUGHT YOU SAID YOUR KNEES WERE SHOT FROM HIGH SCHOOL BALL?
YOU MOVE PRETTY GOOD FOR A GIMP!

YEAH, I'M HOPING THEY'RE BAD ENOUGH TO KEEP ME OUT OF COMBAT DUTY.
THAT'S WHY I KEEP PLAYING!
HA!
R.O.T.C.

I GOTTA GET GOING. ME AND A BUDDY ARE GONNA RENT DIRT BIKES OUT AT THE RESERVOIR.
32
THUD!

I DIDN'T WORK UP MUCH OF A SWEAT, SINCE WE CAN'T PLAY FIVE-ON-FIVE LIKE WE USUALLY DO.
WE'D BE ARRESTED FOR AN "ILLEGAL ASSEMBLY!"
THE EDICT READ ON THE RADIO SAID ONLY TWO STUDENTS TOGETHER AT ANY TIME!
PRRRRRRRRRRRRRRR
S-302550
LORAIN
32

RRRRRRRRRRRR

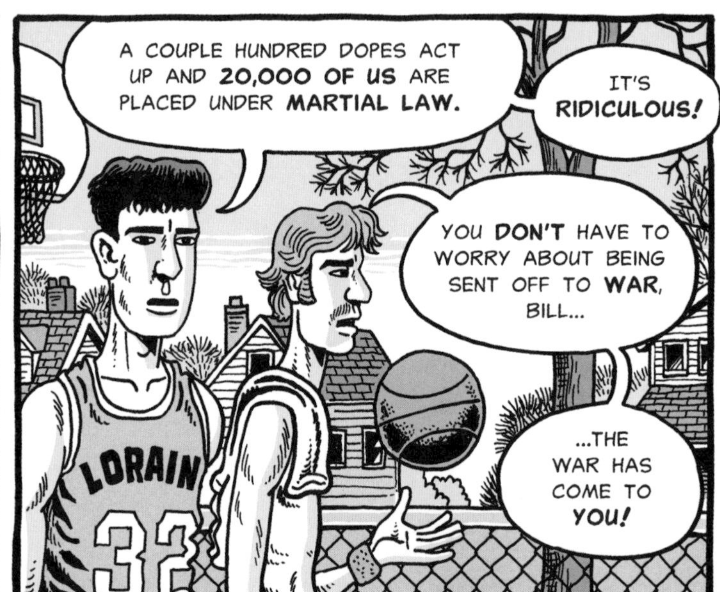
A COUPLE HUNDRED DOPES ACT UP AND 20,000 OF US ARE PLACED UNDER MARTIAL LAW.
IT'S RIDICULOUS!
YOU DON'T HAVE TO WORRY ABOUT BEING SENT OFF TO WAR, BILL...
...THE WAR HAS COME TO YOU!
LORAIN
32

BOOM! SHING! SHING! SHING!
BADA BOOM!
BADA-DADA-BADA
DADA-BADA!
CRASH!
WBAI

HEY, JEFF! OH, YOU GOTTA HEAR THIS, MAN!

I HAD TH' RADIO ON WHILE STUDYING AND HEARD THE LIVE BROADCAST. THEY'RE REPEATING IT NOW...
REEEEEE
...EARLIER TODAY AT A PRESS CONFERENCE...

GOVERNOR RHODES, FLUSHED WITH ANGER AND POUNDING THE TABLE WITH HIS FIST, STATED HE WILL NO LONGER TOLERATE STUDENT RADICALS.
LINCOLN

WE ARE GOING TO ERADICATE THE PROBLEM! THUMP! THUD!
ERADI... IS HE TALKING ABOUT US?
WAIT! IT GETS BETTER!

THEY'RE THE WORST TYPE OF PEOPLE WE HARBOR IN AMERICA!
THUD!
THEY ARE NOT GOING TO TAKE OVER CAMPUS!
LINCOLN

THEY'RE WORSE THAN THE BROWN SHIRTS AND COMMUNIST ELEMENT AND ALSO THE NIGHT RIDERS AND THE VIGILANTES!
FOLLOW YOUR DREAM YOU KNOW WHAT I MEAN?
WHAT TH' HELL ARE NIGHT RIDERS?
INCOLN

UH... THE TOBACCO WARS CIRCA 1905 IN KENTUCKY, IF I REMEMBER MY U.S. HISTORY 300 NOTES.
I KNEW RHODES WAS A GEEZER...
...BUT NOT THAT OLD!

THE GOVERNOR WAS CLEAR WHO HE BLAMES FOR THE TROUBLE AT KENT STATE AND OTHER OHIO UNIVERSITIES.
THERE'S NO SANCTUARY FOR... THUD!... THESE PEOPLE!
IT'S OVER WITH IN OHIO!

WHO DOES HE THINK HE IS, RIPPING US ALL FOR WATER STREET AND THE ROT-SEE BUILDING?
I HAD NO MORE TO DO WITH THAT THAN RHODES DID!
HE'S A NIXON STOOGE. HE'S JUST PARROTING HIS MASTER.
WBAI

MAN! THAT REALLY PISSES ME OFF!
EXPLAINS WHY THE GUARD IS HERE, RIGHT?
US COMMIE STUDENTS HAVE TO BE SHOWN...
...WHO IS IN CHARGE!

BURGER CHEF
HAMBURGERS
WE SELL MILLIONS NATIONWIDE
SHAKES

SLURP!

I NEVER HEARD OF THIS AGENCY, TERRY.
BROOKS DETECTIVE AGENCY
Terry Norman
53- 3318

THAT'S BECAUSE IT DOESN'T EXIST!
"BROOKS" IS MY MIDDLE NAME!
HA!

MAKES ME LOOK MORE LEGIT IF I HAVE A BUSINESS CARD, THOUGH.
RIGHT.

AND YOU TOOK ALL THESE PHOTOS?
YEP. THEY'RE MY SURVEILLANCE PHOTOS OF LOCAL RADICALS.

I USED TO TAKE THEM FOR THE CAMPUS POLICE...
...NOW I TAKE THEM FOR THE FBI!

SHOULD YOU BE TALKING ABOUT THIS STUFF?
ISN'T CLANDESTINE WORK SUPPOSED TO BE... UH... CLANDESTINE?

DON'T WORRY ABOUT IT.
I KNOW WHAT I'M DOING.

SAY... THIS SUMMER YOU GONNA WORK AS A SECURITY GUARD AT BLOSSOM MUSIC CENTER AGAIN?
THINK YOU CAN GET ME A JOB THERE?

WORKING AT AN OUTDOOR AMPHITHEATER SOUNDS LIKE A CUSHY WAY TO SPEND SUMMER BREAK!
YEAH, UNTIL YOU HAFTA PULL HIGH SCHOOL KIDS ON ACID OUTTA TREES!

THAT'S SMALL POTATOES! I HOPE TA BE WORKING FOR THE BUREAU FROM HERE ON OUT!
THIS ISN'T MY FIRST ASSIGNMENT FOR THEM, YA KNOW. I WAS AN INFILTRATOR IN A WHITE SUPREMACIST GROUP IN VIRGINIA LAST YEAR!
NO SHIT!

A BIG **UNANSWERED QUESTION** ABOUT KENT STATE IS HOW MANY **UNDERCOVER OPERATIVES,** FROM PLANTS TO INFORMANTS TO AGENTS PROVOCATEUR, ARE INVOLVED WITH EVENTS THIS WEEKEND, WORKING NOT ONLY FOR LOCAL AND STATE LAW ENFORCEMENT, BUT ALSO FOR **THE FBI, THE CIA, AND MILITARY INTELLIGENCE.** NORMAN, THE LOOSE-LIPPED FBI OPERATIVE, IS AN AMATEURISH EXAMPLE OF THESE INDIVIDUALS.

SOUND ABSURD? JUST TWO YEARS LATER, WITH ANTIWAR TENSIONS STILL SIMMERING, **RON MOHR**, AN AGENT PROVOCATEUR, WAS PUBLICLY EXPOSED TRYING TO PLANT A ROCKET-PROPELLED GRENADE LAUNCHER AND A RUSSIAN AK-47 IN THE OFFICE OF A CAMPUS ANTIWAR GROUP.

IF THIS SOUNDS LIKE THE STUFF OF **SPY NOVELS**, IT WAS! THIS IS THE DEEPEST DEPTHS OF **THE COLD WAR** AND THE U.S. SPY APPARATUS IS OPERATING WITH FEW CONSTRAINTS.

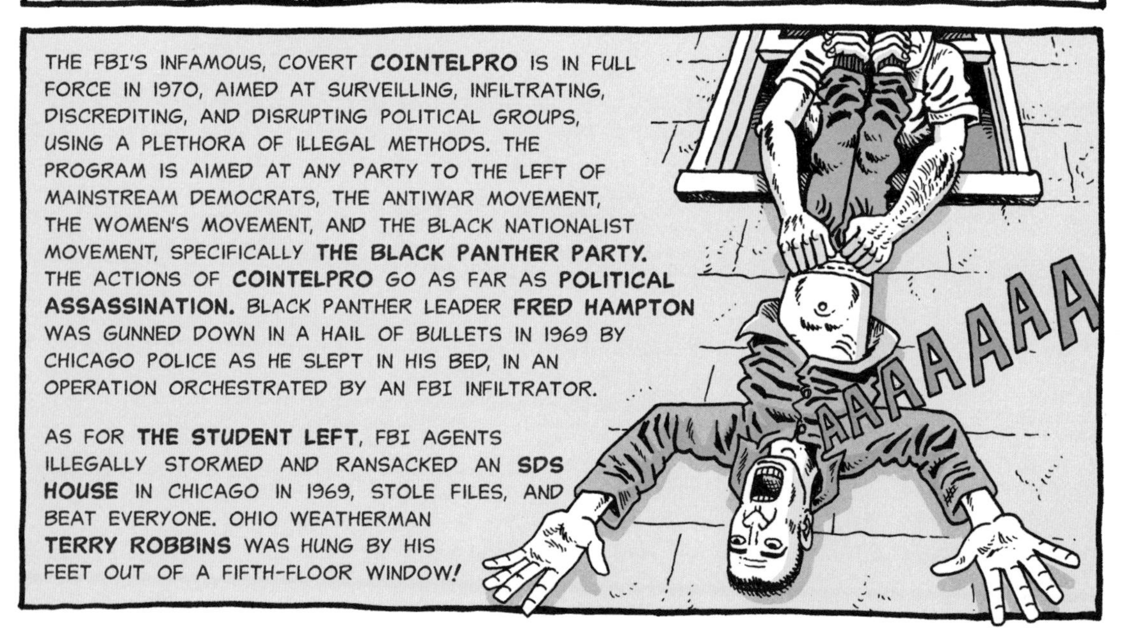

NIXON IS OBSESSED WITH THE STUDENT LEFT. KENT STATE IS THE 24TH LARGEST UNIVERSITY IN THE U.S., LOCATED IN A WEATHERMEN STRONGHOLD, EVEN IF THE STUDENT BODY IS NOT PARTICULARLY RADICAL. IT WOULD BE **UTTERLY NAIVE** TO THINK KENT STATE WAS NOT BEING **CLOSELY WATCHED.**

MANY FORMER STUDENTS INTERVIEWED FOR THIS BOOK SPEAK OF **STRANGERS**, PASSING THEMSELVES OFF AS STUDENTS, AT **EVERY INCIDENT** THIS WEEKEND.

CAMPUS POLICE CHIEF SCHWARTZMILLER WOULD LATER ADMIT THAT HIS OFFICERS AND INFILTRATORS **WORKED CLOSELY** WITH BOTH THE FBI AND MILITARY INTELLIGENCE.

THE CIA IS, BY LAW, FORBIDDEN TO OPERATE WITHIN THE U.S., AND DENIES IT IS DOING SO IN 1970. THIS IS **A LIE.**

OPERATION CHAOS IS A MASSIVE SPECIAL OPS PROGRAM DIRECTED AT THE ANTIWAR MOVEMENT AND THE STUDENT LEFT. ITS OPERATIONS INCLUDE WIRETAPS, READING MAIL, PSYCHOLOGICAL WARFARE, SPREADING DISINFORMATION, SMEAR CAMPAIGNS, AND SPYING ON JOURNALISTS.

SOME OPERATION CHAOS ACTIVITIES ARE **STILL CLASSIFIED**, 50 YEARS LATER. AFTER THE PROGRAM WAS EXPOSED IN 1974, CONGRESS FEARED THAT IF THE PUBLIC KNEW ALL, THE OUTCRY WOULD RESULT IN THE END OF THE AGENCY. WHAT **IS** KNOWN IS THAT OPERATION CHAOS HAD **300,000 CASE FILES** ON AMERICAN CITIZENS AND ORGANIZATIONS DURING THE VIETNAM ERA.

NIXON ALSO ORDERS **THE PENTAGON** TO SPY ON ALL **ANTIWAR GROUPS**, PARTICULARLY AT UNIVERSITIES.
AN OFFICE OF 350 **MILITARY INTELLIGENCE AGENTS** IS ASSIGNED THIS TASK. MORE PENTAGON SPIES ARE COMMITTED TO SPYING ON "SUSPECT" AMERICANS THAN ARE ASSIGNED TO **ANY** HOSTILE FOREIGN GOVERNMENT... INCLUDING THE SOVIET UNION.

ADDITIONALLY, **ROTC FACULTY** AT EVERY UNIVERSITY ARE ORDERED TO FILE **REGULAR REPORTS** TO MILITARY INTELLIGENCE ON STUDENT ANTIWAR ACTIVISTS ON THEIR CAMPUSES. THE KENT STATE ROTC FACULTY IS DOING SO. TURNS OUT SDS-ERS ARE RIGHT TO BE **PARANOID** ABOUT ROTC.
SO WHAT, EXACTLY, ARE THESE **THREE SPY AGENCIES** UP TO THIS WEEKEND? **HOW MANY** OF THEIR AGENTS ARE ON CAMPUS OR INFILTRATING THE PROTESTS? ARE THESE OPERATIVES PROFESSIONALS OR JUST UNSUPERVISED FREE AGENTS? THERE WAS AT LEAST ONE OPERATIVE FROM MILITARY INTELLIGENCE AND ALSO A SQUAD OF UNDERCOVER FBI ON CAMPUS.
THESE ARE **SECRETS** THAT REMAIN **HIDDEN** TO THIS DAY.
TAP
TAPPITY TAPPITY
TAP TAP
TAPPITY
TAP

YOU'RE **A MARKED MAN**, TERRY. WORRIED?

I CAN LOOK AFTER MYSELF.

SLURP!

3:30 P.M.
25 MPH
ATO

DARN IT! I FORGOT TO PUT BASIL ON THE GROCERY LIST. DON'T LET ME FORGET IT.
OKAY.

WELL, HI, POOCH!
AREN'T YOU A FRIENDLY GIRL.

WHAT A SWEETHEART! SHE MUST BE A STRAY, THE POOR THING, AND...OH!... SHE'S PREGNANT!

WE HAVE TO TAKE HER HOME WITH US, BARB.
GROAN. OH, SANDY. REALLY?

YOU **CAN'T** SAVE **EVERY** PUPPY IN THE WORLD.

GIVE ME YOUR **RIBBON.** WE CAN USE THAT AS **A LEASH.** WE'LL GET A BAG OF **DOG FOOD** AT THE STORE.

SIGH.

WHAT SHOULD WE CALL HER? HOW ABOUT **"HEAVY"?**
THAT'S WHAT SHE **IS!**
C'MON, HEAVY!

SNIFF! THIS WHOLE TOWN SMELLS LIKE A **FIREPLACE!** LET'S GO BY **THE ROT-SEE BUILDING** AND CHECK IT OUT.
Fish & Chips
CAMPUS CENTER
CAMPUS HUT

5 P.M.

HI, LADIES!
JEFF! I WAS **HOPING** YOU'D TURN UP!

LEMME GET THOSE FOR YA.

WHAT'S WITH THE PUP?
DON'T ASK.

MMMMM. SMELLS GREAT!
HEY, GIVE ME SOME ELBOW ROOM HERE!

DIDJA SEE THE ROT-SEE BUILDING?
YEAH. WHAT A MESS.

AND DIDJA HEAR ABOUT RHODES'S TEMPER TANTRUM?
OH YEAH!
EVERYONE IS TALKING ABOUT IT.

I GOT STOPPED BY SOLDIERS SIX TIMES TODAY. I HAD GUNS POINTED AT ME TWICE!
BARB AND I GOT STOPPED, TOO.

I'M SCARED TO EVEN LEAVE MY HOUSE. WHICH IS JUST WHAT THAT BASTARD RHODES WANTS!

THERE'S GONNA BE A SIT-IN TONIGHT AT PRENTICE GATE TO PROTEST THE MILITARY OCCUPATION OF CAMPUS.
YEAH?
I'M GONNA CHECK IT OUT. WANNA GO?
CAN'T. I HAVE A BIG TEST TOMORROW.
OOOOKAY, BOOKWORM.
SURE I CAN'T HELP?
GIGGLE. JUST POUR A GLASS OF WINE...
...AND GO READ THE PAPER AND RELAX.
HEY, IS THIS THE NEW PAUL McCARTNEY YOU'RE PLAYING?
YEP! JUST GOT IT. IT'S NOT THE BEATLES, BUT I LIKE IT.
POOR PAUL. EVERYONE IS BLAMING HIM FOR BREAKIN' UP THE BAND.
THEIR FINAL ALBUM COMES OUT LATER THIS WEEK!
I CAN'T WAIT TO HEAR IT.
Z

7 P.M.
fresh POP CORN
I LOVE HOW TH' UNIVERSITY IS SHOWING FREE FILMS TO DISTRACT AND AMUSE US REVOLUTIONARIES!
OKAY BY ME, BARRY. I'D RATHER WATCH W.C. FIELDS SHORTS THAN THROW STONES!

9:30 P.M.

I CAN **HEAR** STUDENTS MOVING AROUND IN **TH' TREES** ON CAMPUS, UP ON THAT HILL.
SOUNDS LIKE A **SHITLOAD** OF 'EM!
YEAH.

I'M **DEAD ON MY FEET**, FRANK. I HAVEN'T SLEPT IN FOUR DAYS! I'VE **HAD IT** WITH THESE ASSHOLES!
IT'S JUST **FUN AND GAMES** TO THEM.

HERE WE COME! HERE WE COME!
ARE... ARE THEY GONNA **CHARGE** AT US?
ON YER TOES!
WE **GASSED** A BIG GROUP OF 'EM ON TH' COMMONS EARLIER... AND **HEADED OFF** OTHERS MARCHIN' TO TH' PRESIDENT'S HOUSE.
LET'S SEE WHAT **THESE** IDIOTS WANT.

THOP THOP THOP THOP THO

HERE WE COME!
HERE WE COME!

HERE WE COME!! HERE

WHAT'S **YOUR** TAKE ON THIS, DETECTIVE?
THEY APPEAR TO BE **PEACEFUL,** MAJOR.
JONES

LET'S SEE WHAT THEY WANT... **WHAT TH' HELL?** THEY'RE ALL **SITTING DOWN!** IN THE MIDDLE OF **MAIN STREET!**

GAS TOWN
TKE
Robin Hood
FISH SPECIAL TONIGHT
GUARD OFF CAMPUS!
GUARD OFF CAMPUS!
GUARD OFF CAMPUS!
GUARD OFF CAMPUS!
U.S. ARMY
PO5000231
107 CAV

GUARD OFF CAMPUS!!
GUARD OFF CAMPUS!!
I JUST GOT HERE. **WHAT'S** HAPPENING?

THEY'VE BEEN **IN THE STREET** FOR OVER AN HOUR. THEY PRESENTED A **LIST OF DEMANDS.**
WHAT **ARE** THEY?
Horn's Captain BRADY
BAKERY
KENT

UH... **NOT** SURE.
THE GUARD MUST LEAVE, THE CURFEW ENDED, NO MORE ROT-SEE, **THAT** SORT OF THING.
THEY WANT **A MEETING** TONIGHT WITH PRESIDENT WHITE, **THAT** MUCH I OVERHEARD.

HEY! THERE'S MY FRIEND BUTLER!

PRESIDENT WHITE HAS JUST **TURNED DOWN** A MEETING WITH THE PROTESTERS, MAJOR.
OKAY, **THAT'S IT!** I'M TIRED OF **BABYSITTING** THESE CLOWNS.
JONES

THE ORDER OF THE DAY IS TO GO EASY ON STUDENTS, TO ENGAGE WITH THEM, AND TALK TO THEM, TO EASE TENSIONS AND DEFUSE THE SITUATION.

MAJOR HARRY JONES HAS NO INTEREST IN EASING OR DEFUSING.

JONES, AGE 43, IS THE 145TH'S FULL-TIME TRAINING OFFICER, IN CHARGE OF THE WEEKEND EXERCISES. KENT MARKS HIS SEVENTH GUARD ACTION. A TENNESSEE NATIVE AND SELF-DESCRIBED "HILLBILLY," HE IS 5'9" AND WIRY, AND IS KNOWN AS A NO-NONSENSE HARD-ASS.

HE JOINED THE GUARD IN 1954 AND IS A VETERAN OF THE VIOLENT CLEVELAND AND AKRON URBAN RIOTS. WHEN HE GIVES AN ORDER, HE EXPECTS IT TO BE FOLLOWED, WITHOUT QUESTION. TODAY IS HIS BIRTHDAY. HE'S NOT HAVING A HAPPY ONE.

11 P.M.

LOOK! A LOT OF THEM ARE ALREADY LEAVING!

YEAH? WELL, I'LL GET THEM TO LEAVE EVEN FASTER!
CLEAR 'EM OUT!
JONES
U.S.ARMY

C COMPANY! BE MEAN AND GREEN! HIT 'EM HARD!!
SANDER

WHAT TH' HELL!
RUN!
AGAIN?

FRIDAY AND SATURDAY WERE STUDENT RIOTS.
EXHAUSTED, FRAZZLED, FED UP AND PISSED OFF, NOW IT'S THE GUARDSMEN'S TURN TO RIOT!

CLEAR THE CAMPUS!
RETURN TO YOUR DORMS!
HHHHHISS
THOP THOP THOP
HHHHHISS

LIARS!
LIARS!
AAAAAAAH!!
US ARMY

KRAK!
RUN!
USAR

WH-WHAT ARE THEY DOING? THAT WAS A PEACEFUL PROTEST!
ERS
ZA
dry

YEAH, GUARD! KICK SOME HIPPIE ASS!
HAW! LOOKIT THOSE WIMPS RUN!
FRAT RAT CREEPS!

HISSSSSSS

YAAAA!! KOFF!
WE'RE ON YOUR SIDE!
SHIT!
HISSSSSS

GAG!
TIME TO GET TH' HELL OUT OF HERE!
SPIT!

I'M GONNA CUT THROUGH BACKYARDS TO GET HOME!
GOOD LUCK!

THERE GOES WHATEVER CHANCE WE HAD TO MAKE PEACE WITH THE STUDENTS.
I FEEL SICK!

US ARMY
LET'S SHOW THESE ASSHOLES WHO IS IN CHARGE!
I HEAR SOME OF 'EM IN BACK OF THE LIBRARY.

RUN!
THERE!

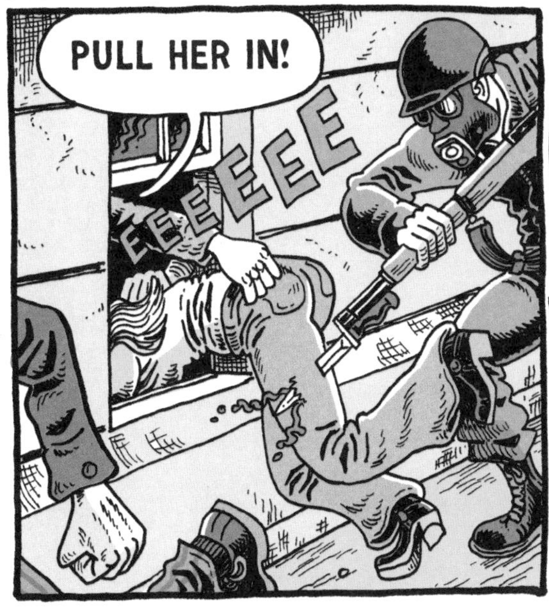
PULL HER IN!
EEEEEEE

AND STAY INSIDE, PUNKS!
U.S. AR

KRAK!

OKAY! OKAY!

N-N-NO!

I KNOW YOUR FACE NOW... BUT YOU DON'T KNOW MINE!
IF I RUN INTO YOU AGAIN, I'LL PUT THIS BAYONET THROUGH YOUR NOSE!

AAAAAA!!
CHOK!!

THUD!

NICE AND CLEAN!
LET'S GO, FRANK.

THOP THOP THOP
STAY INSIDE!
DAMN.

*BLACK UNITED STUDENTS

NOTE: RIOTS IN CLEVELAND.

BACK AT PRENTICE GATE

HEH. SOME **SMARTASS** IS BLASTING THE STONES' **"STREET FIGHTING MAN"**!
TURN THAT SHIT OFF AND ARREST THAT GUY!
U.S. ARMY

BAM! BANG! BAM!
CRUNCH

CLUMP
STOMP
THUD

SCREE!

KRAK!

AAAAAAAA
BUMP! THUMP!

ON THE OTHER SIDE OF CAMPUS, NEAR TRI-TOWERS
THOSE FILM SHORTS WERE GREAT!
WISH IT TOOK MY MIND OFF WHAT'S GOING DOWN HERE.
YEAH.
SIGH. CAN YOU BELIEVE IT WAS ONLY SIX MONTHS AGO WE WERE MARCHING IN WASHINGTON, D.C.?
A MILLION OF US!

IT'S LIKE IT NEVER HAPPENED! THE WAR IS WORSE THAN EVER AND OUR CAMPUS HAS BEEN SEIZED IN A MILITARY COUP!
I KNOW, I KNOW.
IT'S SO DEPRESSING, BARRY.

WHOA!
WH-WHAT'S HAPPENING OVER THERE ON FRONT CAMPUS?

THOP THOP
THOP
THAT... DOESN'T LOOK GOOD.

TROMP! TROMP! TROMP!
OH NO.

ATTENTION! CURFEW IS NOW IN FORCE!

GET INSIDE A DORM IMMEDIATELY OR BE ARRESTED!

FOOSH!

GO!
HHIISSSS
THUD!

IT... IT'S LOCKED! LET US IN! LET US IN!!
BANG! BANG!
THEY'RE COMING!
RATTLE! RATTLE!

GET INSIDE! GET INSIDE!
US ARMY
TROMP! TROMP! TROMP!

C'MON! HURRY!
THE JERK DORM DIRECTOR LOCKED THE DOORS!
VISITORS MUST REGISTER AT THE DESK
THANK GOD!

I TOLD YOU NOT TO LET PEOPLE IN! I'M REPORTING THIS!
THAT WOULD BE A MISTAKE!
GET ME?

WE'RE SAFE. IT'S OKAY.
TH-THOSE HORRIBLE MASKS! THEY LOOK LIKE MONSTERS!

GUESS WE'RE STUCK IN TRI-TOWERS FOR THE NIGHT. I HAVE A BUDDY ON THE FIFTH FLOOR.
LET'S SEE IF WE CAN CRASH WITH HIM.

IN THE NEIGHBORHOOD BORDERING CAMPUS
I WANNA SEE **WHAT'S HAPPENING** ON CAMPUS.
IT'S **AFTER** THE CITY CURFEW.
THIS IS **RISKY**, RITA!

HEY! IS THAT **JEFF MILLER?**
JEFF!

PANT-PANT. YOU GUYS **DON'T** WANT TO BE ON TH' STREET!
THE GUARD HAS GONE **BERSERK!**

THOP THOP THOP THOP
CRAP!
IF THEY SPOT US, **WE'RE TOAST!**

OUR HOUSE IS RIGHT HERE! **C'MON!**

THOP THOP THOP
SOUNDS LIKE IT'S RIGHT **OVERHEAD!**
DID THEY **SEE** US?

THOP THOP THOP THOP
SSSSSSSSS

THUD!

AUGH! GAS!
GAG!
SLAM!

THOP THOP THOP
TH-THEY'RE JUST FLYING AWAY! KOFF! KOFF!
FASCISTS!

MAN! I GOT A GOOD WHIFF OF THAT STUFF! AUGH!
SPLASH!

OH NO! NOAH! THE BASTARDS EVEN GASSED OUR DOG!
WHINE! WHINE!

A HOUSE FULL OF GAS ISN'T MUCH OF A REFUGE.
I'M GONNA MAKE A BREAK FOR HOME.
GOOD LUCK!

GRUNT! JUST ONE MORE BLOCK TO GO.

PANT.

THOP! THOP! THOP! THOP!
DAMN!

THOP! THOP! TH
BUSTED! YOU POOR BASTARDS!

KOFF! GAG!
WHEEZE!
HIIISSSSS

ARRGH! I GOT ANOTHER DOSE OF THAT CRAP!

THOP THOP THOP THOP
FINALLY!

JEFF!
THANK GOD!
BANG!
WHEW!

SPIT! I'M GONNA DEVELOP AN IMMUNITY TO TEAR GAS BEFORE THIS QUARTER ENDS. GROAN.
SPLASH!

PHEW... IT TOOK ME TWO HOURS TO GET FOUR BLOCKS!
EVERYONE ELSE MAKE IT BACK?
STEVE IS STILL OUT THERE.
B21

IT'S UNBELIEVABLE, JOHN. THE GUARD WENT INSANE!
GASSING, BEATING, STABBING!
IT'S A TOTAL MILITARY CRACKDOWN! IT'S NIXON'S WET DREAM!

G-GOD, LOOK AT ME! I'M... I'M SHAKING I'M SO ANGRY!

PROTESTER OR BYSTANDER, IT DIDN'T MATTER. IT WAS A NIGHTMARE! I'VE NEVER SEEN ANYTHING LIKE IT.

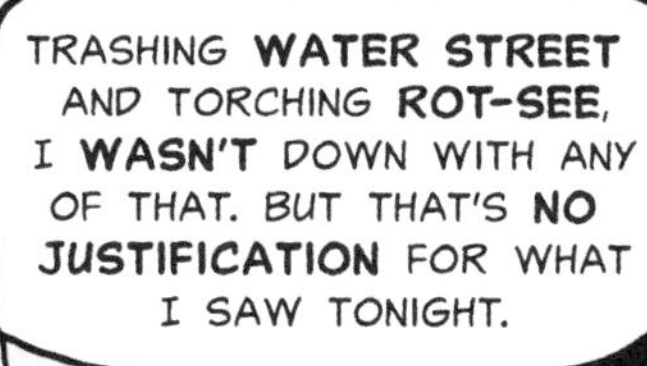
TRASHING **WATER STREET** AND TORCHING **ROT-SEE**, I **WASN'T** DOWN WITH ANY OF THAT. BUT THAT'S **NO JUSTIFICATION** FOR WHAT I SAW TONIGHT.

WORD IS A LOT OF TH' HARD-CORE SDS-ERS BEHIND THAT STUFF HAVE **LEGGED IT** OUTTA TOWN.
GOT **TOO HOT** FOR THEM HERE.
YEAH?

SO THE GUARD BEATS THE SHIT OUT OF **INNOCENT STUDENTS?**

IT'S **NOT** EVEN ABOUT **THE WAR** AND **CAMBODIA** ANYMORE.
IT'S ABOUT THESE **GOONS** WHO HAVE **INVADED OUR CAMPUS!**

I **CAN'T WAIT** FOR THAT **RALLY ON THE COMMONS** TOMORROW!

...THERE HAVE BEEN **DOZENS** OF ARRESTS. THE GUARD IS USING **CAMPUS BUSES** TO TRANSPORT STUDENTS TO THE RAVENNA JAIL...

THAT SOUNDS BAD, BILL.
YEAH. **WAKR** HAS BEEN REPORTING ON IT **ALL** EVENING.
Charles Chips

RHODES AND THE GUARD HAVE TURNED KENT INTO A POLICE STATE! IT'S JUST NOT RIGHT.
IS THIS AMERICA... OR EAST GERMANY?
YEAH.

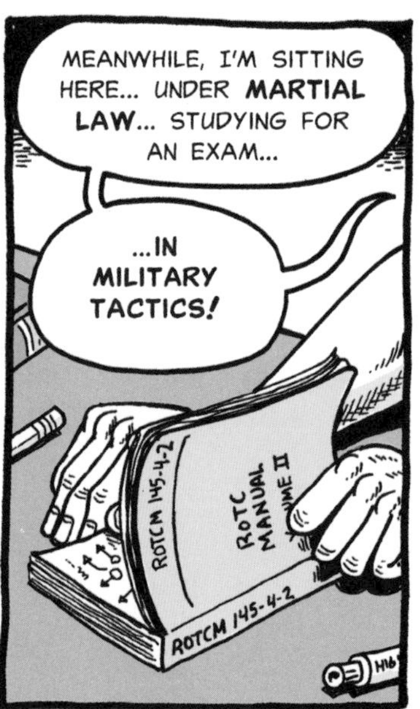
MEANWHILE, I'M SITTING HERE... UNDER MARTIAL LAW... STUDYING FOR AN EXAM...
...IN MILITARY TACTICS!
ROTCM 145-4-2
ROTC MANUAL
ROTCM 145-4-2

WHAT A CRAZY WORLD, LOUIE.
...WE GO NOW LIVE TO CAMPUS...

RING!

HELLO?
HOPE I DIDN'T WAKE YOU, TERRY.
IT'S NO PROBLEM, AGENT CHAPIN.

WE NEED YOU AT THE NOON RALLY TOMORROW. TAKE PHOTOS OF THE MOST VOCAL PROTESTERS.
OKAY.

EWS 20 TIMES DAILY
WAKR
1590 - AKRON
USE YOUR PRESS CREDENTIALS AS A COVER. I'LL NOTIFY THE GUARD YOU'RE WITH US.
BF Goodrich
TIRES
Luigi's

YOU CAN COUNT ON ME.
GET A GOOD NIGHT'S SLEEP.
KLIK

2 A.M.
WALLS SCHOOL
SCHOOL 20 MPH
B-27035-4
ONG
145 INF

SLAM! BANG!
HACK! SNORT!
THOMAS! YER ON GUARD DUTY!
LIEUTENANT! TH' MAJOR WANTS YOU!
SNORT!
GROAN.
UGH.

CRASH!
FRANK. YOU ASLEEP?
SHUT UP!
ARE YOU FRIGGIN' KIDDING ME?

THEY COULD AT LEAST TURN OUT TH' DAMN LIGHTS.
SLAM!
KOFF! HACK!
THUD!
ZZZ!

THOP THOP THOP

THOP THOP THOP

THOP
THOP
THOP
THOP

JEEZUS, BILL. THAT'S THE **THIRD** TIME THAT HELICOPTER HAS **FLOWN PAST.**
I KNOW.

I'M **SCARED,** LOUIE.

THOP
THOP
THOP
THOP
THOP

MONDAY, MAY 4
7:55 A.M.

DAMN! THERE'S A SOLDIER EVERY TEN FEET!
I GO HOME TO CLEVELAND FOR TH' WEEKEND AND COME BACK TO A JOHN WAYNE FILM SET!
YEAH, IT'S NUTS.

HOLY CRAP! WHERE DID ALL THESE STUDENTS COME FROM?

THERE'S THOUSANDS OF THEM!
IS THIS TH' PROTEST WE WUZ WARNED ABOUT?
NO, DUMBASS...

THIS IS WHAT A BIG UNIVERSITY LOOKS LIKE ON A MONDAY MORNING.
THESE ARE KIDS GOING TO CLASS.

THAT SHITHEAD RHODES TELLS US TO KEEP STUDENTS FROM BEIN' TOGETHER...
...THEN REFUSES TO CLOSE TH' SCHOOL...
...SO STUDENTS HAFTA BE TOGETHER!

SO OUR MISSION IS TO DO... WHAT, EXACTLY?
I HOPE THAT CREEP LOSES HIS DAMN ELECTION IN A LANDSLIDE.

BILL! YOU SLEPT THROUGH YER ALARM!

HUH? WHAT TIME IS IT?
8:15? AW, NO!

WOW. THOSE ORANGE CORDS ARE AN EYEFUL!
THEY'RE MY ROLLING STONES PANTS.
LIKE BRIAN JONES WORE.

I LIKE TH' PURPLE FLOWER PIN. IS THAT WHAT ALL TH' ROT-SEE CADETS ARE WEARING NOW?
IT'S MY "PURPLE HEART"!

WILLIAMS ST
25 MPH

OH NO!

HEAVY CHEWED THROUGH HER LEASH!
SHE RAN OFF!

WE HAVE TO FIND HER.
I CAN'T RIGHT NOW. EXAMS.

I'LL HELP LOOK FOR HER THIS AFTERNOON.
YOU HEADING TO CAMPUS?

NOT JUST YET.
OH, AND HEY! IT'S MY PARENTS' ANNIVERSARY TODAY. DON'T LET ME FORGET TO CALL THEM THIS EVENING!
WILL DO, MISS BEACH.

HEY, SANDY!
HI, ELLIS!
WHAT'S HAPPENIN'?
USARMY

JUST ENJOYING A LOVELY SPRING MORNING.
SMELL THOSE LILACS IN BLOOM!

HI, MOM.
HI, HONEY! I'M GLAD YOU CALLED.

I SAW SOMETHING ABOUT KENT STATE ON THE NEWS.
YEAH, THERE WAS SOME TROUBLE.

I HAD AN ADVENTURE LAST NIGHT, BUT NOTHING SERIOUS.

THERE'S A BIG RALLY TODAY ON CAMPUS TO PROTEST THE GUARD OCCUPATION.
I'M GOING TO GO.

DON'T WORRY. I MIGHT GET ARRESTED, BUT I WON'T GET MY HEAD BUSTED.
I'M NOT WORRIED.

BUT WILL THIS ACCOMPLISH ANYTHING?
PROBABLY NOT.

BUT WE HAVE TO DO SOMETHING! THE SOLDIERS HERE ARE OUT OF CONTROL.
THANKS FOR LETTING ME KNOW.

OKAY, MOM. TALK TO YOU SOON.
LOVE YOU. BYE.

DANG IT.... NOW, **WHERE** DID I LEAVE THAT **HEADBAND?**
BINGO!

CHANG!

FOLLOW YOUR DREAM. DO YOU KNOW WHAT I MEAN?

K

HOW'S THE GRUB THIS MORNING, FRANK?
IT'S OKAY.

I DON'T REALLY HAVE MUCH OF AN APPETITE.
I HEAR YA.

I JUST WANT THIS GODDAM MISSION TO BE OVER!
I'VE HAD IT!
I'M BEAT, I'M SORE ALL OVER, AND I HAVEN'T HAD A DAMN SHOWER IN A WEEK!
SQUEAK!

OKAY... LET'S SADDLE UP!
WE'RE HEADIN' TO CAMPUS!
GROAN.

AGAIN WITH THIS SHIT?
DON'T THESE BASTARDS EVER GO TO CLASS?

FULL FIELD GEAR! FORM UP OUTSIDE!
LET'S GO!
AW, JESUS, YA MEAN WE GOTTA LUG AROUND OUR OWN GEAR?
THEY COULD JUST TRUCK THAT STUFF OVER.

THIS IS A TOTAL CHICKENSHIT OPERATION.

THE KENT FIRE STATION
10 A.M.

PRESIDENT WHITE MEETS WITH MAYOR SATROM AND GENERAL CANTERBURY, CONCERNING THE NOON PROTEST RALLY.
IT IS NOT A FRIENDLY CONFAB.

ALL THREE WOULD LATER DISPUTE WHAT WAS AGREED UPON HERE, EACH BLAMING THE OTHERS FOR WHAT WAS ABOUT TO UNFOLD.

SATROM ACCUSES WHITE OF BEING "COCKY." WHITE STATES HE WAS BULLIED BY SATROM AND CANTERBURY. THE GENERAL INSISTS THAT WHITE "BEGGED" HIM TO PREVENT THE RALLY. WHITE ASSERTS HE DID NO SUCH THING.

WHAT IS AGREED IS THAT THE GENERAL TOOK CONTROL.
THE GUARD IS IN CHARGE TODAY!

IT IS A DAY **UNLIKE ANY OTHER** IN THE HISTORY OF THE UNIVERSITY.
U.S. ARMY
12 EG 49
107CAV
E24

ARMED SENTRIES ARE POSTED AT THE ENTRANCE OF EVERY CLASSROOM BUILDING.

REMINDERS OF THE RALLY ARE SCRAWLED ON BLACKBOARDS.
GUARD OFF CAMPUS!! NOON RALLY ON THE COMMONS

MANY PROFS **SCRAP** THE LESSON PLAN SO STUDENTS CAN **DISCUSS AND DEBATE** THE WEEKEND'S EVENTS.

OTHERS PLOW AHEAD WITH SCHEDULED **LECTURES AND EXAMS.**

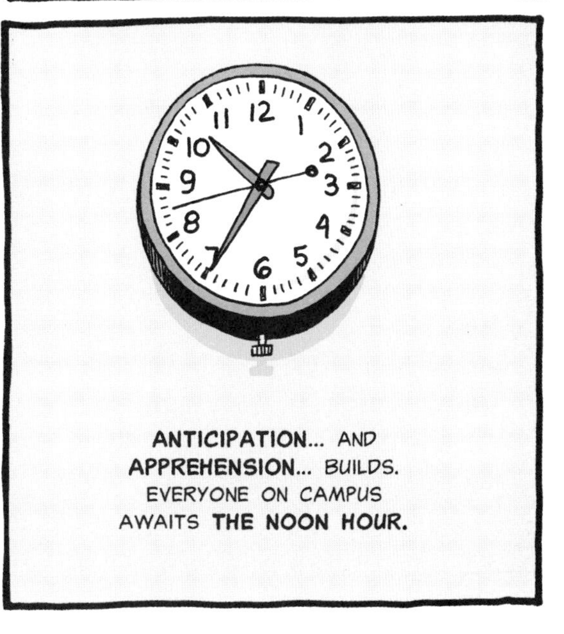
ANTICIPATION... AND **APPREHENSION...** BUILDS. EVERYONE ON CAMPUS AWAITS **THE NOON HOUR.**

MMPH! WINDY!
KENNEDY

KENNEDY

BONNIE? WANNA GRAB SOME LUNCH BEFORE THE RALLY? I'M CUTTING ART CLASS SO I WON'T BE LATE.
TAP TAP

I... DON'T THINK I'M GOING. THOSE SOLDIERS...I HAVE A BAD FEELING ABOUT THIS.

BONNIE! I'M YOUR FRIEND. NOTHING IS GOING TO HAPPEN TO YOU. I WON'T LET IT!

OKAY, OKAY... I LOVE YOU.

IF I SEE YOU WAVIN' AROUND THAT FLAG AT THAT PROTEST, BOY...
...I'M GONNA MAKE YOU EAT IT!

GET TOO CLOSE AND I'LL RAM IT UP YER ASS!

SNAP!

C LOT
STUDENT PARKING...
PERMIT STICKER REQUIRED

AS NOON APPROACHES, **PRESIDENT WHITE** STAYS TRUE TO FORM.
DOES HE PRESSURE RHODES?
DOES HE LOBBY POLITICAL ALLIES?
DOES HE THROW HIMSELF BETWEEN THE GUARD AND HIS STUDENTS?

HE DOES NOT. INSTEAD, IN AN ACT PERFECTLY SYMBOLIC OF HIS LEADERSHIP...
I'M GOING TO **LUNCH,** SHIRLEY.
OKAY, DR. WHITE.

CALL ME AT THE **BROWN DERBY...**
...IF ANYTHING IMPORTANT COMES UP.

STUDENT UNION
EUGENE ISTOMIN
ISAAC STERN
LEONARD ROSE
IN CONCERT, MAY 16

I WISH YOU'D **RECONSIDER,** JEFF...
STUDENT UNION

MY RIDE WILL BE HERE ANY SECOND. THERE'S ROOM IN THE CAR.
THE BUS LEAVES CLEVELAND AT 2 P.M. AND GETS INTO NEW YORK CITY AT 5 A.M.
WE'LL BE HOME IN PLAINVIEW BY BREAKFAST!

IT'S A SCARY SCENE HERE, MAN.
SMARTER TO GET TH' HELL OUTTA KENT UNTIL IT COOLS OFF.
PLEASE COME WITH ME.

NAH, I'M STAYIN', STEVE.
I HAVEN'T TAKEN PART IN ANY PROTESTS SINCE I CAME TO KENT STATE.
NO MORE.

IT'S TIME FOR ME TO TAKE A STAND...

...AND BE COUNTED!

BUTLER! YOU SURVIVED THE NIGHT OF THE HELICOPTERS!
YEAH, THAT WAS SOMETHING.
YOU KNOW PATTY.
SURE.

I ESCAPED TH' GUARD, THEN SPENT TH' REST OF TH' NIGHT CRAWLING THROUGH BACKYARDS DELIVERING MESSAGES TO HOUSES!

HEARD A SHITLOAD OF PEOPLE GOT ARRESTED.
IT WAS CRAZY.
THERE WERE 51 ARRESTS.

SO WHAT'S HAPPENIN' HERE? SHOULDN'T WE HAVE A MEETING OR SOMETHING?
WHOA! CAREFUL!
EXIT
YEAH! WE GOTTA ASSUME THIS ROOM IS FULL OF UNDERCOVER PIGS!
WE'VE BEEN SPEADING TH' WORD ALL MORNING. SO... LET'S JUST GO HAVE A RALLY!

DING!
DING!

DING! DING! DING! DING!
DING! DING! DING!

DING! DING! DING! DING!
DING!
DING!

IT'S AN OK TURNOUT. MAYBE **500** KIDS HERE, TOPS.
I DON'T SEE MANY OF THE USUAL **SDS-ERS.**

YEAH, I ONLY RECOGNIZE ABOUT **TEN PEOPLE!** EITHER A LOT OF APATHETIC STUDENTS HAVE **SEEN TH' LIGHT** AT LAST...

...OR THIS CROWD IS ALL **UNDERCOVER COPS!**

WHO'S TH' BLACK GUY? I THOUGHT **BUS** WAS SITTING THIS ONE OUT.
THAT'S **BROTHER FARGO!**
HE'S A **LONGTIME** ACTIVIST.

BROTHER FARGO!
AWRIIIGHT!

THOP THOP THOP
DING! DING! DING!

THERE ARE LIKE 10 TIMES AS MANY PEOPLE WATCHIN' FROM THE HILLSIDE AS THERE ARE AROUND THE VICTORY BELL!
KINDA LOOKS LIKE MUNI STADIUM DURING A BROWNS GAME!

THERE'S A NICE BREEZE TODAY, TOO. THAT'S GOOD NEWS. IT'LL BLOW AWAY THE TEAR GAS.

GUARD OFF CAMPUS! GUARD OFF CAMPUS!

GUARD OFF CAMPUS!!

KLIK!
KLIK!
KLIK!
SMILE FOR TH' PIG PHOTOG, EVERYONE!

HERE'S A SHOT FOR YA, NORMAN!

THUD!
THUD!

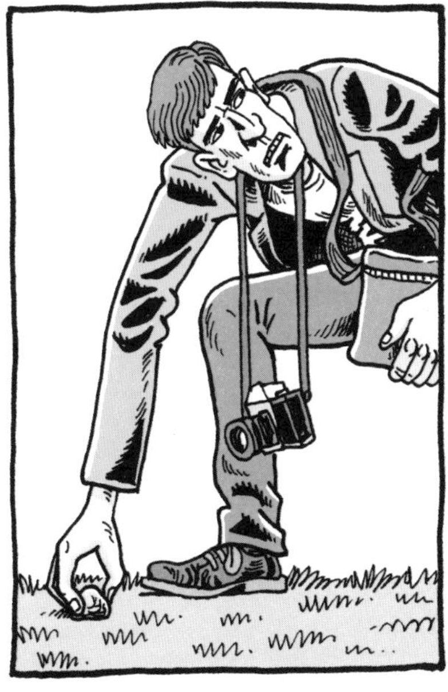

WHERE DID **THAT** IDIOT COME FROM?

...AND **WHAT** IS HE DOING HERE?
THUD!
THUD!

HEY, WANT SOME **"AMMO"?**
UH... YEAH, **SURE!**

GRAVEL... FROM THE **PARKING LOTS!**
RATTLE
KLAK

IT'S ALL WE **PEASANTS** GET!

BARRY!

BONNIE WON'T LEAVE **HER ROOM.**
THESE SOLDIERS HAVE TERRORIZED EVERYONE.
IT MAKES ME SO **FURIOUS.**

HERE. I BROUGHT A **WET RAG!**
FOR **THE TEAR GAS.**
KENNEDY
RIIIIP!

BILL! HEY, BILL!
HIYA, GENE!

YOU GOIN' TO **TH' PROTEST?**
I WANNA **CHECK IT OUT**, YEAH. COME ON. LET'S GO.

I **DOUBT** IT WILL AMOUNT TO MUCH OF **ANYTHING.**

KLIK!

BRIGADIER GENERAL ROBERT CANTERBURY, AGE 55, IS THE ASSISTANT ADJUTANT GENERAL OF THE OHIO NATIONAL GUARD, HANDPICKED BY GEN. DEL CORSO TO BE SECOND IN COMMAND.

CANTERBURY JOINED THE GUARD IN 1949, AFTER BEING A DESK JOCKEY IN WWII FOR THE MERCHANT MARINES AND THE ARMY. HE NEVER SAW COMBAT. HE ROSE STEADILY UP THE GUARD RANKS IN A VARIETY OF BUREAUCRATIC POSITIONS, AT ONE TIME OVERSEEING OHIO'S PLANS FOR POST-NUCLEAR WAR SURVIVAL! HE OWNED A RESTAURANT AND WORKED IN CONSTRUCTION UNTIL HE TOOK A FULL-TIME GUARD JOB IN 1960.

AS A COLONEL, HE LED THE 2,200-MAN GUARD OPERATION THAT CRUSHED THE **HOUGH RIOT** IN INNER-CITY CLEVELAND IN 1966. HE WAS THEN PROMOTED TO GENERAL.

AS THE COMMANDING OFFICER OF THE GUARD ON MAY 4... HE IS A **DISASTER.**

AT THAT MOMENT, THE CLASS PERIOD **ENDS** AND STUDENTS **STREAM** OUT OF EVERY BUILDING ON CAMPUS.
DO YOU HAVE **PLANS** THIS SUMMER, SANDY?
YEAH! A FRIEND AND I ARE HOPING TO GET JOBS AT A SEASIDE HOTEL IN **ATLANTIC CITY.**
WE'LL SPEND THE BREAK WAITING ON **ELDERLY TOURISTS** AND WORKING ON **OUR TANS!**

GUARD! FORM UP IN A LINE!
CHARLIE COMPANY ON THE LEFT FLANK, **G TROOP** CENTER, AND **ALPHA COMPANY** ON THE RIGHT!

KARLOVIC, WE'RE **SHORT ON MEN.** FILL IN THAT GAP OVER THERE WITH **A COMPANY.**
SIR.

WHAT TH' HELL?
IS THAT CRAZY GENERAL **REALLY** GONNA MOUNT **AN ARMED CHARGE** AGAINST A BUNCH OF **CHANTING KIDS?**
PRESS

GUARD OFF CAMPUS!!
THERE WON'T BE ANY VIOLENCE TODAY. EVERYONE GOT THAT OUT OF THEIR SYSTEM.

GUARD OFF CAMPUS!!
I CAN'T WATCH THIS. I HAVE CLASS.
ENNEDY

11:55 A.M.
LOOK AT THAT HILLSIDE! IT'S FULL OF PROTESTERS!

IT'S THE FIRST OF CANTERBURY'S CALAMITOUS BLUNDERS TODAY.
OKAY, THAT'S IT!
THE GENERAL MISTAKES THOUSANDS OF STUDENTS SIMPLY MOVING FROM CLASS TO CLASS, OR PAUSING TO WATCH THE UNFOLDING DRAMA ON THE COMMONS, AS PROTESTERS DEFIANTLY IGNORING HIS EDICT.

AN EDICT AGAINST FREE ASSEMBLY THAT HE HAD QUESTIONABLE LEGAL RIGHT TO ENFORCE.

NO MORE WAR! NO MORE WAR!
CANTERBURY CITES RHODES'S DECLARATION OF MARTIAL LAW, WHICH THE GOVERNOR HAD NEGLECTED TO OFFICIALLY ISSUE, AND THE POWERS THE GENERAL BELIEVES ARE GRANTED HIM UNDER THE OFT-CITED OHIO RIOT ACT, A LAW THAT, IN FACT, DOESN'T EXIST!
47
145 INF
RRRRRRRRR
BUMP! THUMP! BUMP!

THIS IS AN ILLEGAL ASSEMBLY! YOU MUST DISPERSE!
POLICE
U.S. ARMY
2010000013
A MONTH LATER, THE OHIO LEGISLATURE WILL QUIETLY PASS A RIOT ACT.

BOOOOO!!

YOU MUST...
GRR.

...DISPERSE!
KLANG!
U.S. ARMY
2010000013

YAAAAAAAY!!
RRRRRRRRR

IT'S TIME FOR THESE STUDENTS TO FIND OUT WHAT **LAW AND ORDER** IS ALL ABOUT!
BAYONETS! MASK UP!

LOCK AND LOAD!!

U.S. ARMY
THE **M1 GARAND** THAT IS CARRIED BY THE GUARD IS U.S. ARMY SURPLUS.
IT IS THE **ICONIC RIFLE** THAT WAS THE STANDARD-ISSUE COMBAT WEAPON DURING **WORLD WAR II** AND THE **KOREAN WAR.**
IT IS A .30 CALIBER, GAS-POWERED RIFLE, WITH AN EIGHT-BULLET CLIP. THE SEMIAUTOMATIC OPERATION ALLOWS SOLDIERS TO FIRE THE EIGHT ROUNDS AS QUICKLY AS THEY CAN PULL THE TRIGGER. **GENERAL GEORGE PATTON** CALLED THE M1 "THE GREATEST BATTLE IMPLEMENT EVER DEVISED."

THE M1 IS DEADLY ACCURATE AND POWERFUL.
IT FIRES WITH SUCH FORCE, ITS BULLET CAN GO CLEAN THROUGH A FOOT-THICK TREE TRUNK OR THROUGH FOUR MEN STANDING IN A ROW... AND KILL THEM ALL. THE COPPER-JACKETED BULLET IS OVER AN INCH LONG.
HEY! THEY ISSUED ME ARMOR PIERCING AMMO BY MISTAKE.
TOO LATE NOW.
CANTERBURY'S ORDER TO "LOCK AND LOAD" MEANS MEN INSERT A CLIP INTO THEIR GUNS AND HAVE A BULLET IN THE CHAMBER. THE GUN IS READY TO FIRE BY SIMPLY FLIPPING OFF THE SAFETY. PENTAGON GUIDELINES FOR NATIONAL GUARDS SPECIFY SEVERAL CONDITIONS BE MET BEFORE LOCK AND LOAD IS ORDERED. OHIO IGNORES THESE AND HAS ITS OWN GUIDELINES, THE LAXEST IN THE NATION.
ARMY

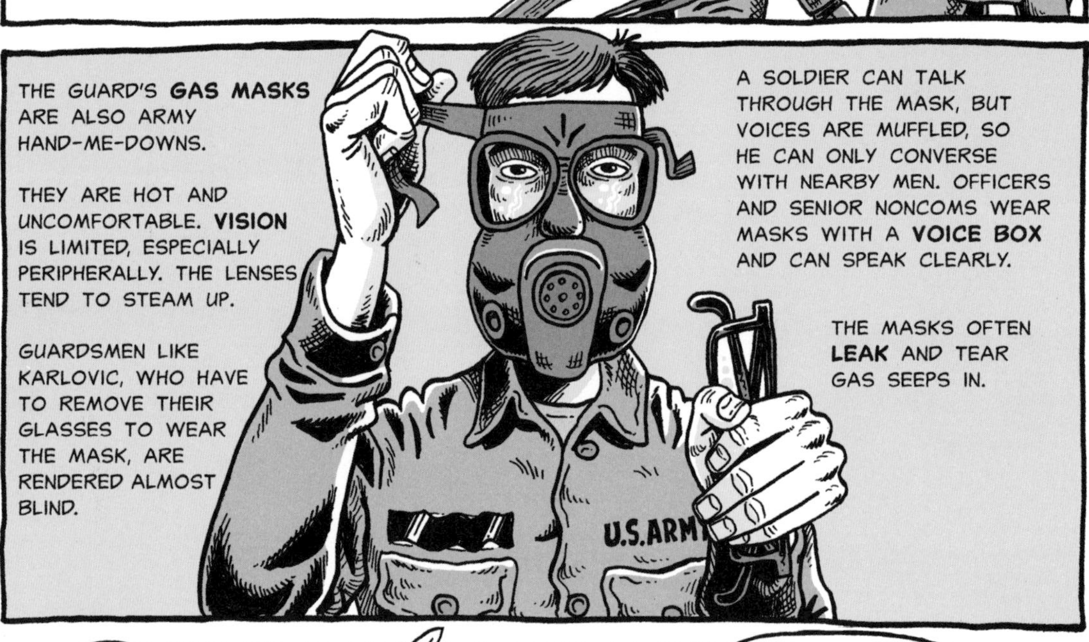
THE GUARD'S GAS MASKS ARE ALSO ARMY HAND-ME-DOWNS.
THEY ARE HOT AND UNCOMFORTABLE. VISION IS LIMITED, ESPECIALLY PERIPHERALLY. THE LENSES TEND TO STEAM UP.
GUARDSMEN LIKE KARLOVIC, WHO HAVE TO REMOVE THEIR GLASSES TO WEAR THE MASK, ARE RENDERED ALMOST BLIND.
A SOLDIER CAN TALK THROUGH THE MASK, BUT VOICES ARE MUFFLED, SO HE CAN ONLY CONVERSE WITH NEARBY MEN. OFFICERS AND SENIOR NONCOMS WEAR MASKS WITH A VOICE BOX AND CAN SPEAK CLEARLY.
THE MASKS OFTEN LEAK AND TEAR GAS SEEPS IN.
U.S.ARMY

FIRE GAS! MOVE OUT!

DING!
DING!
DING!
DING!
DING!

THOOOP!
THOOOP!
FOOOP!

SSSSSSSSS
SSSSSS
HERE IT COMES!
DING!
DING!

DING!
DING!
DING!
DING!
DING!

SIGH.

ARE THE **FACULTY MONITORS** ALL IN POSITION?
YES.

THIS IS **INSANE**, PROFESSOR FRANK!
NO WAY THEY HAVE **LIVE AMMO** IN THOSE GUNS.

FOOSH!

HARRY! WHERE'S YOUR GAS MASK?
JONES
USA
I DIDN'T HAVE TIME TO GO TO SUPPLY.

I'LL BE OKAY.

THOP!

LET'S SPLIT, GENE! YOU DON'T WANT A SNOOTFUL OF THAT STUFF...

...EVEN THOUGH IT'S TOO WINDY FOR GAS TO BE EFFECTIVE.

KOFF!

OW!
BOK!

LET'S GO!

WHY ARE THEY DOING THIS!?!
KENNED

UP THE HILL TO THE RIGHT OF THE BUILDING! CLEAR THE AREA!
U.S.AR

STUDENTS **SCATTER** BEFORE THE ADVANCING GUARD...

ON THE **OTHER SIDE** OF TAYLOR HALL, **C COMPANY** MOVES UP THE HILL THROUGH THE TREES....
KOFF!
THUD!

PIGS...
KOFF!
...OFF CAMPUS!

GIT OUTTA HERE!
YOW!
THWAP!

THE PLAN TO CLEAR THE COMMONS IS A SIMPLE ONE. IN A THREE-PRONGED ADVANCE, THE GUARD WILL USE GAS AND BAYONETS TO HERD STUDENTS OFF THE COMMONS, UP THE HILL TO EITHER SIDE OF TAYLOR HALL, AND DEEPER INTO CAMPUS.
PRENTICE HALL
PARKING LOT
ATHLETIC PRACTICE FIELD
1 C COMPANY TAKES THE LEFT PRONG WITH 30-36 MEN, MOVES UP THROUGH THE TREES, AND SEALS THE GAP BETWEEN PRENTICE AND TAYLOR HALLS.
TAYLOR HALL
PAGODA
TENNIS COURTS
VICTORY BELL
JOHNSON HALL
THE COMMONS
1
2
3
2 G TROOP, WITH 16 MEN, TAKES THE MIDDLE, THEN SWEEPS RIGHT AND MEETS UP WITH A COMPANY.
110 MEN REMAIN IN RESERVE AT THE GUARD LINE.
3 A COMPANY TAKES THE RIGHT PRONG. WHEN IT JOINS WITH G TROOP AT THE TOP OF THE HILL, 76 MEN WILL SEAL THE GAP BETWEEN TAYLOR AND JOHNSON HALLS.
ROTC
STUDENT UNION
A SIMPLE PLAN. AND THEN... IT ALL GOES WRONG.

KARLOVIC STRUGGLES UP THE RIGHT SIDE OF THE HILL WITH A COMPANY...
KOFF!
SPIT! AUGH! GAS IS LEAKIN' INTO TH' MASK.
SWEATIN' MY ASS OFF IN THIS THING.
AND I CAN'T SEE SHIT WITHOUT MY GLASSES!
U.S.A.
U.S.ARMY

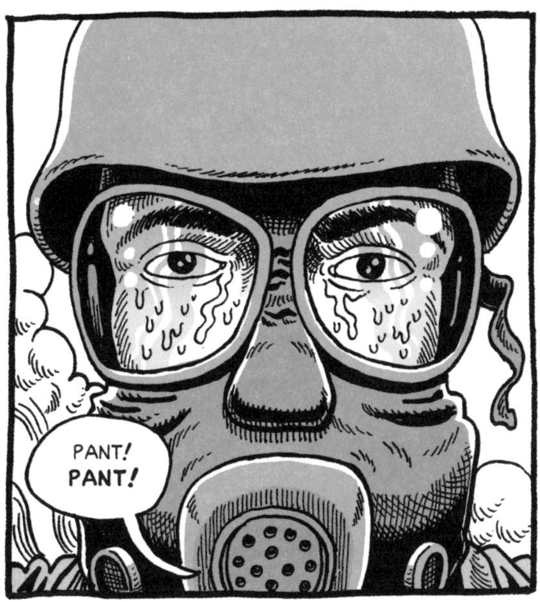
PANT! PANT!

OW! BASTARD!
THUD!

WE CAN GET SOME GREAT OVERHEAD SHOTS FROM THE ROOF, JERRY.

UH... ARE WE ALLOWED UP HERE, PROFESSOR?
THAT'S WHY I CAME WITH YOU.
GOTTA BEND THE RULES SOMETIMES.

GET OFF OUR CAMPUS, YOU PIGS!
C'MON, ALLISON!

YOU FASCIST PIGS!!

THE COMMONS IS CLEAR, GENERAL. C COMPANY IS IN POSITION ON THE OTHER SIDE OF THE BUILDING.
EXCELLENT, COLONEL.
FASSINGER
U.S.

BUT THAT GROUP OF PROTESTERS THERE NEEDS TO BE DEALT WITH.

AND WHAT ABOUT ALL THOSE STUDENTS ON THE TERRACE OVER THERE?
THAT'S A CLASSROOM BUILDING, GENERAL. THOSE KIDS ARE JUST WATCHING. THEY DON'T LOOK LIKE A THREAT.

FINE. BUT I STILL WANT THAT GROUP ON TH' HILL CHASED OFF.

FORWARD! AFTER THEM!

IT WAS YET ANOTHER BLUNDER BY THE GENERAL...
RATTLE!
CLUNK!
RATTLE!
CLANK!
CLUNK!
TROMP! TROMP!
TROMP!
TROMP!
TROMP!
TROMP!
TROMP

3 THE GUARD MOVES ONTO A LARGE ATHLETIC FIELD.
REMAINING PROTESTERS
REMAINING PROTESTERS
2 CANTERBURY LEADS HIS MEN DOWN THE HILL, PURSUING 50 OR SO PROTESTERS.
ACCESS ROAD
PRENTICE PARKING LOT
C COMPANY HALTS IN THE GAP BETWEEN BUILDINGS.
PAGODA
TAYLOR HALL
1 A COMPANY AND G TROOP SHOULD HAVE STOPPED HERE.

...A FIELD RINGED ON THREE SIDES BY A SIX-FOOT-TALL CHAIN-LINK FENCE.

PENNED IN LIKE SHEEP, DUMBASSES!
CHINK! CHINK!

HA HA HA!
BAA! BAAAA!

A SNIPER COULD PICK US OFF ONE BY ONE ON THIS FIELD! SHIT! SHIT! SHIT!
U.S. ARMY

THOSE STUDENTS BEHIND TH' FENCE...
GAS 'EM!

SSSSSS

THUD!

YEAH! NICE THROW!

SSSSSSSSSSSS
THUD!
THUD!

sSSSSSSSSSSSSS

OH FER CHRISSAKE! THEY'RE JUST PLAYIN' CATCH WITH THE GAS!

WHY TH' HELL DID CANTERBURY TAKE THEM DOWN THERE? THEY'RE PINNED!
DAMMIT!

HOLD YER POSITION, RON. I'M GOIN' DOWN TO THAT FIELD.
YESSIR.

GRUNT!

SAVE YER STONES. THOSE GUARDSMEN ARE TOO FAR AWAY. NOT EVEN TH' KENT STATE QUARTERBACK COULD HEAVE 'EM THAT FAR!
OW.

PIGS OFF CAMPUS! PIGS OFF CAMPUS!
KENNED

TROT! TROT! TRO

KLIK!
WHO'S TH' DICK IN TH' SCUBA MASK TAKIN' OUR PICTURES?
IT'S THAT NARC NORMAN AGAIN!

GENERAL CANTERBURY!
U.S. ARMY

IN THE PRENTICE HALL PARKING LOT, HUNDREDS OF STUDENTS MOVE THROUGH, OBLIVIOUS TO THE DRAMA ON THE NEARBY FIELD.
SANDY! WE MEET AGAIN!
AUGH! M-MY GOD! IS THAT TEAR GAS?
OH. HI, ELLIS.
HERE. WIPE YER EYES WITH THIS... A RAG SOAKED IN VINEGAR. A TRIED-AND-TRUE SDS RECIPE!
THANKS.
WHAT'S HAPPENING AT THE PROTEST?
I WAS THERE FOR A BIT. IT'S A FARCE.
I'M ON MY WAY TO MEET MY GIRLFRIEND.
I'LL WALK WITH YOU.
THOK!
OW!

THAT HURT!!

YEAH!
BULL'S-EYE!
WHEN ARE WE GONNA SHOW THESE LITTLE SHITS WHO IS IN CHARGE HERE?

HEY, "GOMER PYLE" WAS CANCELED! DIDN'T YOU EXTRAS GET TH' MEMO?

THE TAUNTS HIT HOME WITH KARLOVIC...
I'M GONNA LAY ONE ON THAT GUY IF I GET TH' CHANCE.
THREE DAYS OF THESE CREEPS!
U.S. ARMY

THAT GENERAL MARCHES US DOWN HERE AND LOOKIT HIM... HE HAS NO CLUE WHAT TO DO NOW!
HIS GODDAM HEAD IS COMPLETELY UP HIS ASS!

WE'RE SITTING DUCKS OUT HERE!

WHAT'S YOUR PLAN HERE, GENERAL?
I... UH... WANTED TO SCARE OFF... ERR...
...THOSE VOCAL PROTESTERS OVER THERE. THEY... UH... SEEM TO BE TH' LEADERS.
JONES

THEN LET'S DO THAT.
JONES

BANG!
WHAT'S HAPPENING OUT THERE, BARRY?
NOT SURE.

WHOA! W-WAS THAT... A SHOT?
ONE OF THOSE GUYS FIRED A PISTOL INTO TH' AIR!

OKAY! LISSEN UP!

KNEEL AND POINT YOUR RIFLES AT TH' PROTESTERS. DO NOT FIRE! WE JUST WANNA SCARE THEM ASSHOLES!
JONES

FLAP! FLAP! FLAP! FLAP! FLAP!

AT THIS POINT, ONLY **20 OR SO** PROTESTERS REMAIN, ON THE EDGE OF THE PRACTICE FIELD.

JEFF, WHO WAS SO HESITANT TO TAKE PART IN CAMPUS PROTESTS, IS ONE OF THOSE **STUBBORN FEW.** THE DISTINCTIVE SHIRT HE CHOSE TO WEAR MAKES HIM **EASY** TO SPOT FROM A DISTANCE.

STAND DOWN, G TROOP!
I CAN'T BELIEVE THIS! THEM JERKS ARE JUST LAUGHIN' AT US!
JONES
US ARMY

HOW MUCH OF THIS SHIT ARE WE GONNA TAKE?
GODDAMMIT! I'VE FUCKING HAD ENOUGH!
THE 16 MEN OF G TROOP ARE VETERANS OF THE RACIAL UNREST AND RIOTS IN CLEVELAND AND AKRON. THEY ARE OLDER THAN THE OTHER GUARD UNITS ON CAMPUS, MID-TWENTIES AND UP, WITH AN AVERAGE OF 3 1/2 YEARS OF DUTY.
MORE EXPERIENCED ...AND ANGRIER.
U.S. ARMY

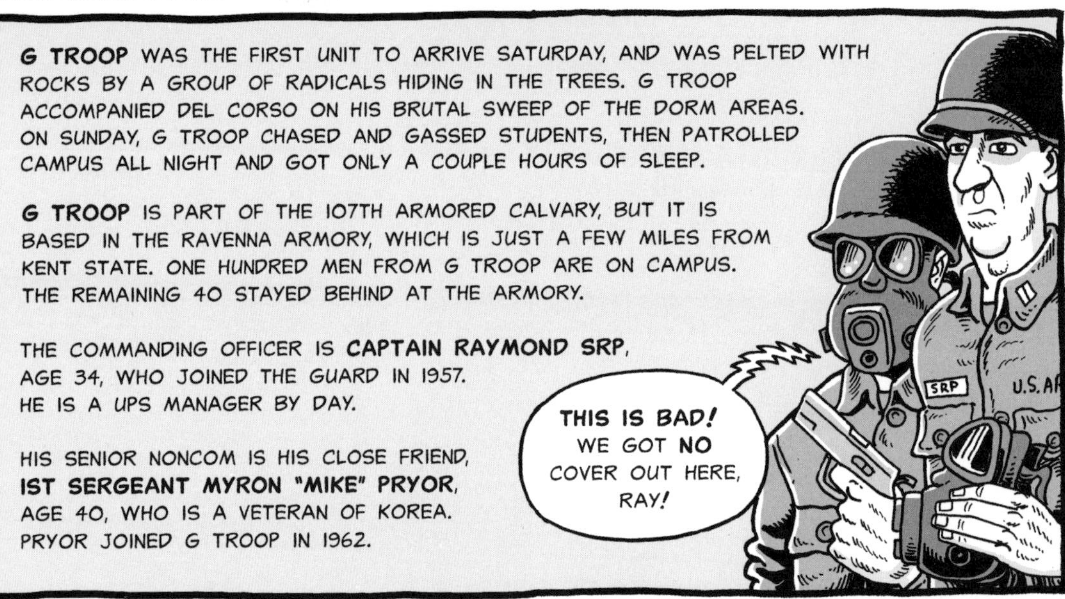
G TROOP WAS THE FIRST UNIT TO ARRIVE SATURDAY, AND WAS PELTED WITH ROCKS BY A GROUP OF RADICALS HIDING IN THE TREES. G TROOP ACCOMPANIED DEL CORSO ON HIS BRUTAL SWEEP OF THE DORM AREAS. ON SUNDAY, G TROOP CHASED AND GASSED STUDENTS, THEN PATROLLED CAMPUS ALL NIGHT AND GOT ONLY A COUPLE HOURS OF SLEEP.
G TROOP IS PART OF THE 107TH ARMORED CALVARY, BUT IT IS BASED IN THE RAVENNA ARMORY, WHICH IS JUST A FEW MILES FROM KENT STATE. ONE HUNDRED MEN FROM G TROOP ARE ON CAMPUS. THE REMAINING 40 STAYED BEHIND AT THE ARMORY.
THE COMMANDING OFFICER IS CAPTAIN RAYMOND SRP, AGE 34, WHO JOINED THE GUARD IN 1957. HE IS A UPS MANAGER BY DAY.
HIS SENIOR NONCOM IS HIS CLOSE FRIEND, 1ST SERGEANT MYRON "MIKE" PRYOR, AGE 40, WHO IS A VETERAN OF KOREA. PRYOR JOINED G TROOP IN 1962.
THIS IS BAD! WE GOT NO COVER OUT HERE, RAY!
SRP

AS CANTERBURY MULLS HIS NEXT MOVE, G TROOP HUDDLES TOGETHER.
THEIR IDENTITIES ARE HIDDEN BY THEIR GAS MASKS AND COVERED NAME TAGS.
GUARDSMEN REFUSE TO DISCLOSE WHAT WAS DISCUSSED. SOME DENY THERE WAS A HUDDLE AT ALL, EVEN THOUGH THERE ARE MANY EYEWITNESSES, INCLUDING FELLOW GUARD.

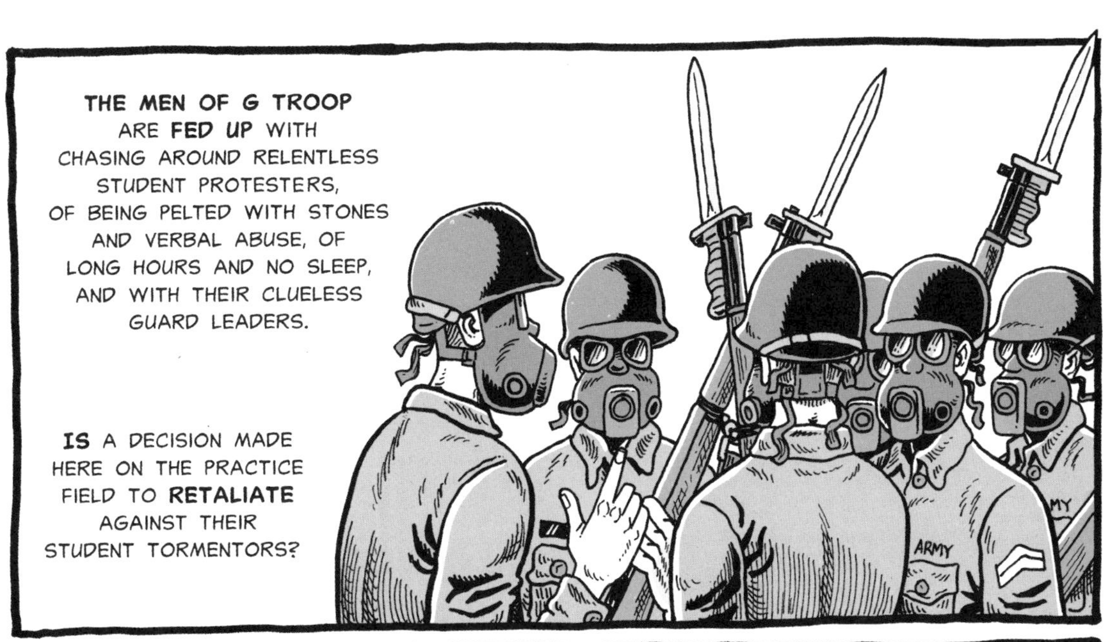
THE MEN OF G TROOP ARE FED UP WITH CHASING AROUND RELENTLESS STUDENT PROTESTERS, OF BEING PELTED WITH STONES AND VERBAL ABUSE, OF LONG HOURS AND NO SLEEP, AND WITH THEIR CLUELESS GUARD LEADERS.
IS A DECISION MADE HERE ON THE PRACTICE FIELD TO RETALIATE AGAINST THEIR STUDENT TORMENTORS?
ARMY

THOP THOP THOP THOP THOP

FASCISTS!
PIGS!!

WE'RE **NOT** ACCOMPLISHIN' A **GODDAM THING** HERE, GENERAL.

WE NEED TO GET TH' HELL OFF THIS FIELD!

THE GUARD HAS BEEN STUCK ON THE FIELD FOR AN INTERMINABLE **10 MINUTES.**
YEAH, YOU'RE **RIGHT,** MAJOR.
LET'S **PULL BACK** TO OUR LINE ON **THE COMMONS.**

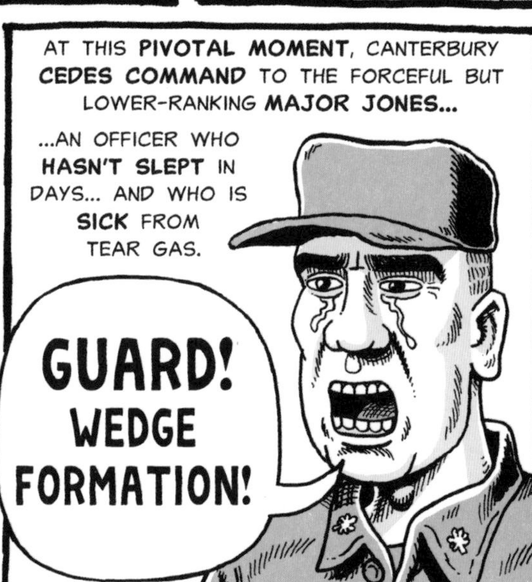

AT THIS **PIVOTAL MOMENT**, CANTERBURY **CEDES COMMAND** TO THE FORCEFUL BUT LOWER-RANKING **MAJOR JONES...**
...AN OFFICER WHO **HASN'T SLEPT** IN DAYS... AND WHO IS **SICK** FROM TEAR GAS.
GUARD! WEDGE FORMATION!

THE WEDGE FORMATION HAS BEEN USED SINCE ANCIENT TIMES. BILL STUDIED THIS IN ROTC CLASS.
OFFICERS IN THE MIDDLE.
MOST IMPORTANT, **G TROOP** TAKES THE RIGHT REAR FLANK.
JONES

JONES LATER DENIES HE GAVE ANY ORDERS ON MAY 4. HIS MEN AND FELLOW OFFICERS STATE OTHERWISE.
CLANK! RATTLE!
(RATTLE!)
CLATTER! CLUNK!
CLANK!
CLATTER! RATTLE!
KLINK! CLANK!
TROMP! TROMP! TROMP! TROMP!
RETREAT! RETREAT!

YEAH!
LOOKIT THEM RUN!

HERE COMES TH' GUARD AGAIN, PROFESSOR!
KLIK KLIK KLIK

WOO!
AWRIGHT! WE'VE WON!
GET OFF OUR CAMPUS, YOU CREEPS!

LOOKS LIKE THEY'RE GOING BACK THE WAY THEY CAME.
YEAH, IT'S OVER. LET'S SPLIT.
KENNEDY
HEY!
WEREN'T YOU SLEEPING ON MY COUCH FRIDAY NIGHT?
WAS THAT YOUR PLACE?
...WITH THE POOL?
HOW ARE YOUR EYES, SANDY?
MUCH BETTER, THANKS.
HI, JOHN!
SANDY!
LOTTA YELLING UP THERE.
THIS WHOLE THING IS A JOKE.
I GOTTA HEAD TO CLASS.
PIGS OFF CAMPUS! PIGS OFF CAMPUS!
GRUNT!
GASP!
UMPH!
CLANK!
CLATTER!
KLUNK!
CLATTER!
TROMP! TROMP! TROMP! TROMP!

NORMAN TRAILS BEHIND THE GUARD UP THE HILL...
SNIFF! KOFF!

...TOO FAR BEHIND.
GASP!
ZIIIIP!

THAT GUY WORKS FOR THE THE PIGS!
YEAH, I KNOW HIM. HE'S A NARC.

WE'RE GONNA SHOVE THAT CAMERA UP YER ASS!

JUST TRY!

KARLOVIC IS ON THE LEFT FLANK, UNABLE TO SEE WITHOUT HIS GLASSES, AND UNABLE TO HEAR OVER THE DIN.
GRUNT! PANT! GASP!

THE GUARD STUMBLES BACK UP THE HILL, ALMOST RUNNING...

YAAAY!!
OINK! OINK!
WOOOOOO!!
IF THEY RUSH US, LET 'EM HAVE IT!
ERG! OOF!
WHO IS THAT UP ON THE ROOF? I-IS IT A SNIPER?
WHEEZE!
CLANK! RATTLE! TROMP!
CLANK! CLATTER! TROMP!
CLUNK! TROMP!

MAJOR JONES THREATENS STUDENTS HE PASSES.
C'MON! C'MON! I'LL FIX YA!
JONES

BEFORE THEM, AT THE CREST OF THE HILL, STANDS THE PAGODA.

HAHAHA!! WHOOP! YAAWR!!
POP! POP! POP! YEEEEAA!
GRUNT! GASP! GODDAMMIT! I'VE HAD IT! I'VE HAD IT!
LISSEN TO THEM JERKS CHEER!
IF THEY GRAB OUR GUNS, WE'LL BE WIPED OUT!
LOOK FER TH' LEADERS IN HEADBANDS!
OOF!
UGH!
US
ARMY
CLINK! RATTLE! CLATTER! CLANK! CLUNK!
TROMP! TROMP! TROMP!

CANTERBURY AND MANY OF THE GUARDSMEN WILL CLAIM A THOUSAND PROTESTERS CHARGED THEM UP THE HILL AND THAT THE "AIR WAS BLACK WITH STONES."
THIS IS A LIE.
HERE, BASED ON PHOTOS AND THE LONE FILM FOOTAGE OF THE EVENT, IS WHAT THE GUARD FACED AT THE TOP OF BLANKET HILL.
ABOUT 50 PROTESTORS ARE AT THE BOTTOM OF THE HILL, CHANTING AND YELLING. SOME WALK TOWARD THE GUARD, BUT THERE IS NO CHARGE. MOST ARE MORE THAN 150 FEET AWAY. AROUND 100 STUDENTS WATCH FROM THE TERRACE OF TAYLOR HALL TO THE LEFT.
IN THE PRENTICE HALL PARKING LOT, SEVERAL HUNDRED STUDENTS FILE PAST, ON THEIR WAY TO AND FROM CLASS.
TROMP!
TROMP!
CLANK!
TROMP!

WHAT HAPPENS NEXT...
...CHANGES THE COURSE OF HISTORY.
CLATTER!
KLANK!
RATTLE!
CLANK!
THUNK!
CLUNK!
CLATTER!
RATTLE!
TROMP!
TROMP!
TROMP!
TROMP!

SOME GUARDSMEN ON THE RIGHT REAR FLANK TAP EACH OTHER ON THE ARMS AND SHOULDERS.
THEY STARE DOWN THE HILL AT THE PROTESTERS.
TAP! TAP!
TROMP! TROMP!

TROMP! TROMP!
SWOSH
MAJOR JONES MAKES A PRONOUNCED MOTION WITH HIS CROP. IS IT A SIGNAL?

YAAAA CLUNK! POP!
AND THEN, OVER THE CLAMOR, AN ORDER RINGS OUT.
RAWR! THUD! BANG!
GUARD! ALL RIGHT... PREPARE TO FIRE! GUARD!....
G TROOP WHEELS COMPLETELY AROUND IN UNISON AND...

POP!
BOOM!
BA
POW!
BADA-BOOM!
BANG!
BOOM!
POW!
BOOM!
BANG!
BANG!

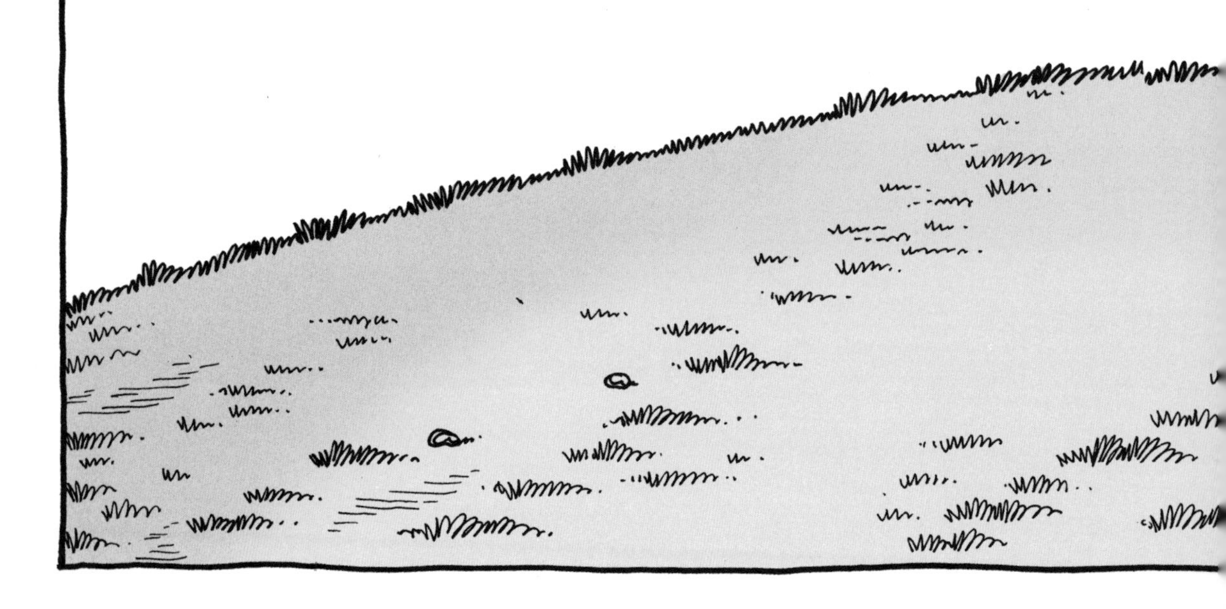

POW!
NG!
BOOM!

OTHER GUARDSMEN PIVOT AT THE SOUND OF G TROOP'S SALVO...
BOOM! POW! POP BANG!
BANG! BOOM

BANG! BOOM! POW!
BANG!
BANG! BOOM! POW!
...AND ALSO OPEN FIRE!
MOST OF THE 28 MEN WHO ADMIT TO FIRING THEIR WEAPONS SHOOT INTO THE AIR, AT THE GROUND, OR UP INTO THE TREES...

...BUT EIGHT TO 10 MEMBERS OF G TROOP FIRE DIRECTLY AT THE STUDENTS AT THE FOOT OF BLANKET HILL...
POW! BOOM!
BANG! POW!
....AND INTO THE PARKING LOT BEYOND.

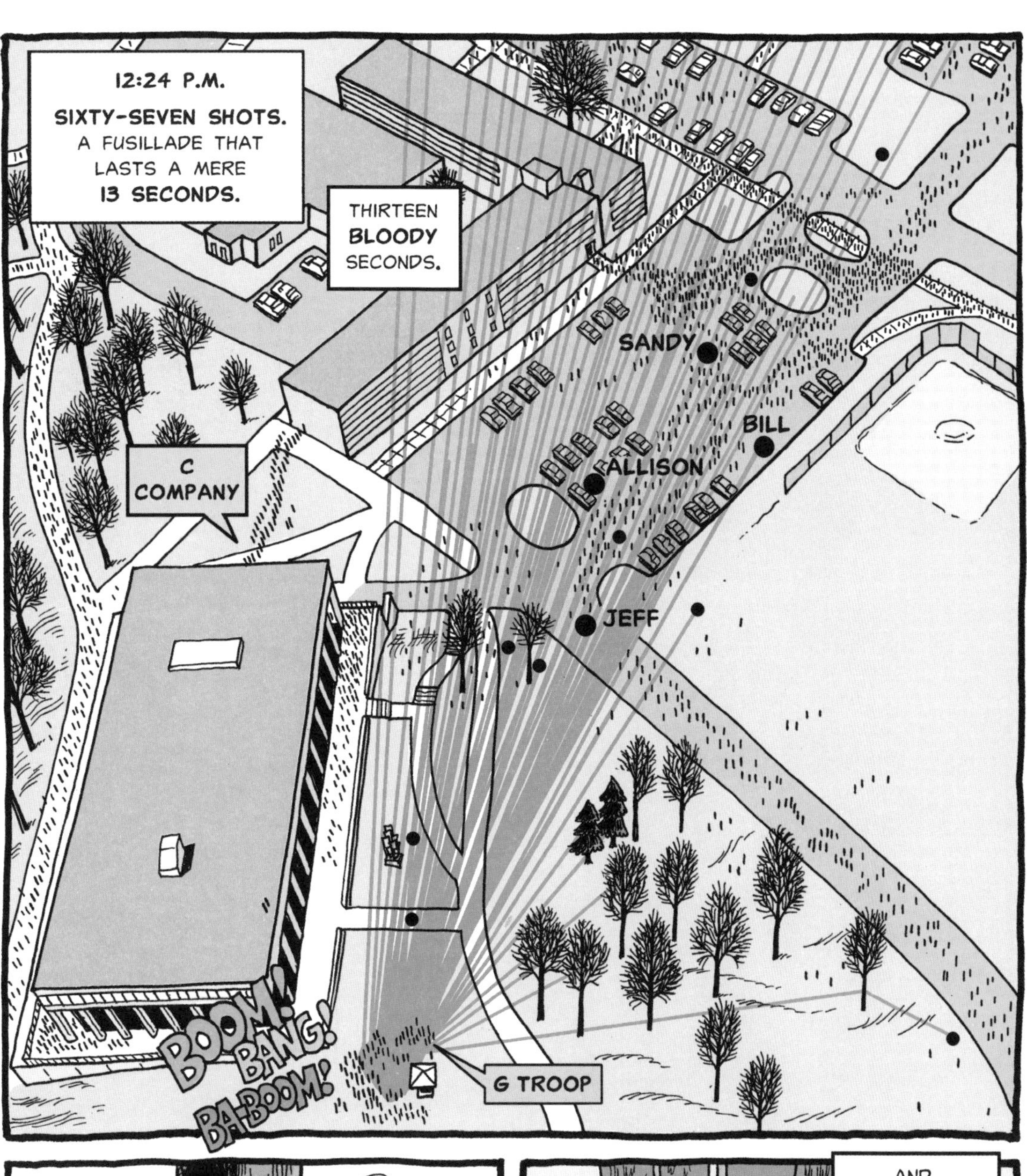
12:24 P.M.
SIXTY-SEVEN SHOTS. A FUSILLADE THAT LASTS A MERE 13 SECONDS.
THIRTEEN BLOODY SECONDS.
SANDY
BILL
ALLISON
JEFF
C COMPANY
BOOM! BANG! BA-BOOM!
G TROOP

THAK!
ZZZZZZ
GASP!
A BULLET RIPS THROUGH A TREE 18 INCHES THICK.

AND THROUGH THE HALF-INCH-THICK STEEL OF A SCULPTURE.
PANG!
AAAAAAA!

GUARD OFF CA...
JEFF IS 265 FEET FROM THE GUARD.
HE IS SHOT THROUGH THE MOUTH.

THE BULLET BLASTS OUT THE BACK OF HIS SKULL AND SEVERS HIS SPINAL CORD AND CAROTID ARTERY.
THE FORCE OF THE SHOT IS SO POWERFUL IT SPINS HIM COMPLETELY AROUND IN A GHASTLY PIROUETTE.

HE IS DEAD BEFORE HE HITS THE ASPHALT.
THUMP!

THE RETICENT PROTESTER,
DREAMER, DRUMMER, EASYGOING FRIEND
TO EVERYONE HE MET...
"HIS EYES WERE
WIDE OPEN TO EVERYTHING,"
SAYS HIS ROOMMATE STEVE.
JEFF IS JUST 20 YEARS OLD.

ALLISON IS
343 FEET AWAY...
BOOM!
BANG!
BANG!
BANG!
THUD!
POW!
BANG!
GET DOWN!

BARRY.
I'M HIT.

WHAT!?!
NO!
I'M HIT.
KENNEDY
THE BULLET ENTERS THE BACK OF HER LEFT ARMPIT AND SHATTERS ON AN ARM BONE. THE SHARDS **RIP THROUGH** ORGANS AND ARTERIES.

SHE NEVER REGAINS CONSCIOUSNESS.
POW! BANG!
BOOM! BANG! BOOM! BANG! BANG!
BANG! POP! POW! BANG!
HELP! HELP!!
TANG!
AAAAA!
BASH!
PANG!
SMASH!
PING!
TAK!
PASSIONATE, SMART, AND COMMITTED,
ALLISON WANTED TO SAVE THE WORLD FROM ITSELF.
SHE IS ONLY 19 YEARS OLD.

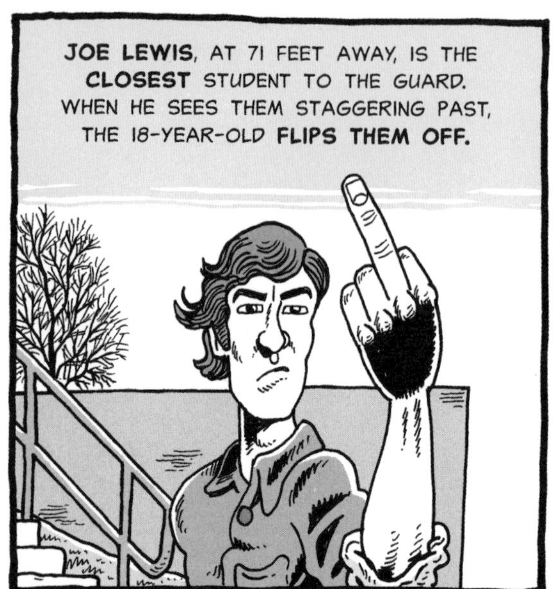
JOE LEWIS, AT 71 FEET AWAY, IS THE CLOSEST STUDENT TO THE GUARD. WHEN HE SEES THEM STAGGERING PAST, THE 18-YEAR-OLD FLIPS THEM OFF.

FOR THAT, HE IS SHOT IN THE GROIN. THE BULLET BLOWS OUT A THREE-INCH HOLE IN HIS BACK AS IT EXITS.
BANG!
BOOM!
BANG!
SQUIRT
THUD!

THEN HE IS SHOT IN THE LEG.
POW!
BANG!
YAARGH!
BANG!
TAK!

BEFORE PASSING OUT, HE CAN ONLY CRY...
BANG!
POW!
BANG!
OH M-MY GOD! THEY SHOT ME!

BANG!
BOOM
POW!
BANG!
PROTESTER TOM GRACE, AGE 20, IS AT THE BOTTOM OF THE HILL, 200 FEET AWAY.
HE TURNS AND FLEES AS THE GUARD OPENS FIRE...
THUD!

HALF HIS FOOT IS BLOWN OFF.
YAAAAA!!
KRAK!

BOOM! BANG!
POW! BANG!
AAAAAAA
WHUMP!

BANG! BANG! BANG!
POW!
STAY DOWN!
ALAN CANFORA, 21, IS GRACE'S ROOMMATE. HE IS 225 FEET AWAY.
SHIT!

BANG! BANG!
BOOM!
AAAAAA!
THAK!
A BULLET TEARS THROUGH HIS WRIST.

THUD!
THUD!
ARRRR!
THE TREE HE HIDES BEHIND LIKELY SAVES HIS LIFE.

UUUUUH!
BANG!
BANG!
POW
BANG!
JOHN CLEARY, 19, IS 110 FEET AWAY. HE PAUSES TO TAKE A PHOTO WITH HIS INSTAMATIC CAMERA AND IS SHOT IN THE CHEST.

DONALD "SCOTT" MACKENZIE, 22, IS 730 FEET FROM THE GUARD, A DISTANCE OF MORE THAN TWO FOOTBALL FIELDS.
GUUH!
HE IS SHOT IN THE BACK OF THE NECK. THE BULLET NARROWLY MISSES HIS SPINE AND BURSTS OUT OF HIS CHEEK.

BANG! BANG! BOOM! BANG!
UH!
THWIT!
GET DOWN, SANDY!

SANDY IS 390 FEET AWAY. THE BULLET TEARS OUT THE RIGHT SIDE OF HER NECK, DESTROYING HER LARYNX AND SEVERING HER JUGULAR.
SANDY! NO! NO!

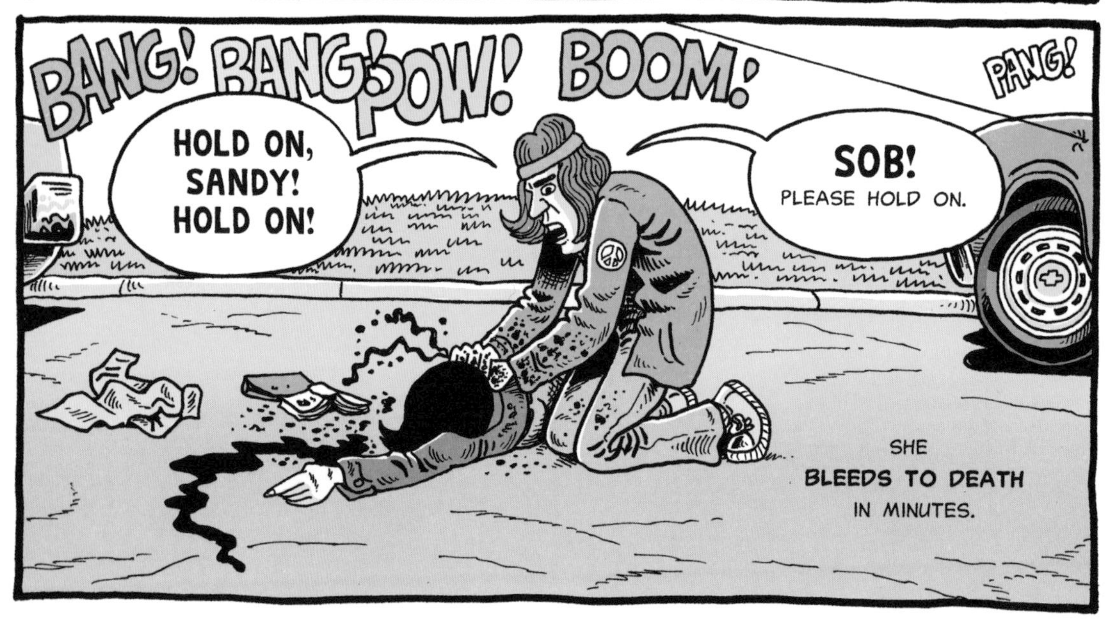
BANG! BANG! POW! BOOM!
PANG!
HOLD ON, SANDY! HOLD ON!
SOB! PLEASE HOLD ON.
SHE BLEEDS TO DEATH IN MINUTES.

SANDY, 20 YEARS OLD, CARING AND EXTROVERTED, DEVOTED DAUGHTER, AND THE BEST FRIEND YOU COULD EVER HAVE...

...IS GONE.

BANG! BOOM!
BANG!
POW!
THUD!
GASP!
DEAN KAHLER, 20, IS WATCHING THE PROTEST FROM THE EDGE OF THE PRACTICE FIELD, 300 FEET AWAY. HE DIVES TO THE GROUND...
...AND A BULLET SLAMS INTO HIS BACK, TEARS THROUGH A LUNG AND HIS DIAPHRAGM, AND SHATTERS THREE VERTEBRAE. HE IS INSTANTLY PARALYZED FROM THE WAIST DOWN.

DOUG WRENTMORE, 20 YEARS OLD, IS ALSO RUNNING AWAY. HE IS 329 FEET FROM THE GUARD...
GAH!
THAK!
...WHEN HE IS SHOT IN THE KNEE. THE BULLET SHATTERS HIS TIBIA.

ROBBIE STAMPS, AGE 19, IS WALKING TO CLASS, 495 FEET AWAY, WITH HIS LUNCH IN HIS HAND.
A BULLET SLAMS INTO HIS HIP.

JAMES RUSSELL, 375 FEET AWAY, IS HIT IN THE FOREHEAD AND THIGH BY A SHOTGUN BLAST THAT RICOCHETS OFF A TREE. HE'S 23 YEARS OLD.
UUH!

LUCKIER STUDENTS, LIKE BUTLER, FIND COVER BEHIND CARS.
KER-RASH!
STAY DOWN!

BANG! BOOM! BANG! BOOM!
POW! BANG! BLAM!
KRASH!
TOK!
AT THE SOUND OF GUNFIRE, **BILL**, THE YOUNG SOLDIER, INSTINCTIVELY **DIVES FOR COVER.**

HE IS **SHOT** IN THE BACK.
PSYCH
AUGH!!
HE IS 382 FEET FROM THE GUARD.
THUD!
SKRIT!
THE BULLET BREAKS FIVE RIBS, TEARS THROUGH HIS LUNG, AND EXITS THROUGH HIS SHOULDER.

BANG! BLAM! BOOM!
POW! POW! BANG!
OMIGOD!
UGH!

THE 19-YEAR-OLD ROTC CADET WITH THE
MIND OF A SCIENTIST
AND THE
HEART OF A PHILOSOPHER...
SOMEBODY C-CALL AN AMBULANCE.
MODERN PSYCHOLOGY
PYSCH
Schroeder
...BILL DIES AT THE HOSPITAL.

BANG! POW! BANG! POW!
KARLOVIC, TOO, RAISES HIS RIFLE AND SHOOTS.
SOLDIER! NO!
US ARMY

DO NOT FIRE!

CEASE FIRE!!
POW!
BANG BANG
JONES
WHAP!
BANG!

CEASE FIRE!
KLANG!
KRAK!

CEASE FIRE!

JONES
US
US ARMY

AFTER THE BARRAGE...

...SILENCE.

THEN COME THE SCREAMS.
OH MY GOD!!

JESUS CHRIST! JESUS CHRIST!
SOB!
GASP!
WE NEED AMBULANCES ...FAST!
AIIIEEEEEEEE
SHRIEEE
ARE... ARE... Y-YOU...

EEEEEEEEEE

EEEEEEEEEEEEEEEEEE
WH-WHAT TH' HELL JUST HAPPENED?
WHY DID THEY SHOOT?
WAS IT PREMEDITATED RETALIATION, AGREED UPON ON THE PRACTICE FIELD?... OR WERE THEY JUST BLINDLY FOLLOWING AN ORDER?
SINCE THERE WAS AN ORDER, AT LEAST ONE OFFICER WAS INVOLVED.
WHO GAVE THAT ORDER TO FIRE?
US ARMY

FIFTY YEARS LATER AND THE GUARDSMEN STILL AREN'T TALKING. MANY HAVE TAKEN THE SECRET TO THEIR GRAVES.
GENERAL, WE NEED TO GET THESE MEN OUTTA HERE! GENERAL!

OFFICERS! CHECK WEAPONS! IF THEY FIRED, MARCH THEM BACK TO ROT-SEE!
JONES

THE REST, MOVE OUT TO TH' BIVOUAC AREA ON TH' EDGE OF CAMPUS!
GO!!
YES, SIR!

SOLDIER, DID YOU FIRE?
I... I...
GOOD. GO WITH TH' REST OF ALPHA COMPANY.

C COMPANY LEAVES THEIR POSITION TO INVESTIGATE. THE ONLY ASSISTANCE THE GUARD OFFERS TO THE DEAD AND WOUNDED...

...IS THE BOOT.

J-JESUS CHRIST, CAPTAIN... IS HE DEAD?
SNYDER
U.S. ARMY
FLIP HIM OVER FOR ME, PRIVATE.

MURDERERS!
END
BASTARDS!
LET'S GET OUTTA HERE.

SSSSSSSS

KOFF!
GAG!
BANG!

CAPTAIN SNYDER LATER PRODUCES **A HANDGUN** AND CLAIMS HE FOUND IT ON JEFF WHEN HE ROLLED HIM OVER. IT IS A LIE.
THE GUN IS AN **UNTRACEABLE THROWDOWN** THAT BELONGS TO SNYDER.
DEAD END
IT WILL BE **FIVE YEARS** BEFORE SNYDER ADMITS **THE TRUTH.**

REEEEEEEREEEEE
BUMP!
WHUMP!

NORMAN FINDS HIMSELF CUT OFF FROM HIS GUARD PROTECTORS...
NARC!
GET THE PIG'S CAMERA!

YAAAA!

RRRRRRR
RRAAWR!!
GASP!

GET BACK!

AUGH!!
SOB!
THE SHOOTERS STUMBLE BACK TO THE GUARD LINE... ...AND COLLAPSE.
U.S. ARMY
GASP! SPUTTER!

STAY IN FORMATION! ST-STAY... IN... F...

THOSE BASTARDS HAD IT C-COMING!

THEY... THEY WERE... SOB!... JUST KIDS! THAT GODDAM GENERAL! THE BLIND FOOL!
SOB!

GET THESE MEN INSIDE A BUILDING. NOW!
JONES
U.S. ARMY
YES SIR, MAJOR.

THERE WAS, OF COURSE, NO SNIPER.

THE GUARDSMAN IS HOSPITALIZED AFTER HAVING A **PANIC ATTACK.** HE IS THE LONE **GUARD CASUALTY** ON MAY 4.

ON THE OTHER SIDE, **FOUR STUDENTS** ARE KILLED, AND **NINE** ARE SHOT AND WOUNDED, TWO OF WHOM ARE CRIPPLED FOR LIFE. ONLY **EIGHT** OF THE 13 WERE PROTESTERS.

MOST WERE **SHOT IN THE BACK** OR WHILE **DIVING FOR COVER.**

STOP THAT MAN!

HE HAS A GUN!

HE HAS A GUN!!

HALT!
HOLD IT! I KNOW THIS GUY!
U.S.ARMY

STOP HIM!
PANT! PANT!

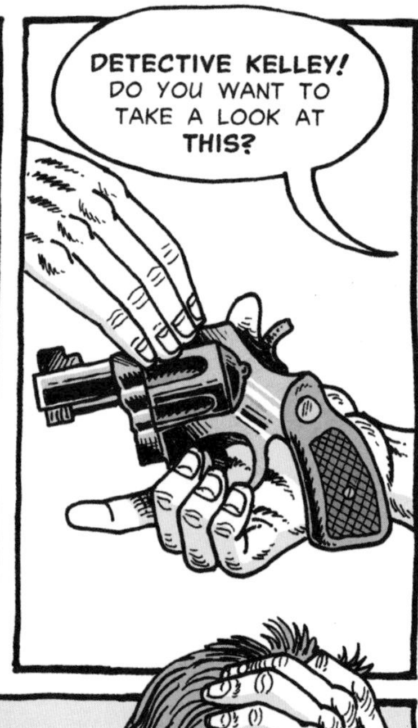

NEARBY PRESS AND GUARDSMEN **DISAGREE** WHAT KELLEY SAID. SOME SWEAR HE BLURTED OUT, "MY GOD, IT'S BEEN FIRED FOUR TIMES!" OTHER WITNESSES CLAIM HE SAID THE GUN HAD **NOT** BEEN FIRED.

NO CREDIBLE EYEWITNESSES COME FORWARD WHO **SAW** NORMAN FIRE HIS WEAPON.

WHAT WERE THE FBI, AND WHATEVER OTHER AGENCY, IF ANY, NORMAN IS WORKING FOR, **THINKING?**

SENDING AN **AMATEUR,** WITH A REPUTATION FOR **BRAVADO, IMMATURITY, AND AGGRESSION,** AND WELL KNOWN AS **A SNITCH,** INTO A VOLATILE PROTEST, ARMED AND UNSUPERVIZED... IS SIMPLY STUNNING IN ITS **RECKLESSNESS.**

ONLY A FEW OF THE SHOOTERS MENTION NORMAN IN THEIR GUARD REPORTS OR IN INTERVIEWS WITH LAW ENFORCEMENT. FIVE YEARS LATER, HOWEVER, GUARD DEFENDERS ARE PUSHING THE THEORY THAT NORMAN **FIRED HIS GUN** AND THE GUARDSMEN MISTOOK NORMAN'S WARNING SHOTS FOR A SNIPER AND **THAT'S** WHY THEY OPENED FIRE.

BUT THE GUARD **DIDN'T** FIRE IN NORMAN'S DIRECTION, AND EYEWITNESSES STATE HE DIDN'T PULL HIS PISTOL UNTIL **AFTER** THE GUARD'S FUSILLADE.

THE FBI **DENIES** NORMAN WAS WORKING FOR THEM. IT IS YEARS BEFORE THE BUREAU ADMITS THE TRUTH. NORMAN FLEES TOWN SHORTLY AFTER MAY 4 AND IS NEVER SEEN AT KENT STATE AGAIN.

MANY STUDENTS STAGGER AROUND IN **STUNNED DISBELIEF** OVER WHAT THEY HAVE JUST SEEN.

OTHERS FLEE. **BUTLER** IS ONE OF THESE. HE HAS **NO IDEA** HIS FRIEND JEFF HAS BEEN SHOT AND KILLED. HE WILL FIRST LEARN THE AWFUL NEWS ON TV THAT EVENING.
RUN!

OH MY GOD! PANT! PANT! OH MY GOD!
WE GOTTA GET OUT OF KENT... FAST!
RRR-RRR-RRR
VROOOM!

STUDENT LOT C
SCREEEEEEE

IN SHOCK, GRIEVING AND AFRAID OF BEING ARRESTED, BUTLER **HIDES OUT** FOR A WEEK AT A FRIEND'S CABIN IN MICHIGAN'S UPPER PENINSULA.
WHEN HE RETURNS TO KENT, THE FBI IMMEDIATELY BRINGS HIM IN FOR **INTERROGATION.** THE AGENT'S FIRST QUESTION?
"SO. HOW WAS MICHIGAN?"
ENTERING SUMMIT CO. LEAVING PORTAGE CO.
50 MPH
ROOOOAARR!!

SCREW THIS! I'M GOING CONSCIENTIOUS OBJECTOR!
GROAN.
I... I... CAN'T BELIEVE IT!
JESUS!
TROMP TROMP TROMP
U.S. ARMY

HOLY CRAP! WHAT HAPPENED UP THERE?
I HAVE NO IDEA.
TROMP TROMP

IT WUZ G TROOP! I HEARD AN ORDER TO FIRE... DID ANYONE ELSE HEAR IT?
I DID!
I DIDN'T HEAR IT.

IF THEM STUDENTS HAD GRABBED OUR GUNS, WE WOULDA BEEN WIPED OUT!
TROMP TROMP TROMP

ANY PUNK KID THAT TRIED TA TAKE MY GUN WOULDA GOT A BAYONET UP HIS ASS!
FUCKIN' A!
U.S. ARMY

THANK GOD I HAD TH' BRAINS TO HOLD MY FIRE!
AN OFFICER GRABBED MY RIFLE.

IF HE HADN'T...
...I WOULD HAVE EMPTIED MY CLIP!

ON THE COMMONS, PROFESSOR GLENN FRANK AND THE FACULTY MONITORS FRANTICALLY TRY TO CALM AN ENRAGED MOB OF SEVERAL THOUSAND STUDENTS WHO ARE NOW OUT FOR BLOOD.

I AM BEGGING YOU RIGHT NOW! IF YOU DON'T DISPERSE RIGHT NOW, THEY'RE GOING TO MOVE IN...

...AND IT CAN ONLY BE A SLAUGHTER!
U.S. ARMY

JESUS CHRIST, I DON'T WANT TO BE A PART OF THIS!!

MIRACULOUSLY, THE RESPECTED PROFESSOR'S RAW EMOTIONAL PLEA WORKS. THE CURSES STOP. ONE BY ONE, THE STUDENTS TURN...
...AND LEAVE.
IT'S OVER.

SEVERAL HOURS LATER. THE WOUNDED ARE BEING TREATED IN THE HOSPITAL.
OUTPATIENT C
THE FOUR DEAD ARE MOVED TO THE HOSPITAL MORGUE.
BARRY SITS ALONE IN THE HALLWAY.

ARE YOU A KENT STATE STUDENT?
YEAH.
WHY ARE YOU HERE?

I'M WAITING FOR PERMISSION TO SEE MY GIRL.

THEY'RE NOT GOING TO LET YOU SEE HER BODY.

THE UNIVERSITY HAS BEEN CLOSED. ALL STUDENTS HAVE TO BE ACROSS CITY LIMITS BY 6 P.M.
YOU HAVE TO LEAVE.

BUT...
...I DON'T HAVE ANYPLACE TO GO.

ROADS INTO KENT ARE CLOSED. PHONE LINES ARE OVERWHELMED AND DEAD.
FRANTIC PARENTS SNARL THE ROADS FOR MILES IN EVERY DIRECTION. MANY STUDENTS JUST WALK OUT OF TOWN.
IT'S A STRANGE, SAD PARADE...

...WATCHED OVER BY SOLDIERS, POLICE, AND SHOTGUN-TOTING LOCALS, SOME NEWLY DEPUTIZED, SOME JUST TAKING THE LAW INTO THEIR OWN HANDS.

KEEP MOVIN'!

A FEW HOURS LATER, THE CAMPUS IS EMPTY.

A SPRING RAIN COMES.

AND WASHES AWAY THE BLOODSTAINS ON THE PAVEMENT.

THE SIGN-OUT RECORDS OF G TROOP—USED WHEN SOLDIERS ARE HANDED THEIR GUNS—DISAPPEAR AND ARE NEVER SEEN AGAIN. COUPLED WITH THE SLOPPY HANDLING OF THE RIFLES, THERE IS NO WAY TO DETERMINE WHICH GUARDSMEN FIRED THE FATAL SHOTS.

GUARDSMEN RELOAD THEIR CLIPS TO MAKE IT APPEAR THEY DID NOT FIRE. GUNS ARE DITCHED OR SWITCHED. WITHIN AN HOUR, THE SHOOTERS ALL ADOPT THE SAME DEFENSE: "WE WERE IN FEAR FOR OUR LIVES, WE FELT WE HAD NO CHOICE." GUARD LEADERS ADVISE THEM TO LAWYER UP. THE FBI NOTES IN ITS REPORT LATER THAT FALL THAT MANY GUARDSMEN LIED IN THEIR INTERVIEWS WITH AGENTS.

JIM RHODES, WHO HAD BEEN TRAILING BADLY IN HIS REPUBLICAN PRIMARY RACE, SURGES AND ALMOST WINS HIS PRIMARY ELECTION ON MAY 5, 1970, LOSING BY LESS THAN ONE PERCENT, A MERE 5,300 VOTES. AFTER SITTING OUT A TERM, RHODES IS TWICE REELECTED GOVERNOR.

GENERAL DEL CORSO AND GUARD SUPPORTERS CLAIM THAT A SNIPER SET OFF THE SHOOTINGS. NINETY FBI INVESTIGATORS SCOUR THE CAMPUS FOR WEEKS. IN OCTOBER, THE FBI CONCLUDES UNEQUIVOCABLY, "THERE WAS NO SNIPER."

LIEUTENANT COLONEL FASSINGER DESCRIBES GENERAL CANTERBURY, POST-SHOOTINGS, AS "A BASKET CASE." CANTERBURY'S MILITARY CAREER IS OVER. IN 1971, WHEN DEMOCRATIC GOVERNOR JOHN GILLIGAN TAKES OFFICE, DEL CORSO AND CANTERBURY ARE REPLACED.

THE FIRST LETTER DEAN KAHLER RECEIVES WHILE RECOVERING IN THE HOSPITAL READS "DEAR COMMUNIST HIPPIE RADICAL, BY THE TIME YOU READ THIS, I HOPE YOU ARE DEAD."

ELAINE HOLSTEIN, JEFF'S GRIEVING MOTHER, RECEIVES HATE MAIL SMEARED WITH FECES.

A GALLUP POLL TAKEN THE FOLLOWING WEEK SHOWS 58 PERCENT OF AMERICANS BLAME THE STUDENTS WHO WERE SHOT FOR THE SHOOTING, AND ONLY 11 PERCENT BLAME THE GUARD WHO SHOT THEM.

ON MAY 8, NEW YORK CITY MAYOR JOHN LINDSAY, A REPUBLICAN, ORDERS THE FLAG AT CITY HALL FLOWN AT HALF MAST FOR THE FOUR DEAD, ESPECIALLY NEW YORKER JEFF MILLER. ANTIWAR PROTESTERS HOLD A RALLY IN FRONT OF CITY HALL. THEY ARE ATTACKED BY HUNDREDS OF CONSTRUCTION WORKERS, WHO SAVAGELY BEAT PEOPLE WITH HARD HATS AND CLUBS, THEN STORM CITY HALL AND RAISE THE FLAG TO FULL MAST. SYMPATHETIC POLICE DO NOT INTERCEDE. THE HARDHATS THEN BURST INTO NEARBY PACE UNIVERSITY AND SEVERELY BEAT ANY STUDENT THEY ENCOUNTER. SEVENTY PEOPLE ARE INJURED. IT IS NAMED "THE HARDHAT RIOT." NIXON IS OVERJOYED AND INVITES THE HARDHAT LEADERS TO THE WHITE HOUSE.

ELEVEN DAYS LATER, ON MAY 15, 1970, TWO STUDENTS ARE KILLED AND 12 INJURED DURING CAMPUS UNREST AT JACKSON STATE COLLEGE IN MISSISSIPPI. POLICE OPEN FIRE INDISCRIMINANTLY ON A DORMITORY. STUDENT PHILLIP LAFAYETTE GIBBS, AGE 21, AND A VISITING HIGH SCHOOL STUDENT, JAMES EARL GREEN, 17, ARE KILLED. POLICE AGAIN CLAIM A SNIPER SET OFF THE BARRAGE. NO EVIDENCE OF A SNIPER IS FOUND.

FOLLOWING THE SHOOTINGS, COLLEGE CAMPUSES THROUGHOUT THE COUNTRY EXPLODE IN PROTEST. MORE THAN FOUR MILLION STUDENTS AT MORE THAN 800 UNIVERSITIES AND COLLEGES TAKE PART IN STUDENT STRIKES, WALKING OUT OF CLASSES. MORE THAN 400 SCHOOLS CLOSE. DOZENS OF ROTC BUILDINGS ARE ATTACKED. THERE ARE VIOLENT CLASHES BETWEEN STUDENTS AND POLICE AT 26 SCHOOLS, AND NATIONAL GUARD UNITS ARE MOBILIZED ON 21 CAMPUSES IN 16 STATES.

KENT STATE DOES NOT REOPEN UNTIL JUNE. PROFESSORS ALLOW STUDENTS TO COMPLETE THEIR CLASSES BY CORRESPONDENCE. SOME HOLD CLASSES IN THEIR HOMES OR BACKYARDS. ALMOST NO STUDENTS FAIL CLASSES OR, MOST IMPORTANT, LOSE THEIR DEFERMENTS.

A WEEK AFTER THE SHOOTINGS, A LARGE HOUSE AD RUNS IN THE *KENT RECORD-COURIER* SIGNED BY PUBLISHER ROBERT DIX, WHO WAS ALSO A UNIVERSITY TRUSTEE. IT READS "THANK YOU, OHIO NATIONAL GUARD."

THE FOLLOWING QUARTER, 50 UNDERCOVER FBI AGENTS ARE ENROLLED IN KENT STATE CLASSES.

THAT FALL, NIXON FORMS A PRESIDENTIAL COMMISSION, KNOWN AS THE SCRANTON COMMISSION, TO EXAMINE THE KENT STATE SHOOTINGS AND CAMPUS UNREST. ITS FINDINGS ARE SURPRISINGLY FRANK. "THE INDISCRIMINATE FIRING INTO A CROWD OF STUDENTS AND THE DEATHS THAT FOLLOWED WERE UNNECESSARY, UNWARRANTED, AND INEXCUSABLE."

KENT STATE PRESIDENT ROBERT WHITE STEPS DOWN THE FOLLOWING FEBRUARY.

IN 1974, EIGHT GUARD SHOOTERS ARE INDICTED ON FEDERAL CHARGES FOR THE SHOOTINGS. JUST TEN DAYS INTO THE TRIAL, THE JUDGE THROWS THE CASE OUT OF COURT AND ACQUITS THE GUARDSMEN.

AFTER BEING ACQUITTED, FOUR OF THE GUARDSMEN AUTOGRAPH AN ENLARGED TRIAL EXHIBIT PHOTO OUTSIDE THE COURTROOM OF THE GUARD OPENING FIRE ON STUDENTS.

THE VIETNAM WAR GRINDS ON FOR ANOTHER FIVE YEARS. FROM 1970 UNTIL THE LAST CHOPPER OUT OF SAIGON ON APRIL 29, 1975, 9,477 U.S. SERVICEMEN LOSE THEIR LIVES.

IN 1979, AFTER YEARS OF LEGAL WRANGLING, A SETTLEMENT IS REACHED BETWEEN THE PARENTS OF THE FOUR KILLED AND THE NINE WOUNDED STUDENTS, AND THE STATE OF OHIO. GOVERNOR RHODES, BY THEN BACK IN OFFICE, AND THE GUARD ACCEPT NO BLAME, BUT EXPRESS "REGRET."

NO SHOOTER, OFFICIAL, OR POLITICIAN IS HELD ACCOUNTABLE FOR THE KENT STATE SHOOTINGS.

NOTES

My primary source was the May 4 Collection at the Kent State University Library, an impressive archive of all things concerning the 1970 tragedy. Of particular value were the oral histories—first-person recorded accounts by participants and witnesses of the events of May 1–4. There are over one hundred of these in the May 4 Collection. An additional fifty oral histories were available (but have since been taken down) from the Kent State Truth Tribunal, a project spearheaded by Laurel Krause, Allison's sister. I listened to every one of these recordings. It was a real luxury to have all of these interviews readily available—some with people no longer alive, since the project was started in 1990.

There is also a May 4 Visitors Center at Kent State, located on the ground floor of Taylor Hall, devoted to the shootings. This is separate from the May 4 Collection.

I also used materials from the Kent State Collection at Yale University. This consists of seventy-six boxes of legal documents, letters, film, and memorabilia from 1970. Established in 1977, this large archive was donated by the lawyers and families of the four slain students, as well as by several authors who wrote books on the shooting—the families did not want the material kept in Ohio or at Kent State.

I interviewed some key student activists and other contemporaries. A huge thank you to Chris Butler, a friend of Jeff Miller's, who has detailed memories of the events of all four days; Steve Drucker, Jeff's roommate and also a former boyfriend of Sandy Scheuer; Neil Phillips, a close friend of Jeff's at both Kent State and in high school on Long Island; Thomas M. Grace, the leading expert on student activism at Kent State; and Alan Canfora, an activist and archivist of all things May 4. Grace and Canfora were also two of the nine students shot and wounded on May 4.

There were several official investigations into the shootings of May 4, 1970. The first, by the FBI in 1970, is remarkably frank, considering the politics of the era and the FBI's obvious involvement in the tragedy. Nixon also ordered a formal investigation, which became known as the Scranton Commission. Its report was issued in September 1970. Both are found in the May 4 Collection and the Kent State Collection at Yale University (which I refer to as the Yale Collection going forward).

There were three trials. The first was a short federal criminal trial against eight guardsmen in 1974. All were acquitted. A civil trial, brought by Arthur Krause, Allison's father, and joined by the other parents of the dead students and by the wounded students, occurred in 1975. A jury ruled in favor of the State of Ohio, but that verdict was tossed out on appeal and a new trial was ordered in 1978. The second civil trial ended just as it convened in January 1979, in a settlement. These trials were the only time that state officials, officers, and guardsmen were publicly questioned under oath, or in many cases, questioned at all. Their transcripts are a treasure trove of information and are also found in the May 4 Collection and the Yale Collection.

I also relied on several of the (many) books written about the shootings. The best of these is *Thirteen Seconds: Confrontation at Kent State* (Dodd, Mead, 1970) by Cleveland reporters Joe Eszterhas and Michael D. Roberts. These gentlemen covered the event for the *Cleveland Plain Dealer* and knew the lay of the land and the players involved as only local reporters can. They wrote their book because they were unhappy with the paper's bungled coverage of May 4 (an editor decided protests at Kent State weren't worth covering, so there were no reporters on campus on May 4 or on the days leading up to it, and the paper had to scramble when the shootings happened).

An ebook in the May 4 Collection by Charles A. Thomas, *Blood of Isaac* (1999), provides an excellent timeline of events, with footnotes referencing the original source material. This saved me a lot of legwork, so a big thank you to Charles.

The most famous book on the shootings is James A. Michener's *Kent State: What Happened and Why*, written by the star author and his team of investigators in the months after the shootings and rushed into print by Random House in April 1971. It's more a political period piece than accurate history, and is full of ridiculous communist plots involving secret radical SDS (Students for a Democratic

Society) cells. Some of it is outright bullshit. But it does contain much useful information. At the time, *Thirteen Seconds* was a counterpoint to Michener's book, when controversy about the shootings still raged. In fact, according to *Blood of Isaac,* there was an infamous on-air shouting match between Michener and Eszterhas and Roberts during a segment on the *Today* show on May 4, 1971.

Kent State: Death and Dissent in the Long Sixties by Thomas M. Grace (University of Massachusetts Press, 2016) is the go-to resource on the history of student activism at Kent State.

The Kent State Coverup by Joseph Kelner and James Munves (HarperCollins, 1980) is a detailed summary of the civil trial of 1975. Kelner was the lead attorney for the plaintiffs.

Mayday: Kent State by J. Gregory Payne (Kendall Hunt Publishing, 1981) is full of wonderful accounts from family and friends of the victims.

The Truth About Kent State: A Challenge to the American Conscience by Peter H. Davies (Farrar Straus Giroux, 1973).

I used news accounts from 1970, particularly those of the *Akron Beacon Journal* (*ABJ*), which won a Pulitzer for its coverage. The *Beacon* published the most detailed (at the time) account of the events of May 4 and the days leading up to it, in a multiple-story special report, "The Tragedy at Kent State," in its May 24, 1970, issue. The report was written by an *ABJ* team and other reporters and editors from Knight Newspapers. Breaking news stories are tricky as resources, because the facts come out piecemeal and are often mixed with spin and falsehoods. This was especially true at Kent State, as the Guard, state authorities, and law enforcement concocted all sorts of wild claims and outright lies to justify the shootings. It would be many years before these fabrications were either abandoned or debunked. Some still aren't. On the other side, student activists, many facing indictments and fearful of government retaliation, either vanished, went silent, or purposely misled the media. That's not a criticism of the reporters—it's just the nature of breaking news. But with careful reading, breaking news stories can produce useful details, and the *Beacon*'s coverage was excellent throughout, and was the first media to question the official narrative that the students were solely to blame. Owner and publisher John S. Knight often recounted how many subscriptions the paper lost for its reporting of May 4.

The digital archive of the *Daily Kent Stater* (*DKS*) was a source I used repeatedly, both for accounts of events leading up to May 4, but also for details on student life, and campus and local events in 1970. Ditto the digital archive of the *Chestnut Burr,* the university yearbook.

The settings in this book are based on live sketches I made at Kent State. I coupled these sketches with reference photos and maps from the day to re-create both the 1970 university and the town. Photos came from the *DKS* digital archive, the *Chestnut Burr* yearbook archive, and the photo archive at the Kent State University Libraries—as well as from the voluminous personal collection of Jason Prufer, a senior library associate there, who deserves special thanks.

PROLOGUE

Pages 1–7: The account of the Teamsters strike is pieced together from my own recollections, the oral histories in the May 4 Collection of two guardsmen who were on duty, and news accounts from the *ABJ*. My otherwise quaint hometown had a dozen ugly truck depots on the southern edge of the village, built on former farms. The depots moved in when two major interstates were carved through town in the early sixties. Town leaders tried to keep them out, but the trucking industry, considered vital to the nation by Congress, enjoyed immunity from local zoning laws. The Guard was dispatched to Richfield, Ohio, on Wednesday, April 29, 1970.

Page 5: The Terry Point Inn was one of two raucous trucker bars in this part of town, the Clearview Inn being the other, along Cleveland-Massillon Road. The teamsters spent the day inside, boozing it up, until one of their posted watchmen alerted them that a truck convoy was leaving the depots. They would then pour out and leap in their pickup trucks to intercept the convoy. The Guard quickly figured out if they just surrounded the bars, the teamsters would be hemmed in.

Page 7: The account from Guardsman Frank

Karlovic comes from a lengthy oral history and an earlier written account, both in the May 4 Collection. Karlovic is a fake name. In the archive, he is listed only as "Anonymous Guardsman." It wasn't hard to figure out his real identity, but I've left it masked out of respect for his willingness to talk.

The two oral histories are the only detailed day-to-day accounts of the experiences of a shooter during this event. Most refused to speak following May 4, and have refused to speak since. Karlovic's account of the Teamsters strike in Richfield, and of the events of Saturday and Sunday, are wonderfully descriptive and ring true to my research.

Karlovic exaggerates about the student protestors, however. His tales of "bags of urine and feces" being hurled at guardsmen were refuted by the FBI in its report, and by historians and reporters. The National Guard insisted they were pelted with feces for three days, yet could not produce a single scrap of evidence. It didn't happen. This was a common charge leveled against the "dirty" radicals of the era. He's bit of a braggart, too, and his descriptions of the Guard's prowess and efficiency are clearly disputed by the debacle of the Kent State action and by the comments of other Guardsmen.

I realize using the Anonymous Guardsman's account is controversial. Nevertheless, most of his account, outside of the shooting itself, is remarkably detailed and blunt. I really had no choice here. None of the other Guard on Blanket Hill have broken their silence to this extent. I felt it was vital to show this perspective.

Pages 8–9: Sources for Nixon's speech: Transcript from the Nixon Library; network TV schedule for 1970.

FRIDAY, MAY 1

Page 12: The transcript of this protest on the Commons is available from several sources.

The Victory Bell was donated to the university by the Erie Railroad in 1950. An architecture student designed the brick structure. Source: Kent State website.

Page 14: Bill Schroeder's views on the war. Sources: "A Boy Who was Just There Watching It and Making Up His Mind" by John Pekkanen, *Life* magazine, May 15, 1970; Gene Pekarik account, *Lorain Journal,* May 5, 1970; Lou Cusella account, *Communication Quarterly,* 1982; Payne, 1981.

Sources for summary of the Cambodia Invasion: "Nixon Authorizes Invasion of Cambodia, April 28, 1970," by Andrew Glass, *Politico,* April 28, 2015; *New York Times* (*NYT*), May 1, 1970.

Page 15: Flyers calling for the torching of ROTC began appearing around campus at this time. Source: William A. Gordon, *The Fourth of May* (Prometheus Books, 1990).

Terry Norman's cover as a yearbook photographer. Sources: The first detailed profile of Norman, by Janis Froelich in the *Tampa Tribune,* "Kent State: A New Look," April 30, 2006; "Does Former Informant Hold the Key to the May 4 Mystery?," *Plain Dealer,* December 19, 2010; *ABJ Special Report*; Butler, 2017; Drucker, 2017.

Norman was a recognized informant. In a letter to *DKS* in 1969, Norman complains of being ejected from an SDS meeting. "I would like to know what the SDS had to hide," he writes. Source: *DKS,* May 9, 1969.

A few days later, Chris Butler writes a letter in rebuttal. "I cannot conceive how Terry Norman cannot see SDS's paranoia, when he told me and others on two occasions that he is working as an informer for campus police." Source: *DKS,* May 15, 1969.

Page 16: This excerpt comes from the *DKS,* May 1, 1970 (the last issue that would be published that academic quarter). The *DKS* published Tuesday through Friday in 1970, so there was no edition for Monday, May 4. Once the university was closed that afternoon, the paper could no longer publish. Source: *DKS* digital archive.

Pages 17–18: Source of poll: *DKS,* May 1, 1968. The history of the university comes from the Kent State University website and the *ABJ,* May 24, 1970.

The black squirrels were imported in 1961 from Canada by the head groundskeeper, per the Kent State website.

Page 20: Sandy's house on East Summit Street is still standing. Her nickname, "Sandy Beach," was given to her by Steve Drucker and used by friends and colleagues. Many phone messages to Sandy at the Speech Lab are addressed to "Sandy Beach" or simply "Miss Beach." Sources:

"Sandy's Scrapbook," a 2018 exhibit in the May 4 Center, Kent State University; interview with Drucker, 2017.

As a speech pathology major, Sandy was assigned to work with a student from Kent State who had a speech impediment. Source: May 4 Collection.

Sources for wedding announcements from Sandy's mom: Michener, 1971; Eszterhas and Roberts, 1970.

Page 21: The blood bank was near Sandy's house on East Summit Street.

Page 22: Jeff's house is still standing, at the end of a long, unnamed alley a block from campus. Jeff's drum kit was loaned to him by Butler and was later confiscated by the FBI. When it was returned to Butler months later, the tom-tom drum was missing. Butler never got it back. Sources: Interview with Butler, 2017; Drucker, 2017.

Page 23: The boys always practiced to *Live/Dead*, released in November 1969. Sources: Butler, 2017; Drucker, 2017.

Jeff was lured to Kent by friends Drucker and Neil Phillips, all of whom attended the same high school in Plainview, on Long Island. Jeff transferred to Kent over Christmas break and started there in January 1970. Sources: Interviews with Drucker and Phillips; speech by Russ Miller, YouTube.

Page 24: Orville's is repeatedly mentioned in many source materials and often cited by interviewees. It was Seaver's up until sometime in 1969, then was rechristened Orville's. It was renamed Walter's a few years later and stayed open into the eighties. Students from this era refer to it by all those names, sometimes in the same conversation. The building at 252 North Water Street still stands, although it has been empty for some time. Sources: Butler, 2017; Canfora, 2017; Kent city directories.

Ohio's drinking age in 1970 was eighteen for so-called "low" beer, which had an alcohol content of 3.2 percent. You had to be twenty-one to purchase wine, regular beer, or hard liquor. This was, of course, based on my experience in the seventies, loosely enforced and easily skirted. Source: *DKS*, October 17, 1968.

Page 25: Source for this conversation and the details of Jeff's departure for his date: Butler, 2017.

Page 26: Sources on the SDS: *The Weather Underground* documentary (2002); United Press International reports of the convention (September 1970); SDS files, May 4 Collection; *SDS (Students for a Democratic Society)* by Kirkpatrick Sale (Vintage Books, 1974); *The Port Huron Statement* by Tom Hayden (Public Affairs, 2005); *Encyclopedia Britannica*; *Fire in the Streets: America in the 1960s* by Milton Viorst (Touchstone, 1979); Todd Gitlin, "What Was the Protest Group Students for a Democratic Society?," *Smithsonian* magazine, May 4, 2017.

Carl Ogelsby, who grew up in my hometown and graduated from my alma mater, Revere High School, became president of SDS in 1965, and offers a great history of SDS in the sixties. He was purged by the Weathermen in 1969. Source: *Ravens in the Storm* by Carl Ogelsby (Scribner, 2008).

Sources on Kent SDS: *ABJ*, various articles (1970); *DKS*, various articles (1968–70); Thomas M. Grace, *Kent State: Death and Dissent in the Long Sixties* (University of Massachusetts Press, 2016); James A. Michener, *Kent State: What Happened and Why* (Random House, 1971); police files in the May 4 Collection.

Source for induction numbers: U.S. Selective Service.

The SDS flyer is modeled after an image from *The Big Us*, an SDS-affiliated newspaper based in Cleveland, January 1969.

Sources on the end of Kent SDS: *DKS*, 1969; Grace book, 2016.

The "Kent State Four"—Rick Erickson, Howie Emmer, Colin Neiburger, and Jeff Powell—served six months starting on October 29, 1969. They were released April 29, 1970. Source: *DKS*, 1970.

Seventy-two other SDSers were charged and all entered plea bargains. A dozen were jailed for fifteen to forty-five days, including Weathermen leader Terry Robbins. Authorities apparently had no clue who he was! Sources: Grace book, 2016; Cathy Wilkerson, *Flying Close to the Sun* (Seven Stories Press, 2007).

SDS member Ken Hammond confirms there was little left of the Kent State chapter by 1970. "We didn't have the troops." Source: Oral history, May 4 Collection.

Page 27: The Pit was a large, round structure in the middle of the three dorms that comprised the Tri-Towers. It was a popular student hangout with a large sunken lounge area (thus the name). Jeff's birthday was March 28. His draft lottery number was 223. Source: U.S. Selective Service.

Page 28: Sources for draft figures: American War Library; U.S. Selective Service; "The Military Draft During the Vietnam War," an article in a history project, *Resistance and Revolution: The Antiwar Movement at the University of Michigan,* the University of Michigan website.

Sources on Trump and Clinton: "Donald Trump's Draft Deferments: Four for College, One for Bad Feet," *NYT*, August 1, 2016; "Bill Clinton's Vietnam Test," *NYT*, February 14, 1992.

The Draft Lottery was held on December 1, 1969, at Selective Service National Headquarters in Washington, D.C. There were 366 blue plastic capsules containing birth dates placed in a large glass container and drawn by hand to assign order-of-call numbers to all men between the ages of eighteen and twenty-six. The lottery was televised and watched by millions of nervous draft-eligible men. Sources: May 4 Collection; U.S. Selective Service; various news reports.

Page 29: Congress passed the Twenty-Sixth Amendment on March 23, 1971, lowering the voting age to eighteen. The states promptly ratified it on July 1, 1971 (the fastest an amendment has been ratified in U.S. history). Source: *NYT,* July 6, 1970, and May 19, 2019. This scene is based on the recollections of Russ Miller, Jeff's brother, from the May 4 Collection, as well as my interview with Butler.

Page 30: Allison's attempt to send a telegram to Nixon. Source: Eszterhas and Roberts, 1970. The Western Union office was at 150 North Water Street, two blocks south of the bar district. Source: Kent city directory, 1970.

Page 31: Sources on Terry Norman: The definitive profile of Norman is by Janis Froelich, "Kent State—A New Look," *Tampa Tribune,* April 30, 2006; profile of Norman by John Mangels, "Kent State Shootings: Does Former Informant Hold the Key to the May 4 Mystery?," *Plain Dealer,* December 19, 2010; Taylor Rogers and Emily Inverso, "Who Is Terry Norman?," *KentWired,* November 16, 2010; Eszterhas and Roberts, 1970.

Page 32: Source on campus police: *DKS,* January 23, 1969.

Source on county sheriff and highway patrol: Scranton Commission Report, 1970.

Source on city police: Testimony of Chief Roy Thompson, 1975.

Sources on FBI and military intelligence: Morton H. Halperin, Jerry J. Berman, Robert L. Borosage, and Christine M. Marwick, *Lawless State: The Crimes of the U.S. Intelligence Agencies* (Penguin, 1976); Clay Risen, "Spies Among Us," *The American Scholar,* December 2008.

The presence of undercover agents was covered by the *ABJ* on March 31, 1974. It was confirmed in 1983 by Lieutenant Colonel Fassinger of the 107th, who told author William A. Gordon in an interview that a military intelligence agent was present in the Guard's command post throughout the occupation of campus. Fassinger also revealed that there was a direct line to the Nixon Justice Department, and that the Guard phoned in frequent updates.

Page 33: Water Street 1970 was re-created with the help of Jason Prufer, who works at the Kent State University Libraries and is a photo archivist. To the north of Main and Water, past the banks and the towering William Brothers Mill silos, was the popular cluster of bars depicted here. The Ron-de-Vou Lounge was an old-timey, blue-collar liquor joint that pulled in some students. JB's was renowned for its live music. The subterranean Kove also had bands. Orville's was the hipster and intellectual hangout, but you could also find bikers and townie barflies there. Big Daddy's and the Pirate's Alley were typical college beer halls. There were also a few scattered bars along Main Street, downtown, and then farther east, bordering campus. Student Joe Lewis, who was shot on May 4, states there were twenty-eight bars spread over five blocks in Kent. Sources: Various interviews; photographs; Kent city directory, 1970.

The Lakers-Knicks 1970 NBA Finals, eventually won by the Knicks in Game 7, is considered one of the greatest championship series in NBA history. Nearby Cleveland, along with Portland and Buffalo, had just been awarded an expansion team, christened the Cavaliers, and would be filling its roster with a draft the following week, so interest in the NBA was at an all-time high in northeast Ohio. It's unclear which bar Bill was in to watch

Game 4 of the series. Sources: *NYT*; Eszterhas and Roberts, 1970; various interviews and news accounts.

Page 34: Allison was placed on Water Street by several books and news accounts, and by the accounts of Barry Levine and Bonnie Henry. The radical musing about bank windows was described by Alan Canfora in a 2017 interview.

Pages 34–35: Officer Ron Craig and the beer bottle come from interviews with Butler and Canfora. The detail of the Stroh's bottle comes from Canfora, who recently asked the thrower of said bottle (who we'll leave anonymous here) what brand it was.

Page 36: Details of Water Street on May 1 come from interviews with eyewitnesses Butler, Canfora, Drucker, and Chas Madonio (a musician playing in one of the clubs that night), numerous oral histories at the May 4 Collection, and news reports from 1970.

Page 37: Chief Roy Thompson, fifty-nine years old, is an old-school, small-town cop. He was born and raised in West Virginia. He became chief in 1962, and was respected and liked by the Kent townsfolk and businessmen. He threatened to retire at the end of 1969, fed up with court rulings about civil liberties, but changed his mind when hundreds signed a petition urging him to stay. Thompson was a fervent anti-communist and saw a pinko plot behind every bush, a paranoia that was almost comical at times. He had grown increasingly alarmed by antiwar activists at Kent State. Sources: Thompson civil trial testimony, Kent police intelligence reports, May 4 Collection; Eszterhas and Roberts, 1970.

Page 38: Jerry Rubin and Nancy Rubin spoke at Kent State on Friday, April 10, at a noon rally on Front Campus. A local jug band, featuring Chris Butler, was the opening act. A crowd of two thousand witnessed the speech. Campus police patrolled the fringe, dozens of plainclothes cops infiltrated the crowd, and a highway patrol plane circled overhead, but there was no trouble. "Being young in America is illegal," said Rubin. "We are a generation of obscenities." Buckets were passed throughout the crowd to help raise money for the jailed Kent SDS leaders. Sources: *DKS*, April 18, 1970; Butler, 2017.

Sources on the Yippies: "The Chicago 10/ The Yippies," PBS's *Independent Lens* (2008); "The Battle for Chicago: From the Yippies' Side," *NYT*, September 15, 1968; Paul Krassner, *Confessions of a Raving, Unconfined Nut: Misadventures in Counter-Culture* (Touchstone, 1994).

Sources on Donald L. Schwartzmiller, chief of the campus police: May 4 Collection; *DKS*, 1970.

Page 39: The "bonfire" in the street was greatly exaggerated by Mayor LeRoy Satrom. Eyewitnesses describe it as the contents of several trash cans. The lone rooftop photo of the blaze shows it to be quite small. Source: Photo in 1971 Kent State yearbook, the *Chestnut Burr*, digital archive, Kent State Libraries.

Page 40: The campus prank club was the Mobrobrious Pit. Sources: *DKS*, April 30, 1971; oral history of Ronald Sterlekar, leader of the Pit in 1970, from the May 4 Collection.

Page 41: The first window hit was the Krahling Loan Company at 303 North Water Street, directly across from the bars. Sources: News reports; interview with Alan Canfora, 2018; Kent city directory, 1970.

A total of fifty-six windows were smashed. Source: *ABJ*, May 24, 1970.

Bill and Al's "rescue" of the two girls from Akron comes from several news sources and books, and from the account of Bill's friend Al Springer. It was also confirmed by the account of Elissa Shockley, one of the girls. Source: *ABJ*, May 18, 2019.

Pages 42–43: The Guard camped in a large open rec field behind Richfield Village Hall. Some guardsmen mistakenly recall camping at the grade school, which was right across the street and plainly visible, so that probably accounts for the error. I was attending that school in May 1970 and remember the Guard camp. It was endlessly fascinating to us schoolkids. Sources: Richfield Historical Society; firsthand observations.

Source for Karlovic's conversation: Anonymous Guardsman oral history, May 4 Collection.

The Hough Riot in 1966 was crushed by 1,700 guardsmen, including the 145th and 107th. During the Glenville Riot in July 1968, the Guard occupied the city again. Both incidents took place in Cleveland, with whole sections of the inner city in flames. Also in July 1968, the Wooster Avenue Riot took place in Akron, and the 145th, headquartered then in downtown Akron, rushed in to contain it. Sources: Cleveland Memory Project, clevelandmemory.org; *Plain Dealer*; *The Encyclopedia of Cleveland History*; *ABJ*, 1968.

Source for the number of soldiers deployed to Vietnam: American War Library ("The World's Oldest and Largest On-line Military, Veteran, and Military Family Registry"), amervets.com.

Page 44: Details of the riot come from interviews with Canfora, Madonio, and Butler, several oral histories in the May 4 Collection, and news reports.

Page 46: The Chosen Few fled as soon as the cops moved in. None were arrested. Sources: Several oral histories, May 4 Collection.

Kent student David Scroggy describes using the tracks to escape from Water Street and skirt the police blockade at Water and Main. He lived on Franklin Street, as did Bill. It makes sense that Bill would have taken this route as well.

Page 47: Jeff and Sandy had just started dating in May 1970 (according to Drucker, Phillips, and Canfora). Drucker, Jeff's housemate, had dated Sandy in their freshman year, and the two remained friends. Phillips describes it as a natural pairing. "They were so much alike," he explains. "Both were these really extroverted, idealistic people." Jan Reinstein, one of Sandy's housemates, also speculates that "the relationship was growing into something more." Source: letter to May 4 Center, 2007. Previous books have described their relationship as platonic, but it was obviously more than that. Probably not serious either, just two kids enjoying each other's company.

Jeff left Chris Butler at Orville's bar because he had a date that evening. Sandy was roller-skating "with friends" at the Moon-Glo Rink, which was a few blocks east of campus on Main Street. Sources: *ABJ*, May 24, 1970; Michener, 1971. This scene is an extrapolation pieced together from these and other accounts.

Pages 48–50: Bill's evening and opinions are described in several matching accounts. His love for the Rolling Stones is recounted by friends, roommates, and family. *Let It Bleed* was released in December 1969. His record player, pictured here, was on display in a 2019 exhibit in the May 4 center, "Bill, an All-American Boy."

Bill's house on Franklin Street still stands.

The poster of Bill is described in several news accounts and the recollections of Bill's friends. This is a re-creation, since the original no longer exists.

Page 51: Allison lived in a single room in Engleman Hall, a lovely art deco dorm in the center of campus, overlooking the Commons. She moved there at the beginning of spring quarter. Her first two quarters she lived with three roommates in Metcalf Hall, one of a cluster of eleven newly built dorms on the far southeastern edge of campus. Known as the Short Group, these dorms have either been demolished or repurposed. Source: *ABJ*, 1970.

The cat came from a floormate, who illegally kept it in her room and was being forced to get rid of it. Allison defiantly took in the pet. Classmates describe her walking around campus with the kitten in her arms. It's unclear what happened to Yossarian after May 4.

Allison, like many, enjoyed pot. Barry, in a later account, describes going back into her room after the FBI had searched it, and finding her small stash still in its hiding place!

Page 52: Mayor LeRoy Satrom had just taken office in January 1970, having previously served as a city councilman and the city engineer. He was at his weekly poker game with friends when he got word of the riot. Sources: News reports; LeRoy Satrom papers, May 4 Collection.

According to the *ABJ*, fourteen people were arrested.

Pages 52–56: Sources on the riot: Various eyewitness oral histories, May 4 Collection; Butler, 2017; Canfora, 2018; *ABJ*, May 2, 1970, and May 24, 1970.

SATURDAY, MAY 2

Page 60: Several oral histories and news accounts describe armed men standing guard atop buildings on Water Street in the days that followed the riot.

Page 61: Norman was a gun aficionado. He often bragged about working undercover with the FBI. Sources: *Plain Dealer*; *Tampa Tribune*; Butler, 2017.

Norman said the silver-plated Smith & Wesson Model 36 handgun was acquired from an Akron police officer. This may or may not be true. The officer purchased it from the Akron Police Department. Source: *Tampa Tribune*.

Page 63: Sandy was assigned a single student with a lisp to work with in the Speech Lab. Source: *ABJ*, May 24, 1970.

Pages 63–64: Sources: Written recollections of Bill's parents, May 4 Collection; Yale Collection; Payne, 1981; *Lorain Journal*, May 5, 1970.

There are conflicting accounts of Bill's whereabouts Saturday morning and afternoon. Some have him in Akron, not returning until Sunday. There's no way of knowing for certain. Akron was a mere fifteen to twenty minutes away.

Pages 65–68: These pages are based on interviews with Butler and Drucker and the recollections of Russ Miller. The pool was filled in years ago, but its cement outline is still visible.

According to Drucker, he rescued Mary Ann Vecchio, a teenage runaway, when the riot broke out on Water Street. She slept on their couch at least that night. In the afterword of Michener's *Kent State: What Happened and Why*, she confirms this. "They had a swimming pool in the back, but I don't remember who they were." It's a safe assumption that there wasn't another student hovel in Kent with a pool.

Pages 69–70: Allison's opinions on Water Street come from various oral histories and the account of Barry Levine.

Source for Allison's assessment of Kent SDS: "Tragedy at Kent," *Life* magazine, May 1970.

Page 71: The plan to burn the ROTC building was spread by word of mouth on May 2. Sources: Canfora, 2017; Grace book, 2016; Butler, 2017.

Sources on ROTC in the Vietnam era: Encylopedia.com; National Archives, archives.gov; *ROTC Manual*, 1968, American Legion, legion.org.

Sources on ROTC at Kent State: "ROTC at KSU," *DKS*, May 20, 1969; *ABJ Special Report*; website for Kent State; Grace book, 2016; Michener, 1971; *NYT*, October 25, 1981; *Harvard Crimson*, March 14, 1968, and January 10, 1969.

Source for Bill's details: His parents' account, May 4 Collection.

Page 72: Sources on ROTC building: Michener, 1971; *ABJ*; *DKS*.

Source for ROTC information: American War Library, America Legion, legion.org.

Sources on protests: Various news accounts.

Page 73: Satrom was sworn in as mayor in January 1970. Previously he served as city engineer and as a city councilman. A conservative Democrat, Satrom had long-standing animosity for student antiwar activists, and paranoia about SDS and Weathermen infiltrators. It's worth noting that Satrom's engineering firm was housed in the First Federal Bank building on South Water Street, which had all its windows broken on May 1. Sources: 1970 Kent City Directory; *ABJ Special Report*.

Chief Thompson's fantastically inaccurate intelligence on local radical activities comes from a variety of sources, particularly police files in the May 4 Collection and Eszterhas and Roberts's *Thirteen Seconds*. Reports from the Intelligence Office of the Ohio Highway Patrol located in the Yale Collection are even more outlandish.

The Kent State Four—the SDS leaders convicted and jailed for the confrontations and building occupation of April 1969—were released from jail on April 29, 1970, after serving their six-month sentences in Portage County Jail. Erickson admits he was in Kent on May 1, at Orville's for "perhaps two minutes" in the afternoon, and was warned to leave and not come back. Kent State police chief Schwartzmiller says the SDS leaders were not seen on campus that weekend. Source: *ABJ*, 1970.

Kent newspaper publisher Robert Dix, who was also a university trustee, however, believes the four planned the entire uprising from jail. There is zero evidence of that and none of the former SDS leaders were charged with any crime relating to May 4. Most left Kent after the shootings. Source: *ABJ*, 1970.

Page 74: SDS was thrown off campus after two incidents on campus in April 1969. The first, on April 8, was an attempt to present a list of demands to President White. Police barred the entrance to the Administration Building and a shoving match resulted. Six SDS leaders, including Erickson and Emmer, were charged with assault. All were immediately barred from campus and the SDS charter was revoked and all members were suspended. Source: Grace book, 2016.

The second incident, referenced in the note for page 26, occurred on April 16. Several hundred members and supporters stormed the Music and Speech Building to halt secret expulsion hearings for two of the SDS leaders. Chanting, "Open it up or shut it down," around one hundred SDSers broke into the building through a side door and occupied the third floor. Highway patrol and campus police arrested sixty, including Weathermen leader Terry Robbins, who gave a fiery speech that whipped up the crowd. The rest escaped through an unguarded freight elevator. Source: *DKS*, April 17, 1969.

Campus police chief Schwartzmiller later revealed it was a setup. His agents provocateur in SDS revealed where the hearing was being held and led the march to Music and Speech. Source: *DKS*, April 14, 1971. Schwartzmiller had also personally recruited fraternity members to lay in wait for the march, resulting in a fistfight and the immediate arrest of SDS members. Source: *DKS*, May 14, 1969.

Fifty-nine more SDSers were suspended, pending expulsion. A week later that number was reduced to twenty-eight. Source: *DKS*, April 21, 1969. As a result, SDS was finished at Kent State.

Mayor Satrom first contacted the Guard during the Water Street riot. He officially requested them at 5 P.M. the following day, without consulting the university administration. Source: *ABJ*, May 24, 1970.

Sources on Thompson's crazy rumors: May 4 Collection; Michener, 1971; Eszterhas and Roberts, 1970; *ABJ*, May 24, 1970.

Page 75: Sources on the history of the Weathermen: Harold Jacobs, *Weatherman* (Rampart Press, 1970); Mark Rudd, *Underground: My Life with SDS and the Weathermen* (William Morrow, 2009); Bill Ayers, *Fugitive Days* (Beacon Press, 2001); Cathy Wilkerson, *Flying Close to the Sun* (Seven Stories Press, 2007); Milton Viorst, *Fire in the Streets: America in the 1960s* (Simon and Schuster, 1979).

Sources on Weathermen activity in Cleveland and Kent: Grace book, 2016; Canfora, 2017; several oral histories; *The Big Us*, September 30, 1968, and January 25, 1969; several Cleveland SDS members I interviewed who wish to remain anonymous.

The *Thinker* bombing has never been solved. The explosion at 1 A.M. was heard for miles and brought hundreds of curious students from nearby Case Western Reserve University to the art museum plaza to survey the damage. The feet were blown off *The Thinker* and the rock on which he sits was mangled. Cast by Auguste Rodin and purchased from the artist by a Cleveland art collector, the statue was donated to the museum in 1917. The museum has another, smaller version, also cast by Rodin.

"This is the first cultural institution in the United States that has been so attacked," said a horrified Sherman E. Lee, director of the Cleveland Museum of Art in 1970. After debating several restoration options, the museum decided to leave it as is and reinstalled the damaged work, where it sits to this day. Sources: Cleveland Museum of Art, clevelandart.org; *Cleveland Press*, March 25, 1970; *Plain Dealer*, March 25, 1970.

In 2017, Cleveland police received a tip as to the identity of the bomber. No arrest has been made as of this writing. Source: *Plain Dealer*, August 31, 2017.

Page 76: Source on SDS: *Smithsonian* magazine, April 7, 2017.

John Jacobs infamous quote is reported in many books and articles stretching all the way back to 1969. I used *Bringing the War Home: The Weather Underground, the Red Army Faction, and Revolutionary Violence in the Sixties and Seventies*, by Jeremy Varon (University of California Press, 2004).

Sources on Terry Robbins's pipe bomb: Rudd, 2009; Wilkerson, 2007.

Of all the top Weathermen, Terry Robbins is particularly fascinating. Short and intense, he was originally from Queens and attended tiny Kenyon College in central Ohio for two years starting in the fall of 1964, where he was radicalized at age eighteen. Robbins was an English major. He never explained his political transformation. Kenyon was a pretty sleepy place, with no SDS activity at all. In fact, Robbins founded the Kenyon chapter. It had one member—him. He dropped out of school after the spring semester of 1966 and moved to Cleveland, where he joined a large and active SDS chapter based on the east side of the city near University Circle and a cluster of small colleges. Robbins worked in an SDS community-organizing project (where he first met some of the Kent activists), and for the SDS-affiliated newspaper, *The Big Us*. In the January 1969 issue, "Terry Roberts" is listed in the masthead.

In 1968, he befriended future Weathermen Bill Ayers and Jim Mellon and relocated to Ann Arbor, Michigan, where he joined a radical SDS faction called "The Jesse James Gang," which pioneered the uncompromising, disruptive tactics the Weathermen would later use to seize control of all of SDS. In 1968, they started infiltrating the National SDS organization. Sources: "The Rise and Fall of the Weather Underground," *Rolling Stone*, September 30, 1982; Wilkerson, 2007.

Robbins impressed leadership with his passion and work ethic, so they sent him to nearby Kent, where he helped start up the Kent State chapter and befriended the local leaders. He then became a Regional Traveler for SDS, visiting and advising all the chapters in the Rust Belt, which again brought him regularly to Kent State. Robbins is an ever-present figure in the short, rocky history of Kent SDS.

Robbins helped write the infamous *Weatherman Manifesto*, the turgid, fifteen-thousand-word declaration that was published in *New Left Notes* before the SDS National Convention in July 1969. It was Robbins who named the group the Weathermen, based on the Bob Dylan lyric "You don't need a weatherman to know which way the wind blows," from "Subterranean Homesick Blues" (1965).

After the Weathermen seized control of the remnants of SDS, Robbins was their most extreme leader, purging anyone who failed to meet his strict ideological standards. Source: "SDS Convention Split," *The Heights* (Boston College), July 3, 1969. Robbins was convicted for his part in the storming and occupation of the Music and Speech Building at Kent State during the hearings for SDS leaders in April 1969. He rallied the members with a fiery speech beforehand and threw punches when the brawl began. He served his sentence, starting in December 1969, and was released in early February 1970. Sources: Wilkerson, 2007; Viorst, 1979; *DKS*, April 18, 1969. Robbins immediately went underground, moving to New York City, where he set up a Weather collective, but one that operated autonomously, led by John "J.J." Jacobs and Robbins—the two most violent radicals in Weather. Their safe house at 18 West Eleventh Street in Greenwich Village was owned by the parents of Cathy Wilkerson, another member of the Weather collective (Dustin Hoffman lived next door). Their first action was firebombing a judge's house, which did only minimal damage. Robbins apologized to the other Weather leaders for his "incompetence."

Robbins was building pipe bombs, packed with dynamite and roofing nails, in a makeshift basement bomb factory. The target, reportedly picked by Robbins, was a dance for noncommissioned officers at Fort Dix. If successful, scores of people would have been killed or maimed. "We wanted to deliver the most horrific hit America had ever suffered on its soil," said Brian Flanagan, another member of the collective. Source: *The Weather Underground* (2002).

Robbins had no electrical experience. The bomb went off accidentally, killing Robbins and Diana Oughton, who were both in the basement, and Ted Gold, who was coming through the front door and was crushed by rubble. The basement was packed with fifty-seven sticks of dynamite, four other pipe bombs, and a World War I antitank bomb.

There were three large, successive explosions as the boxes of dynamite all went up. Two other Weathermen staggered from the wreckage unharmed, and escaped before the entire town house collapsed.

There wasn't enough left of Robbins's body to identify (he had been totally obliterated). Oughton's torso was found, peppered with roofing nails from the bomb. A few days later, her thumb was discovered and used to identify her. And so ended Terry Robbins's career as a revolutionary, at age twenty-two. Almost no photos of him exist—not even, curiously, mug shots. His family has never revealed any details of his life. On May 25, 1970, the Weathermen released a communiqué confirming Robbins's death in the town house. Jacobs was expelled from Weather in April and lived on the run until his death in 1997. Sources: Wilkerson, 2007; Ron Jacobs, *The Way the Wind Blew: A History of the Weather Underground* (Verso, 1997); Harold Jacobs, 1970; Rudd, 2009; various issues of the SDS newsletter *New Left Notes*, 1969–70; Terry Robbins and Lisa Meisel, "The War at Kent State" (1968), May 4 Collection; "You Don't

Need a Weatherman to Know Which Way the Wind Blows," the Weatherman manifesto, 1969; "John Jacobs: The Last Radical," *Vancouver Magazine*, November 1998.

Page 77: Sources: Recollections of Sandy's mom, June 1977, Yale Collection; Payne, 1981. The painting by Jeff and Sandy, titled *Who Is To Say?*, was taken by one of Sandy's roommates after her death. She donated it to the May 4 Collection in 2007.

Page 78: The details of Allison's call home come from Barry. Sources: "Behind the Scenes with a Witness at Kent State," *Seventeen* magazine, August 1970; "The Tragedy at Kent State," *Good Housekeeping*, October 1970. Arthur Krause, a longtime Ohio resident (before jobs took him to other states), was no fan of Governor Jim Rhodes. Krause would soon become Rhodes's archnemesis.

Page 79: Source: Anonymous Guardsman.

Page 80: Sources: *ABJ*, May 3, 1970; *ABJ Special Report.*

Page 81–82: *The Serpent*, written by Jean-Claude van Itallie, is a renowned work of experimental theater, originally staged in 1968, that explores the biblical Book of Genesis by comparing it to modern experiences. It was performed by the Kent State Improvisational Theater on May 1, 2, and 3 in Nixson Hall on campus, starting at 8:30 P.M. Butler was in the troupe. Sources: *DKS*, April 30, 1970; Butler, 2017.

Page 83: The timeline from Saturday night is all over the place, varying from source to source. I went with the one in Michener, 1971. The initial protest around the Victory Bell came together organically, through word of mouth. Participants Alan Canfora and David Scroggy describe it as leaderless, since, as noted earlier, those heading up the SDS had all been banished, or left town voluntarily. Sources: Canfora, 2017; Grace, 2018; Scroggy, 2019; *ABJ Special Report.*

Page 84: Allison watched the assault on the building from her dorm, which was nearby Engleman Hall. The crowd tried for over an hour to set the building on fire.

Sources for scene with Professor Glenn Frank: Frank's written account, submitted to the Commission on KSU Violence, convened on May 8, 1970 by Kent State President Robert White to collect information about the events leading up to the shootings; Michener, 1971.

Source for campus police details: *ABJ Special Report.*

Page 85: The police response has always generated conspiracy theories. Many believe it was a setup by the university administration, or the campus cops, or by the FBI. It is certainly a head-scratcher why the campus police were seemingly so ill-prepared for an assault that everyone on campus knew was coming. Sources: *DKS*; Michener, 1971; various oral histories.

However, in an interview in the *DKS*, November 18, 1971, following his dismissal as chief, Donald Schwartzmiller explains that his entire force was at the ROTC building. The plan was to wait until the arrival of the highway patrol, who were delayed for unspecified reasons. Sheriff's deputies, however, did rush to campus to assist. When they arrived, the protesters were driven away with tear gas. Sources: Grace book, 2016; Michener, 1971; news accounts.

Later investigations made Schwartzmiller the scapegoat for the evening. The photographs he provided for the *DKS* piece counter the findings of those investigations. Professor Jerry Lewis, a faculty monitor and eyewitness, also agrees with Schwartzmiller. One of the photos shows cops stepping over fire hoses right beside the ROTC building, which is smoking, so clearly they were indeed on the scene and moving in. Source: *DKS*.

Why the sheriff's deputies weren't called in earlier has never been explained.

Page 86: President White, in the first of his failures of leadership, left town despite obvious rising tensions for a scheduled conference in Iowa. Vice President Matson was caught completely by surprise at the Guard's arrival. Matson and White talked on the phone at least once. There are conflicting accounts of when. Sources: *ABJ*, May 24, 1970; Eszterhas and Roberts, 1970.

Page 88: This is one of the big unanswered questions. There are many who think the fire was deliberately rekindled by clandestine law enforcement operatives as an excuse to crack down on student protesters. Sources: Butler, 2017; oral history of Rob Fox, May 4 Collection.

Anything is possible during this era, of course, as proven by the mid-seventies revelations about the FBI's sweeping illegal activities through its COINTELPRO (COunter INTELligence PROgram) during this time. FBI agents were under orders from President Nixon and J. Edgar Hoover to disrupt and destroy any and all groups deemed a threat, which—given the political paranoia of those two—was a long list of "enemies." Military intelligence was also heavily monitoring the protest movement, especially the student left, also under orders from Nixon's White House. The CIA's full role is still unknown since much of its Operation Chaos program remains classified.

Some have pinned the fire on the university administration itself. The ROTC building was slated for eventual demolition, and it was damaged in the student assault, so why not burn it as a reason to retaliate against the remaining campus radicals? The administration in 1969 had successfully entrapped and banished SDS leadership. Why not do it again? But this seems preposterous, as fires have a way of spreading and the nearby student union and power plant were crucial structures, and the fire department was not on the scene from the start.

Still others pin it on the state highway patrol, since the building conveniently burst into flames shortly after they arrived to take control of the scene. The theory here is that Governor Rhodes needed an excuse for the Guard, which was mere minutes from arriving in Kent, to occupy the campus, so he ordered the patrol to torch the damaged building. Rhodes, a Nixonian strongman, was itching to stamp out a student uprising as a grand show of force to GOP voters, having suffered a political humiliation at Ohio State the previous week.

It's more likely that the fire inside the building was still smoldering when the fire department fled earlier, and when it reached some of the estimated one thousand rounds of ammunition that were stored inside, it all went off in a fireball. None of the students at the time knew of that arms cache. Fifty years later, questions remain.

Page 89: ROTC in flames. Sources: Canfora, 2017; Scroggy, 2019; Grace book, 2016; account of Barry Levine, May 4 Collection.

The ROTC building had two thousand rounds of ammo. Source: FBI memo, May 5, 1970, Yale Collection.

The National Guard approached campus from three different directions. The main force came up Main Street from downtown. Karlovic's Guard unit, the 145th Infantry, approached Kent from I-76, traveling east from Akron, then took Route 43 north into Kent. Source: Anonymous Guardsman.

Page 92: Sources: *ABJ*, May 3, 1970, and May 24, 1970; Canfora, 2017; Michener, Eszterhas, and Roberts, 1971; *Blood of Isaac*, 1999.

Page 93: Sources for Bill's evening: *ABJ*, May 18, 2019; Eszterhas and Roberts, 1970.

Page 96: In an interview, Butler describes walking out of Nixson Hall and finding the entire horizon aglow. Nixson is just to the east of the Commons, over the hill that rings it. The flames shot seventy-five feet into the air. Source: *ABJ*, May 3, 1970.

Pages 96–97: The Guard swept campus from Prentice Gate and from the Commons. Sources: Various oral histories; Butler, 2017.

Page 98: Several faculty monitors were mistaken for students and beaten. Sources: Various news reports; *Blood of Isaac*, 1999.

Page 99: Source: Anonymous Guardsman.

Page 100: Sources for biography of General Sylvester Del Corso: *NYT* obit, April 11, 1998; Michener, 1971; Eszterhas and Roberts, 1970.

Pages 101–03: Sources: Butler, 2017; Canfora, 2018; Michener, 1971; various oral histories; *ABJ*, May 3, 1970; *ABJ Special Report*.

Page 104: Source: *Blood of Isaac*, 1999.

Pages 105–06: Source: Anonymous Guardsman.

SUNDAY, MAY 3

Pages 111–13: We don't have an exact total for the Guard force. The number on campus was either 800 or 850. All were not on duty at the same time, of course. The in-house documentary in the May 4 Visitors Center lists the total on campus and in the city as 1,200. The scene on campus Sunday. Sources: various oral histories; Canfora, 2017; Butler, 2017; *ABJ Special Report*; Davies, 1973; Michener, 1971.

Page 114: Source: Anonymous Guardsman.

Page 115: Sources: Oral histories of Anonymous Guardsman and Captain Ronald Snyder, May 4 Collection; news reports.

Chief Robert Chiaramonte's advice. Source: Scranton Commission Report.

The rumors in this chapter came from oral histories of Captain Ron Snyder, Anonymous

Guardsman, Albert Van Birk, and Winona Vannoy. It's worth noting that many locals who lived through the events *still* believe these rumors to be fact, even though all were thoroughly debunked by law enforcement who descended en masse on Kent State after May 4.

Page 116: Sources on covering of name tags: Anonymous Guardsman; testimonies of Guardsmen James McGee and Barry Morris, 1975 civil trial.

Page 117: Source: Oral history of Lillian Tyrrell, wife of a Kent professor.

Pages 119–20: Sources for Ohio National Guard facts: News accounts; Michener, 1971; Grace book, 2016; *ABJ*, 1970. The old 107th headquarters are, in fact, two blocks from where I write this. Guard pay. Source: *ABJ Special Report.*

Source on Guard training: Accounts of Captain Ron Snyder.

Pages 120–21: Sources for Guard facts: Grace book, 2016; *ABJ*, 1970; Michener, 1971. The average age of Guardsmen involved in the May 4 action was twenty-seven and a half.

Rhodes was first elected to the Columbus City School Board in 1937 at age twenty-eight. He was subsequently elected city auditor, before serving two terms as mayor, ten years as state auditor, and becoming governor in 1962. Source: Ohio History Central, ohiohistorycentral.org.

Rhodes and the Guard. Source: *ABJ Special Report.*

Page 121: The televised Taft vs. Rhodes debate took place at the Cleveland City Club on Saturday afternoon, May 2. Sources on the Rhodes vs. Taft primary battle: *ABJ*, April 28, 1970, and May 2, 1970; *Rolling Stone*, June 11, 1970.

Pages 121–22: The Six-Hour War at Ohio State is based on my own research while a journalism student at Ohio State in 1982. Sources: *The Ohio State Makio Yearbook*, 1970; *Ohio State Lantern*, April–May 1970; interviews with Ohio State students and professors, William J. Shkurti, *The Ohio State University in the Sixties* (Trillium, 2016).

Ohio State had a combined undergrad and grad student body of 47,738 in 1970. Source: Website for Ohio State University, osu.edu.

Pages 123–24: This incident was recounted by several eyewitnesses. A photo of the soldier with the flower is in the 1970 *Chestnut Burr* yearbook. Allison's statement became her epitaph: "Flowers are better than bullets" is carved on her tombstone.

Page 125: Bill was a star basketball player for Lorain High School. His number was 32. He shot hoops almost daily and had a weekly game with friends. Source: Statement from his parents, May 4 Collection.

Governor Rhodes banned "assemblies" in Kent. When asked by Guard leaders what that meant, Rhodes growled that more than two students together at a time was an "assembly." The Guard then took him at his word and informed local media. Rhodes, of course, had no legal right to do this. Source: Kelner and Munves, 1980.

Pages 127–29: Rhodes's press conference was held at the Kent Fire Department. His speech for this scene was pulled from the transcript of the event, which was archived by the May 4 Collection. All interviewees describe how Rhodes's incendiary rant sparked anger in students. Source: *ABJ*, May 24, 1970.

Page 128: Burger Chef was a popular fast-food spot directly across from campus on Main Street.

Sources on the Brooks Detective Agency: Profile of Terry Norman, *Tampa Tribune.*

Norman frequently boasted of his undercover activities to other students, according to interviewees. He showed Butler his binder of photos at a student function at the union and bragged about his undercover work. He was often spotted photographing protests on campus. Source: Butler, 2017.

Norman worked as a security guard at Blossom Music Center, a popular amphitheater in the rural countryside north of Akron, which was the summer home of the Cleveland Orchestra and which also hosted large rock concerts. He worked there in the summer of 1968 and '69 (at least). Sources: *Plain Dealer*; Eszterhas and Roberts, 1970; Michener, 1971; *ABJ*.

Page 130: Interviewees recount that everyone on campus knew Norman was working for the cops, and student activists would often mock or threaten him. Drucker took karate class with him, and other classmates warned Drucker that Norman was "a narc." No one knew he was armed.

There's some dispute where the snub-nose .38 Smith & Wesson came from. According to Janis Froelich of the *Tampa Tribune*, Norman told some he acquired it "in trade" from Akron police officer Bruce Van Horn. Other sources state a campus police detective gave Norman the gun for protection.

Tom Grace, in my interview with him, recounts that most of the people at the May 4 rally were not the familiar campus activists. Were most of them students who previously didn't take part in protests like Jeff Miller? Or was the crowd packed with undercover cops and plants? Or a combination of both?

After the events of May 4, the town and campus filled with undercover operatives, all seeking information as the government tried to build a case that it was all a grand Weathermen/communist conspiracy directed from the outside. Several interviewees describe Orville's bar being full of strangers, dressed as student radicals, offering to buy students drinks.

Sources on the FBI, COINTELPRO, and Fred Hampton: FBI.gov, *FBI Records: The Vault*; *NYT*, May 15, 1975; *The Weather Underground* (2002); Brian Glick, *The War at Home: Covert Action Against U.S. Activists and What We Can Do About It* (South End Press, 1989); *Chicago Reader*; *1971: The Citizens Who Exposed COINTELPRO*, PBS's *Independent Lens*.

Source on agent provocateur Reinhold "Ron" Mohr: *DKS*, April 26, 1972.

Sources on Terry Robbins and the FBI raid on the SDS house: *The Weather Underground* (2002); several previously cited Weathermen memoirs and lectures.

Page 131: Sources on the FBI's successful scheme to destroy SDS by supporting the Weathermen: Glick, 1989; "The FBI and the Shattering of Students for a Democratic Society," Truthout.org, October 2, 2014; "SDS Scores Big Gains But Faces Many Problems," *NYT*, May 5, 1969.

With a large field office in Cleveland, a smaller one in nearby Akron, several hundred agents and an unknown number of undercover operatives, the FBI easily swooped into Kent in force.

Chief Schwartzmiller's confession about undercover operations. Source: "Former Chief Reveals Agents were at KSU," *DKS*, May 14, 1971. Schwartzmiller was made a scapegoat for the burning of ROTC and was replaced in June 1971. Source: *DKS*, March 31, 1971. He was bitter about this and revealed many details about police operations.

Sources for the details of the CIA's Operation Chaos: *NYT*, December 22, 1974, and June 11, 1975; Walter L. Hickson, *Military Aspects of the Vietnam Conflict* (Taylor and Francis, 2000); Verne Lyon, "The History of Operation Chaos," Covert Action Information Bulletin, Summer 1990.

Page 132: Sources on the details of the Pentagon's surveillance operation: Christopher H. Pyle, *Military Surveillance of Civilian Politics, 1967–1970* (Garland, 1986); *ABJ*, March 31, 1974.

Page 133–34: The scene of Sandy Scheuer and her dog, Heavy. A photo of Sandy and Heavy by the ROTC building, taken on Sunday, May 3, was published in *Time* (May 18, 1970), so the dog and her outfit are accurately depicted. Sandy used a ribbon as a leash, which is visible in the photo. The quote about "saving all the puppies in the world" is how Steve Drucker described Sandy. It seemed apt to put it here. Source: Drucker, 2016.

Pages 135–36: Jeff Miller had dinner at Sandy's house. Sandy, an excellent cook, regularly made a big communal Sunday meal for her housemates and friends. Sources: Michener, Eszterhas, and Roberts, 1971; *ABJ Special Report*.

Anger against the Guard's occupation of campus grew steadily during the day, as students bristled at checkpoints and shakedowns, and exhausted guardsmen grew more short-tempered. Sources: Anonymous Guardsman; Butler, 2017; Canfora, 2017.

Sandy listened to Paul McCartney's new solo album this week. The first McCartney album was released April 17, 1970. McCartney stunned the world when he announced via press release on April 9 that he was leaving the Beatles. Secretly, John Lennon had already informed the band *he* was quitting, but McCartney was savaged by fans and press for breaking up the band. Source: "Why the Beatles Broke Up," *Rolling Stone*, September 3, 2009.

The Beatles's final album, *Let It Be*, was released on May 8, 1970, in the U.S. Jeff would never hear it. The single, however, was released on March 6 and was in heavy rotation on the radio.

The university hastily arranged all manner of entertainment for students over the weekend—dances, free concerts, and films every evening. Sources: Various oral histories; Michener, 1971.

Pages 137–39: Sources: Anonymous Guardsman; Canfora, 2017; Butler, 2017; various news accounts.

The sit-in. The exact time this occurred is hard to pin down, with sources offering a swath from 8:45 P.M. until 10:00 P.M. I went with 9:30 P.M. based on the reporting of the *ABJ*, which was on the scene. Source: *ABJ*, May 4, 1970.

Page 140: Major Harry Jones was presented a list of demands—a rather broad wish list: The Guard was to vacate campus, and the curfew was to be immediately suspended. They insisted on amnesty for all students arrested on Friday and Saturday. ROTC was to be thrown off campus, as was the Liquid Crystal Institute, a research lab that did work for the Pentagon. Additionally, more black students and faculty were to be recruited, and a cultural center for African American students was to be built. Protesters also demanded a meeting that evening with President White. Sources: *ABJ*, May 24, 1970; interviews with Butler and Canfora, 2017, 2018; Michener, 1971; Grace book, 2016.

White insists he never received the request. It was relayed through Vice President Matson, who rejected it, figuring White would. Source: *ABJ*, May 24, 1970.

Page 141: Sources for Major Jones's biography: 1975 civil trial testimony; obit, *Citizen-Tribune* (Morristown, TN), January 9, 2011; Michener, 1971.

Jones insists, in his 1975 testimony, that he was not on the street on Sunday night, and instead was monitoring operations from the Guard field headquarters. However, several news and eyewitness accounts place him there, as does Michener. Jones denies he made any command decisions at all throughout the Guard occupation. Other guardsmen and officers dispute this. Campus police chief Schwartzmiller states Jones was on the scene.

Pages 142–44: The charge of the Guard and injuries to students. Sources: Interviews with Butler and Canfora, 2018; various oral histories; *ABJ*, May 4, 1970, and May 24, 1970.

The growing aggressiveness and frustration of the Guard. Sources: Accounts of Guardsman Larry Shafer, Anonymous Guardsman.

Frat boys, whose houses bordered campus, were indiscriminately gassed. Canfora conjectures that many of them crossed over to "our side" because of this.

It's known as the Night of the Helicopters. Three choppers scoured campus and the town. By day, they were parked at the Kent State football stadium, south of campus.

Pages 145–47: The two bayonetings depicted here are recounted in great detail in the oral history of the Anonymous Guardsman. As many as ten students were bayoneted and an unknown number slashed. Many, fearing arrest, did not have their wounds treated at Kent hospitals.

The girl who was stabbed in this scene gave a statement to the Commission on KSU Violence, Davies 1973. Her account corroborates that of the Anonymous Guardsman.

Page 148: The Black United Students (BUS) leadership refused to take part in the antiwar protests. Most of the African American students at Kent came from inner-city Cleveland and Akron and were teenage eyewitnesses when the Guard crushed unrest in those cities in 1966 and 1968. Sources: Oral histories of Curtis Pittman (BUS member), Napoleon Peoples (professor), E. Timothy Moore (BUS member), May 4 Collection.

Pages 149–50: This incident was recounted to me by eyewitness Butler.

Page 150: Allison and Barry traveled together to Washington, D.C., to take part in the Moratorium to End the War in Vietnam on Saturday, November 15, 1969, which attracted more than half a million protestors to the National Mall. This was preceded by two days of smaller marches. On Friday, a contingent of Weathermen battled police, which further isolated them from the main antiwar movement, but otherwise the vast majority were peaceful. It's unclear if Allison took part in these earlier marches, although some accounts have her talking of tear gas, which would have placed her at the Friday demonstration, where gas was used against rioting Weathermen. President Nixon said he was "not affected by [the protest] whatsoever," and bragged he watched football in the White House residence that day. However, aides later said he was alone in the Oval Office brooding, and was close to a breakdown. Sources: *NYT*, November 14, 1969; *New Left Notes*; *The Nation*, January 12, 2010.

The area in front of Tri-Towers was a construction zone in May 1970. Mounds of dirt and piles of gravel are visible in several photos in the May 4 Collection. This is where protesters loaded up on gravel to throw at the Guard.

Page 151: In various interviews, Barry Levine recounts being chased into Tri-Towers. Captain Snyder led the Guard sweep of this area and he talked of gassing students on the campus. Source: Oral history, Ronald Snyder.

Page 152: Sources: Eszterhas and Roberts, 1970; Michener, 1971.

Pages 153–57: The source for this scene was my email interview with Rita Rubin, who confirmed and expanded upon her account in *The Middle of the Country: The Events of May 4th as Seen By Students & Faculty at Kent State University*, edited by Bill Warren (Avon Books, 1970). Drucker and Butler both say Jeff did not take part in the sit-in, but was observing. Lincoln and Main, where the standoff took place, is roughly four blocks from Jeff's house, in an unnamed alley off Summit Street. There are two likely possibilities for the location of his vantage point: the city curfew was at 8:00 P.M., far earlier than the campus one, so Jeff logically would have been watching either from a spot on Front Campus near Prentice Gate or, if he was across the street in the city proper, from someone's front yard. Residents were permitted in yards, but not on sidewalks or in the street. The Guard was amassed at Lincoln and Main. Rita Rubin's house was farther south, not far from Jeff's house in the alley, so Jeff would likely have circled through the backyards west of campus, although this is just a guess, obviously.

Sunday night is cited over and over again by interviewees as the tipping point. What had been an antiwar protest became, with the crackdown, a protest against the National Guard—their actions and their occupation of campus. A large number of students went home for the weekend and returned Sunday evening surprised to find Kent State now under martial law. Naturally, this did not sit well with a vast majority of students who had nothing to do with the unrest of the previous nights and now found themselves facing tear gas, bayonets, and rifle butts. Almost all of the more vocal radicals left town after the Guard moved in on Saturday. The Guard, for its part, did not realize, or did not particularly care, that the troublemakers had left and the students they were hounding had little or nothing at all to do with the events that had brought the Guard to campus. This was yet another failure of intelligence—the worst blunder so far. Sources: Canfora, 2017; Butler, 2017; Grace book, 2016.

Pages 157–58: Source: Account of Bill's parents, Yale Collection.

Norman lived in downtown Akron, in an apartment on North Main Street. His number was unlisted. Source: Akron telephone directory, 1969.

Most of this area has been demolished.

Norman's contact was FBI Agent William Chapin of the Akron field office. Source: *ABJ*, August 4, 1973. Norman's press credentials were given to him by the campus police during earlier undercover assignments. Source: *Tampa Tribune*, 2006.

Page 159: Source: Anonymous Guardsman.

Page 160: Sources for the account of Bill's roommate Lou Cusella: *Lorain Journal*, 1970; *Cincinnati Enquirer*; Payne, 1981.

MONDAY, MAY 4

Page 164: Rhodes's insistence on keeping the university open while stripping students of their right to assemble freely was completely illogical and probably illegal. How could the Guard enforce his order that no more than two students could be together at the same time, when 21,000 students were moving en masse about campus?

County Prosecutor Ron Kane begged Rhodes on Saturday to close the university for a few days until passions cooled. Rhodes brushed off his advice, wanting to play the tough guy for Republican voters. Sources: *ABJ Special Report*; Davies, 1973. Rhodes did not consult President White on this decision.

Page 165: Sources for Lou Cusella's account: *Lorain Journal*, 1970; "A Boy Who Was Just There Watching It and Making Up His Mind," *Life* magazine, May 15, 1970; Payne, 1981.

There is one photo of Bill on May 4. His outfit is based on that photo. Source: May 4 Collection.

Page 166: Eszterhas and Roberts detail Heavy's escape. Ellis Berns, in his oral history in the May 4 Collection, describes Sandy enjoying the morning from her front porch.

There is a photo of Sandy on May 4, and her outfit here is based on that reference. Source: May 4 Collection.

Lilacs. Source: Payne, 1981.

Page 167: This scene depicts Jeff's call home and the last words his mother, Elaine Holstein, heard him speak. Her account was first reported in an article in (of all places) *Good Housekeeping*, "The Tragedy at Kent State" by Thomas Gallagher, October 1970.

Jeff's distinctive outfit is based on photos from May 4. Source: May 4 Collection.

Page 168: The quote pinned to the wall with a wad of bubble gum is a Jefferson Airplane lyric, from the 1967 song "My Best Friend," written by drummer Skip Spence. Source: Eszterhas and Roberts, 1970.

Page 169: Sources on the Guard on Monday morning: Anonymous Guardsman; May 4 Collection; "A Pitiful, Helpless Giant," *Rolling Stone*, June 11, 1970; "The Guardsmen's View of the Tragedy at Kent State," *NYT*, June 11, 1970.

Page 170: The meeting at the fire station was described in the Scranton Commission Report; Eszterhas and Roberts, 1970.

Page 171: Multiple oral histories describe campus the morning of May 4. Source: May 4 Collection.

Page 172: Source of Bonnie Henry's account: Oral history, Kent State Truth Tribunal, truthtribunal.org.

Allison's outfit is described in several accounts. "Kennedy" is not one of the politicians, it was the name of her high school. Sources: May 4 Collection; Yale Collection.

Page 173: Alan Canfora arrives on campus with his famous black flag. Source: Canfora, 2019.

Page 174: Norman carried his .38 handgun in a shoulder holster. Source: "Kent State Shootings: Does Former Informant Hold the Key to the May 4 Mystery?," *Plain Dealer*, December 19, 2010.

Page 175: President White's lunch plans are mentioned in *Communication Crisis at Kent State: A Case Study* by Phillip K. Tompkins and Elaine Vanden Bout Anderson (Gordon Breach, 1971).

Pages 175–76: Jeff and Steve outside the Student Union. The union is now named Oscar Ritchie Hall, home of the Department of Pan-African Studies. Source: Kent State Libraries.

Concert on sign. Source: *DKS*, April 30, 1970.

According to Drucker, these are the last words he heard his roommate utter. Source: Drucker, 2017.

Page 177: Sources: Butler, 2017; Michener, 1971.

Sunday night is still known as the "Night of Helicopters" in Kent.

Arrests. Sources: *ABJ*, May 4, 1970; Scranton Commission Report.

Page 178: The Victory Bell was donated in 1950 by the Erie Railroad. It was historically rung after football victories. Source: "Kent State History," Kent State website.

Page 179: Grace recalls many strange faces at the rally. Brother Fargo, aka Dwayne White, was a former leader with Black United Students. Sources: Canfora, 2018; Grace, 2019; Grace book, 2016; Michener, 1971; various news accounts.

Page 181: Norman's antics are recounted in several news sources, photographs, and film footage. Apparently some, but not all, of the Guard officers and many of the campus police were told that Norman would be taking pictures during the rally. Sources: *Tampa Tribune*; *Plain Dealer*; *ABJ*, 1970.

Page 182: The protesters armed themselves with stones. Brigadier General Robert Canterbury claimed later they were the "size of grapefruits," which was a preposterous exaggeration. Nor were any such rocks collected by FBI investigators as evidence. Sources: "Rocks," FBI memorandum from Charles Stein to Matthew Byrne Jr., August 29, 1970; Thomas, 1999; May 4 Collection.

Immediately after the shootings, guardsmen were ordered by officers to gather up any and all weapons and projectiles found on campus. They brought in a large array—bricks, boards, large stones—and displayed them on long folding tables. But no attempt was made to log where these items were found. The suspicion was that the guardsmen had pulled these items from areas of campus far from the protest site, from campus construction sites, from inside buildings, even from off campus, in an attempt to justify the shootings. The FBI quickly discounted this alleged arsenal, and it was apparently disposed of by the Guard. Sources: Testimony of Captain Snyder, civil trial, 1975; *ABJ*, 1970.

Kent is a grassy campus. There were few rocks, and no brick walkways, like at Ohio State. Some suggested radicals snuck in wheelbarrows of large rocks and left piles of them at predetermined spots on campus, as if it were possible to cart wheelbarrows laden with stones past 1,200 guardsmen. Sources: Scranton Commission Report; Butler, 2017; Canfora, 2017.

What was available was driveway gravel from the new parking lots and the construction site near Tri-Towers—the likely source. This would have been be no. 3 grade base gravel, made from limestone and ranging in size from one to two inches. Source: Landscape supplier Braen Stone, braenstone.com, located in Haledon, New Jersey.

Page 183: Sources of Barry Levine's account: Payne 1981; May 4 Collection; Yale Collection. Source of Bill and the rally: Account of Gene Pekarick; *Lorain Journal*, 1970; *Life* magazine, 1970.

Page 184: There are conflicting accounts on Major Jones. He was either ordered by Lieutenant Colonel Fassinger to report to campus or he volunteered himself when an exhausted Major Wallach asked for relief from duty. Sources: *ABJ*, May 24, 1970; Jones, Fassinger depositions and testimonies, 1974 criminal trial.

Brigadier General Canterbury's decisions were described by the Scranton Commission Report as "highly questionable." His decision to break up the rally was "a serious error," and the manner in which he did so was "disastrous."

Sources for Canterbury's biography: Testimony of Brigadier General Robert Canterbury, civil trial, 1975; *ABJ*, May 24, 1970; Michener, 1971.

Source on the Hough Riot: Ohio History Central.

It's unclear why Canterbury decided to squash the rally. He insisted he was acting under orders from "his superiors." He had only two superiors, however: the governor and General Del Corso, who both insisted it was Canterbury's call. Governor Rhodes, in his testimony in the civil trial, stated he gave no order to break up protests. Source: May 4 Collection.

Page 185: Source for Sandy's summer plans: Sandy Scheuer Exhibit, May 4 Visitors Center.

Karlovic's addition to A Company is cited in the Anonymous Guardsman's oral history.

Page 186: Jeff was in the thick of the crowd at the Victory Bell. Allison seems to have stayed near the Pagoda at the top of Blanket Hill. Bill and Sandy watched briefly from the hillside, then departed. Sources: Photographs, May 4 Collection; various oral histories and news sources.

Page 187: Sources: *ABJ Special Report*; photographs, May 4 Collection; various other news sources.

The campus riot act passed. Source: ABJ, June 6, 1970.

Page 188: Archived in the May 4 Collection is a photo of Jeff near the Victory Bell, flipping off the Guard announcement with both fingers. The jeep is described in various news accounts and oral histories, plus interviews with Canfora and Butler. Campus police officer Harold Rice made the announcement.

Page 189: Sources on the M1 Garand: Gun Collectors Association; *Gun Digest*; *ABJ*, 1970.

Lock and load. Sources: Snyder testimony, 1975; Michener, 1971; Davies, 1973.

Page 190: Sources on armor-piercing ammo and gas masks: *ABJ Special Report*; Anonymous Guardsman.

A few details about gas masks: Many media reports and a few of the books state that the masks completely muffled voices and made communication impossible for soldiers wearing them. This is not true, based on my experiments conducted with a Vietnam-era mask similar to those worn on May 4. The voice is somewhat muffled, but can be clearly heard and understood, using normal volume, from thirty feet away. Guardsmen could easily converse with one another while wearing masks. Officers and some noncoms had gas masks fitted with voice boxes, which allowed commands to be given loud and clear. There was also the assertion that wearing a mask "distorts" hearing. This is also inaccurate. Hearing is unimpaired.

Source on Guard regulations: Scranton Commission Report; "My God! They're Killing Us!," *Newsweek*, May 18, 1970.

Pages 191–95: Sources: Various news reports; photographs, May 4 Collection; several oral histories.

Page 193: Oral history of Captain Snyder, May 4 Collection. Major Jones testimony, 1975 civil trial. Source for account of Gene Pekarik: *Good Housekeeping*, October 1970.

There is also a photo of Bill in a cluster of students on the hill around the Commons, fleeing the tear gas. Source: May 4 Collection.

Page 194: Jeff threw some stones and stayed in the thick of the protesters. Source: Oral history, student Eldon Fender, May 4 Collection.

Account of Barry Levine. Sources: Letter from Levine to Arthur Krause, Yale Collection; Payne, 1981.

Page 195: Jones did not have time to check out a weapon during the Teamsters strike in Akron. Captain Snyder loaned Jones a .22 Beretta pistol and a plastic riot stick, and Jones kept them when the Guard moved into Kent. Jones also failed to check out a gas mask on May 4. Sources: Snyder, 1975; Jones, 1975; various other sources.

Page 196: Major Jones stated he drew up the plan before dawn on May 3. Source: Jones testimony, 1975.

The aerial view is based on the 1970 campus map and Google Earth.

The Guard numbers are hard to pin down. We don't have an exact number for C Company. G Troop is consistently described as being sixteen men. The total number of G Troop plus members of A Company (and two members of C) on the right prong is listed as anywhere from sixty-six to seventy-seven men in various source material. The FBI and the Scranton Commission Report, which had access to Guard reports and records, lists this force as seventy-six men, so that's what I decided to go with. Sources: Scranton Commission Report; radio log, 145th Infantry, May 4, 1970, by way of *Blood of Isaac*, 1999; *ABJ Special Report*; Michener, 1971; Grace book, 2016.

There are *ten* officers accompanying this force—Brigadier General Canterbury, Lieutenant Colonel Fassinger, Major Jones, three captains, and four lieutenants—yet the operation was total confusion.

Page 197: Sources: Anonymous Guardsman; oral history of Captain Ron Snyder, May 4 Collection.

The man with the camera on the roof of Taylor Hall was student Jerome Stoklas, a photographer for the *DKS*. Source: Scranton Commission Report.

Page 198: Although Allison was definitely a protester, she stayed at the top of Blanket Hill. There is a final photo in the May 4 Collection of her near the Pagoda, fleeing a cloud of gas.

Was she a rock thrower? It's uncertain. The Scranton Commission Report says "small pieces of concrete" were found in her jacket pocket. Barry said several times that they threw "some" stones, but in a later letter to Arthur Krause he wrote, "I never saw Allison throw stones." Barry consistently describes her as being filled with rage and screaming at the Guard and that he had to drag her away more than once. Source: Yale Collection; Payne, 1981.

Pages 199–201: These pages depict the disastrous march to the practice field. Sources: *ABJ*; *NYT*, 1970; all other book sources; several oral histories, photo archive, May 4 Collection; online photo collection of former *ABJ* photographer Paul Tople, then a photographer for the *DKS*. The website was taken down after Paul's death in 2018.

Page 201: Jeff is described in several news stories from 1970 as throwing back tear gas canisters. Sources: *ABJ*; *NYT*.

Page 200: Student protestor Jerry Casale describes Jeff as one of the more vocal on the practice field. Source: Oral history, Kent State Truth Tribunal.

Page 203: Norman followed the Guard down to the practice field and positioned himself between the soldiers and protesters. There are photos of him wearing his scuba mask while taking photos. Sources: *Plain Dealer*; May 4 Collection.

Page 204: Sandy had left the Music and Speech Center and was on her way to another class. Her likely path took her through the Prentice Hall parking lot and down the access road bordering the practice field, right into the remaining protesters. Sources: Oral history of student Lloyd DeVos, who was walking with her; oral history of Ellis Berns, May 4 Collection; campus map, 1979; *ABJ Special Report*.

Page 205: There was half a brick that was apparently thrown several times. Sergeant

Larry Shafer of G Troop, who shot student Joe Lewis, claims he was hit by it. Source: Shafer's testimony, 1975.

Karlovic picked out Jeff in the group of protestors. Source: Oral history of the Anonymous Guardsman.

Canterbury claimed that protesters also threw pieces of lumber with nails driven through them, pieces of rebar and lead pipe, and a fire hydrant! As confirmed by many news reports, no evidence was collected that could prove any of this.

Furthermore, since fire hydrants weigh from 350 to 800 pounds, it's utterly preposterous that a student "threw" one.

Karlovic's growing anger. Source: Anonymous Guardsman.

Gomer Pyle, U.S.M.C. last aired on May 2, the end of the 1969 season. Source: Internet Movie Database, imdb.com.

Page 206: There is a dispute over who fired the pistol shot, either as a warning or to get the attention of other guardsmen. Sergeant Barry Morris initially said it was Sergeant Myron Pryor, carrying a .45, who fired. Professor Richard Schreiber seconds this. Pryor denied firing, under oath during the civil trial, as he denied virtually everything. The Scranton Commission Report, however, describes a .22 being fired and a cartridge found the next day on the practice field. Major Jones was the only guardsman carrying a .22. Jones denied under oath that he fired. Michener reports that Sergeant James Farris, with A Company in its position back at Taylor Hall, saw a guardsman fire a .45. If so, the casing disappeared. All this is par for the course in the immediate aftermath. No attempt was made by the Guard or police to secure the scene or properly log ballistic evidence. A tricky scene to reconstruct here, but an important one because it demonstrates the guardsmen's growing anxiety. Sources: Scranton Commission Report; *NYT*.

This scene unfolds according to Major Jones's testimony in the 1975 civil trial.

Page 207: Sources: Various news accounts and oral histories; Canfora, 2018; Butler, 2017

Pages 208–09: Sources for G Troop facts: Michener, 1971; Grace book, 2016; *ABJ Special Report*; testimonies of Captain Raymond Srp and Sergeant Myron Pryor, civil trial, 1975.

The mysterious huddles are described by various eyewitnesses. Accounts of Joe Lewis, Robbie Stamps, *Mayday: Kent State* (Payne, 1981), and confirmed by Srp of G Troop in his civil trial testimony, although he denies taking part in them. G Troop huddled, as did other smaller groups of guardsmen. Srp admits to conferring with Sergeant Pryor. Officers huddled with one another, then with some of the men. Pryor was seen tapping guardsmen on the helmet as they were pointing their rifles at protesters, to get their attention, then talking to them individually and in a small group. Pryor denied this when questioned under oath. The suspicion is, of course, that the members of G Troop decided at this time to open fire on protesters if the order was given, or perhaps *when* the order was given. Jones was also seen talking to G Troop during its stay on the practice field. But we have no proof of what was said. The members of G Troop have maintained their silence about was discussed on the field.

Page 210: Sources: Testimonies of Jones, Canterbury, and Fassinger, civil trial, 1975; eyewitness accounts; oral history of protestor Ken Hammond, May 4 Collection; *U.S. Army Field Manual.*

Why did Canterbury and Fassinger let the lower-ranking Jones take charge? Both Canterbury and Fassinger were from the 107th. The bulk of the men in that group of guardsmen were from the 145th, Jones's unit. He knew the men; they knew him.

In a 1983 interview with author William A. Gordon, *The Fourth of May,* Fassinger expressed frustration at Canterbury taking command of the operation. So it must have been Canterbury's call to let Jones take over. Canterbury, in his 1975 testimony, insists it was Fassinger who gave all the orders. Almost all other Guard witnesses dispute this. Jones claims, in his testimony, that he gave no orders at all during the operation, which other officers and most guardsmen strongly dispute. In a brief clip of footage taken by Cleveland's WKYC television station, before the sweep of the Commons began, a short officer in a soft cap (Major Jones) can be seen and heard barking orders.

Page 211: Sources: Various oral histories; 1975 testimonies of Srp, Fassinger, Pryor.

Page 212: Sources: Payne, 1981; *Seventeen*; Oral history of Berns and Casale; *Good Housekeeping*;

Life; Butler, 2017; Canfora, 2018.

Page 213: Norman trailed the Guard from the practice field. Sources: "May 4 Answers Lost in the Chaos," *ABJ*, April 30, 2000; *Plain Dealer*, 2010; *Tampa Tribune*, 2006.

Pages 214–15: Sources: Anonymous Guardsman; Shafer, "Guardsman Ends 10-year Silence on KSU," *ABJ*, May 4, 1980; various student oral histories of the Guard retreat, May 4 Collection and Kent State Truth Tribunal.

Jones's threats are recounted by several eyewitnesses, and the 1975 testimony of Captain Srp.

The Pagoda was a guerrilla class project by five architecture students who erected it, without permission, in the middle of the night, shortly before the events depicted in this book. They constructed the sculpture with materials pilfered from the many construction projects on campus. Had it not been for May 4, the Pagoda likely would have been removed by semester's end. Instead it stands to this day, and is now part of the National Historic Landmark. Sources: Michener, 1971; May 4 Visitors Center.

Page 216: Leaning out his dormitory window on the fifth floor of Wright Hall (one of the Tri-Towers, approximately six hundred feet from the Prentice Hall parking lot), student Chris Abell shot the 8mm film. The angle is from the back of the parking lot, looking upward at the guard, but clearly shows the number of protesters and their position, especially filmed as it was from high up. This footage completely debunks the Guard's assertion that they were "surrounded" and in danger of being overrun. As of this writing, the footage is on YouTube, titled "Kent State Shooting Enhanced Audio Home Movie, May 4,1970."

When you stand at the Pagoda and look down toward the parking lot, it's striking how far away it is. The conclusion of both the FBI Report and the Scranton Commission was that there was no reason for the Guard to open fire. Had the guardsmen simply kept marching, in another few seconds they would have vanished around the side of Taylor Hall and could have returned back to the safety of the Guard line without difficulty.

Sources: Scranton Commission Report; FBI Report; photographs, May 4 Collection.

Page 217: This is the enduring mystery. Unless there is a deathbed confession, and many of the shooters and most of the officers have already died, it will remain so. Several students and faculty saw Pryor tap guardsmen as they neared the Pagoda, and observed the Guard on the rear right flank staring down the hill, while the rest of the Guard were looking ahead as they marched. Several saw Jones make a pronounced movement with his riot stick.

The order to fire is on the Strubbe Tape, a cassette copy that was discovered by Alan Canfora in the Yale Collection in 2007. It was a recording made by student Terry Strubbe, who dangled a microphone out his dorm window and let his reel-to-reel tape deck run for thirty minutes, throughout the entire event. The recording, which is of horrible quality, was then restored and enhanced, with extraneous noise stripped away by audio engineers.

There are two restorations and enhancements of the tape. The first, by record producer Ian MacKaye at the behest of Canfora in 2007, revealed the order. Sources: "Ian MacKaye on the Kent State Tape," *Washington City Paper*, May 9, 2007; NPR, May 1, 2007; Yale Collection.

A second team, forensic audio experts Stuart Allen and Tom Owen, were hired by the *Plain Dealer* in 2010. Their restoration reveals a slightly different command of "Guard! All Right . . . prepare to Fire! Guard . . ." The explosion of gunfire immediately follows, presumably on the command "Fire!," which is drowned out by the barrage. This is the command to fire that I depict. Sources: *Plain Dealer*, May 9, 2010; *CBS News*, May 8, 2010.

We don't know who gave the order. There is some question as whether it was one officer, or several, giving different parts of the order. Remember, the Guard was moving rapidly, so the order could have rolled down the line.

The big question remains: Why? Was it premeditated, agreed upon by the members of G Troop in their huddle on the practice field? Was it supposed to be warning shots into the air, over the heads of protesters, and it went horribly wrong? Or was it a combination of those things? That G Troop all turned in unison, in the same direction, has always pointed to either a signal or an order.

Nixon's secretary of labor, George Schultz, who went on to be Ronald Reagan's secretary of state, was a captain in the Marines during World War II. When Schultz watched the news footage and heard the barrage, he said simply, "That was a salvo." Sources: Reagan Library; William Safire, *Before the Fall* (Belmont Tower Books, 1975).

There has been speculation about the order to fire right from the beginning. Sources: *ABJ Special Report*; "Kent Student Suggests Officer Gave Signal to Shoot," *NYT*, August 20, 1970.

Guardsmen Robert James, Roger Maas, Lloyd Thomas, James McGee, and Lieutenants Dwight Cline and Howard Fallon, all admitted to hearing an order to fire. Guardsmen Richard Love and Charles Deegan heard an order to "form up." Source: Grace book, 2016.

Guard leadership vehemently denied there had been an order. Some Guard supporters speculated it was a student radical who shouted out the order, a line later picked up by one of the shooters, Sergeant Matthew McManus, who was indicted for shooting James Russell. Sources: Historian William A. Gordon, blog post, "Two Guardsmen Finally Talk: Both Insist There was No Order to Fire at Kent State," kentstatedevelopments.blogspot.com, August 19, 2011.

The Anonymous Guardsman heard no such order. Sources: Anonymous Guardsman.

When the Strubbe Tape came to light, Lieutenant Colonel Fassinger dismissed it, insisting that the phrasing of the order to fire is not a standard command an officer would give, as if *anything* the Guard did on May 4 followed standard procedure. Source: *Plain Dealer.*

All the officers in 1970, and when questioned directly in the civil trials in 1975, denied giving any such order. There is no conclusive proof of who shouted that order. Both Pryor and Jones are dead (2002 and 2011, respectively). At this point, it seems this is one of the questions that will never be answered.

The eight identified shooters who fired into the crowd all clammed up within hours of May 4. Guard leadership advised the shooters to lawyer up. After they did, they all started reciting the same story. "We were in fear for our lives," "The protesters were charging us." The FBI, in its 1970 report, suspects that the shooters all agreed on a story *after* the shootings. They stuck to that story all through the investigations and trials. Most will not speak to media.

The Guard's report after the shooting was so badly bungled, we're not even sure what weapons were fired. The Scranton Commission Report lists sixty-one total shots. This was later revised to sixty-seven shots. Most came from M1s. Two to five shots came from one, possibly two, .45 pistols. One or two came from shotguns. Ballistic evidence is almost nonexistent. Sources: Scranton Commission Report; *ABJ*.

Page 220: Several guardsmen, in statements and testimonies, describe firing in a panic at the sound of the opening volley by G Troop. Eight to ten guardsmen fired into the crowd. The remaining twenty shooters, from A and C Company, likely fired into the air or into the ground. Twenty-eight guardsmen admitted firing their weapons. Source: Scranton Commission Report.

Page 221: Sources for aerial view: Campus map, 1970; Google Earth.

Sources for shooting pattern: May 4 Visitors Center; news sources.

Page 222: Sources: *ABJ*; *NYT*, 1970; Jeff Miller's autopsy report, Yale Collection; Davies, 1973.

The distances of the victims from the Guard vary by a few feet in source material—I looked for consensus.

Pages 224–25: Sources: Account of Barry Levine and Allison Krause's autopsy report, Yale Collection; Davies, 1973; Scranton Commission Report.

Pages 226–27: Sources: "Blood Brothers," *KentWired*, May 4, 2015; filmed accounts by the wounded during the thirtieth anniversary commemoration, Kent State University Libraries; Grace book, 2016; Canfora, 2019; various news sources; Davies, 1973.

Pages 228–29: Sources: Ellis Berns oral history, May 4 Collection; *ABJ*, May 24, 1970; Sandy Scheuer's autopsy report, Yale Collection; various news sources; Davies, 1973; Scranton Commission Report.

Page 230: Sources: Pittman, 2015; filmed accounts by the wounded during the thirtieth anniversary commemoration, Kent State University Libraries; Grace book, 2016; Canfora, 2019; Butler, 2017; various news sources; Davies, 1973.

Pages 231–32: Sources: Oral history of student Henry Mankowski, May 4 Collection; news accounts; Davies, 1973; Kelner and Munves, 1980.

We have no idea who killed the four students or shot eight of the nine others. The only guardsman who admitted shooting a student was Sergeant Larry Shafer, who confessed to shooting Joe Lewis at least once. Source: Scranton Commission Report.

Bullet fragments taken from the bodies of the dead and wounded could not be matched to any gun by the FBI. Source: FBI Report.

Eight guardsmen were eventually identified by federal investigators as having shot into the crowd and were charged and indicted on March 29, 1974: Shafer, James McGee, William Perkins, James Pierce, Ralph Zoller, Matthew McManus, Barry Morris, and Leon Smith. After a two-week trial, all eight were acquitted for lack of evidence on November 8, 1974. Judge Frank Batista scolded federal prosecutors over the weakness of their case and decided the defense didn't even need to present its case. The Guard and law enforcement had so bungled the documentation on May 4, and had so contaminated the scene, that no shooting could be pinned on any one guardsman. Source: *NYT*, March 30, 1974, and November 9, 1974; May 4 Collection.

The FBI noted that several guardsmen were likely lying under questioning. Many guardsmen had hastily reloaded their clips. Some ditched their guns and grabbed other guns. All eight of the acquitted guardsmen would be named as defendants in the civil trials. Sources: FBI Report; Scranton Commission Report; Davies, 1973.

Page 233: Cease fire. Sources: 1975 testimonies of Jones, Srp, Canterbury; Oral history of the Anonymous Guardsman.

The Anonymous Guardsman (aka Frank Karlovic in this book) insists in his oral history that he did not fire, and the official Guard report that day does not list him as a shooter. The Guard report is infamously inaccurate, however, as it also fails to list Sergeant Larry Shafer (who later admitted to shooting Joe Lewis) and Specialist Leon Smith (who was indicted for shooting James Russell).

The C Company guardsmen on Blanket Hill, one of which was the Anonymous Guardsman, admitted to the FBI that they fired their weapons. Sources: FBI Report; Davies, 1973. The Anonymous Guardsman later flatly states in his oral history that he did not, but would have, had an officer not "grabbed my gun."

Additionally, Captain Ron Snyder, the commanding officer of C Company, testified in the 1975 civil trial that his men on Blanket Hill fired their weapons, a single shot each. Snyder ordered them to replace the discharged bullets in their clips so it would appear they did not fire.

Karlovic fired. So I drew him both firing *and* as having an officer grab his gun. Not a perfect solution, but the one I made.

Other sources: *ABJ Special Report*; news accounts.

Page 234: Sources: Various oral histories, May 4 Collection; Kent State Truth Tribunal; Butler, 2017.

Page 236: The iconic photo of Mary Ann Vecchio screaming in horror over Jeff Miller's body was taken by *DKS* student photographer John Filo, who was also on the photo staff of the *Valley Daily News*, outside Pittsburgh. Filo won the Pulitzer Prize for this photo. Sources: *CBS News*; *CNN*; Filo's speech, thirty-ninth May 4 Commemoration.

Page 237: Source: Anonymous Guardsman.

Pages 238–39: Sources: Oral history of Captain Ronald Snyder; photographs, May 4 Collection; accounts of several students; oral histories of Professor Jerry Lewis and student Carol Mirman, May 4 Collection.

Rolling over Jeff. Source: Michener, 1971.

The planted gun. Source: Snyder testimony, 1975.

Page 240: Terry Norman's actions have been the subject of heated debate for decades. The *Plain Dealer*, in another analysis of the Strubbe Tape, this time by forensic audio expert Stuart Allen, working alone, uncovered what Allen claims are four pistol shots, seventy seconds before the Guard opened fire at the Pagoda. The story raises the possibility that Norman's shots panicked the guardsmen and they opened fire.

There are several problems with this. There is no clear evidence that these sounds are pistol shots—it's one man's opinion. No witness has come forward who saw Norman fire his gun. Even if he had, trailing the Guard from the practice field, wouldn't the Guard turn toward the sound of the noise? Instead, they wheeled to their right and shot into the parking lot. Sources: Mickey Porter, column, "Norman Didn't Fire a Shot," *ABJ*, October 11, 1973.

The seventy-second delay is the primary argument against gunfire. Isn't a panicked response immediate, within a second or two? The Guard had to think it over for more than a minute? Count off seventy seconds and see just how long this is in real time. Source: *Plain Dealer*, 2010.

Lieutenant Colonel Fassinger, with the shooters at the Pagoda, claimed he heard a single shot before the Guard volley. If so, what about the other three? Source: *Tampa Tribune*, 2006.

Pages 241–42: Sources: *ABJ Special Report*; Canterbury testimony, 1975; *NYT*, May 7, 1970; FBI Summary, 1970.

The initial narrative by Guard leaders Canterbury and Del Corso was that a thousand students were charging the Guard up Blanket Hill and hurling large rocks and other projectiles. The guardsmen, fearing for their lives, had no choice but to shoot. The rocks, by Canterbury's description, kept getting ever larger. They went from being the size of baseballs to the size of grapefruits, even though an Olympic shot-putter couldn't heave a rock that size one hundred yards or more—the distance the protesters stood from the Guard. They both also claimed there was a sniper on the roof of Taylor Hall—in reality, it was likely the student photographer and his professor. Source: *ABJ*, August 22, 1970.

When that theory didn't pan out, it changed to a sniper in a nearby dorm. Guard leadership stuck to the sniper claim for months until the FBI flatly rejected the possibility. "There was no sniper," the Bureau's investigators wrote in their 1970 report.

Syndicated columnist Clayton Fritchey summed it up best, pointing out that every time law enforcement fires into an unarmed crowd, an "invisible sniper" is always cited as the reason. Source: Clayton Fritchey, column, *Cleveland Press*, May 28, 1970.

It's worth noting, however, that during the Hough Riot in 1967 and the Glenville Riot in 1968 in inner-city Cleveland, actions in which most members of G Troop and the older members of the 145th had taken part, a number of snipers were encountered. Source: *Plain Dealer* coverage of those events, 1967 and 1968.

The FBI collected 340 stones and rocks, mostly large driveway gravel, from the area of conflict on campus. It's unknown how many were used as weapons or were just part of the landscape. Also collected was a brick; two smaller pieces of brick; a 2 x 2 piece of lumber, twenty-two inches in length; and a dead tree branch, twenty inches long. There was no fire hydrant, no pieces of steel rebar, no boards with nails driven through them, no wrenches and hammers, and no bags of feces—all weapons the Guard claim were used against them. Source: Scranton Commission Report.

The sniper theory, along with the other exaggerated claims by the Guard, was dutifully reported by the media. Over time, all these claims have been proven to be false, or absurdly inflated, given film footage, photos, eyewitness accounts, and even testimony from some of the Guard themselves. This, however, was reported in the form of follow-up stories that came out months or years after the event; they weren't front-page news, so the original falsehoods stuck.

The central question here is, why fabricate things if you have nothing to hide? Isn't the truth always the best defense for the innocent?

Officers and guardsmen began turning on one another shortly after May 4. Individual guardsmen were extremely critical of Canterbury. The general insisted he was not in charge on May 4 and pinned all the field decisions on his junior officers. Those officers all denied making those decisions and blamed Canterbury and each other. Sources: Various news stories; testimonies from the civil trials.

Sergeant Dennis Breckenridge, twenty-six, was the fainting guardsman. Source: *ABJ*, September 26, 1970. Sergeant Larry Shafer later had his arm in a sling and insisted it was "nearly broken" by a thrown brick while he was on the practice field. This, however, did not stop him minutes later from raising his nine-pound rifle and shooting Joe Lewis. Sources: Thomas, 1999; Kelner and Munves, 1980.

Bill Schroeder and Dean Kahler were literally shot in the back, and Douglas Wrentmore, Tom Grace, and Scott Mackenzie were shot as they ran away. Robbie Stamps was hit, unexpectedly, in his hip as he walked away from the protest with his lunch in his hand. Allison Krause was shot in the side as she dove for cover. Of the thirteen victims, Jeff Miller, Allison Krause, Jim Russell, Tom Grace, and Alan Canfora were protesters. Robbie Stamps, Joe Lewis, and Dean Kahler were either at the noon rally or took part in the protest for shorter periods of time. Eight total protesters. The remaining five victims were bystanders, either watching from a distance, or walking to class. Only two of those shot, Miller and Lewis, were actually facing the Guard when hit. Sources: *ABJ*, May 24, 1970; Canfora, 2019; Eszterhas and Roberts, 1970; Michener, 1971; Grace book, 2016; Thomas, 1999; Davies, 1973.

Pages 243–44: Norman's mad dash across the Commons was filmed by a cameraman for WKYC News in Cleveland. I have seen the footage.

Most of the account here comes from the oral history of Bill Barrett (the editor of alumni publications), and the account of instructor Harold Reid, both of whom saw Norman pull his gun and chased him as he sprinted for the Guard line. Sources: May 4 Collection; *Plain Dealer*; *ABJ*; *Tampa Tribune*.

Did Norman fire his gun? Barrett, who was witnessing the confrontation, said no. Campus police detective Tom Kelley, Norman's handler with the campus police, who examined the gun when it was taken from Norman, said no. Patrolman Harold Rice wrote in his report that the gun was fully loaded when taken from Norman. Student Tom Masterson, one of the protesters threatened by Norman, also said Norman did not fire, as did Alan Frank who was nearby when the scuffle occurred Sources: *ABJ*, 1974; *ABJ*, April 30, 2000; *Plain Dealer*, 2010; oral histories of Bill Barrett, William Heasley, May 4 Collection.

On the other hand, TV newsman Fred DeBrine and Joe Butano of WKYC, student Joe Sima, and Guard sergeants Mike Delany and Richard Day all heard Kent State police detective Tom Kelley exclaim, when first examining Norman's gun back at the Guard line, "My God! It's been fired four times!" Kelley later denied saying that and officially stated in his report that the gun had *not* been fired. Sources: Oral history of Joe Sima, Kent State Truth Tribunal; oral history of Marvin Perry, May 4 Collection; *Plain Dealer*, 2010; *Tampa Tribune*, 2006.

Then it gets weird. Norman's gun was confiscated on May 4 by campus police. At some point, they sent it to Smith & Wesson who had it replated. It was not tested beforehand. In 1973, Smith & Wesson reported the gun had been confiscated by the FBI, but by then it was useless as ballistic evidence. Sources: "Who Fired First?," *ABJ*, April 30, 2000; *Tampa Tribune*; "Who is Terry Norman?," *KentWired*, November 16, 2010.

Norman gave one brief interview to the *ABJ* on May 4, and hasn't spoken about it since. In that interview, he denied working for the police and FBI, and claimed he was merely an "amateur photographer." Norman claimed guardsmen were surrounded by one thousand protesters and pummeled with "baseball-size rocks," which felled and injured many guardsmen. At this point, only Norman knows the truth about his role, and he isn't talking.

The FBI denied for three years that Norman worked for them on May 4, or had ever worked for them. In truth, he had a rather long relationship with the Bureau, working undercover for them at least twice. Sources: "No Campus FBI Men," *ABJ*, November 17, 1970; "FBI: Cameraman at KSU Not an Agent,"*ABJ*, July 24, 1973. The FBI certainly behaved as if it had something to hide. There are also indications Norman had ties to the CIA. Sources: *ABJ*, April 30, 2000; *Plain Dealer*, 2010.

What Norman best demonstrates is the chaotic and reckless undercover operations that various law enforcement agencies employed at Kent State in spring 1970. The important point is that the FBI inexplicably dispatched him into a volatile situation, unsupervised and armed. It's a jaw-dropping decision. The campus police are also complicit, and even though Chief Schwartzmiller ordered his men to stop employing Norman, Detective Kelley apparently ignored that order.

Alan Canfora, a wounded student who has been the driving force behind all things May 4, dismisses Norman as "irrelevant" and points out that it was years after the shootings before the Guard started pointing to Norman as the probable cause.

If nothing else, Norman is an example of the right-wing students at Kent State, of which there were many, even though he was an extreme example.

All the conflicting stories succeeded in muddying up the truth about Norman's role, and, more important, that of law enforcement, especially the FBI. And we have no information at all about the still-classified activities, if any, of the CIA or military intelligence as they relate to Kent State and May 4.

In August 1970, Norman was hired as an undercover narcotics agent by the Washington, D.C., police department, at the behest of the FBI. In 1973, he was stripped of his gun and reassigned to a desk job—reason unknown.

Norman quit the force in 1983 and moved to California to work for a data firm. He embezzled more than $675,000 to fund a lavish lifestyle. He was arrested as he was preparing to flee the country. In 1994, Norman pled guilty and served more than three years in federal prison. After release, he moved around a lot, up to ten residences in eight years, before settling in rural North Carolina. Source: *ABJ*, April 30, 2000; *Tampa Tribune*, 2006.

Page 245: Source: Butler, 2017.

Page 246: Source: Anonymous Guardsman.

Page 247: Source: Audio recording of Professor Frank's plea, glennwfrankmay4.com.

Page 248: This is based on Barry Levine's account, which was published in the August 1970 issue of *Seventeen*, as well as on an interview with Alan Canfora, who spoke with Barry at the hospital. Michener describes it, too.

Pages 249-51: Guardsmen in jeeps used bullhorns to order students to leave campus. Many fled immediately, others dragged suitcases. Sources: Oral histories of Christopher Marek, May 4 Collection; oral history of Casale, Kent State Truth Tribunal; Michener, 1971.

The following day, County Prosecutor Ron Kane ordered police officers to search the university's 3,616 dorm rooms for weapons and drugs. No search warrants were obtained. Drugs were found, of course—mostly pot—and a few "weapons," such as a squirrel gun, baseball bats, starter pistols, a toy plastic pistol, and hunting and pocketknives. Also confiscated and displayed were a majorette's baton, art supplies, and a laundry bag stuffed with porno mags. "It's a circus!" yelled one professor at the news conference. Source: "KSU Rooms Yield 36 Knives, Drugs," *ABJ*, May 16, 1970. The ACLU filed suit. Kane brought no charges against students. There was, however, one charge that stuck. One of the campus policemen stole $30 while rifling through the dorm rooms! He was sacked and charged with petty theft. Source: "Says Officer Stole During KSU Search," *ABJ*, June 5, 1970.

The rain and the blood. Graduate assistant Napoleon Peoples was allowed to stay on campus to secure the dorm where he worked. He describes the scene. Source: Oral history of Peoples, May 4 Collection.

Page 252: Paragraph 1: Testimony of Captain Raymond Srp, 1975 civil trial. Paragraph 2: FBI Report. Paragraph 3: *ABJ*, May 6, 1970; obit, *NYT*, March 6, 2001. Paragraph 4: "Del Corso Says Sniper Fired Before Guard," UPI wire service, May 5, 1970; *ABJ*, May 24, 1970; *DKS*, May 4, 1995; FBI Report. Paragraph 5: William A. Gordon 1983. Paragraph 6: "Shots Still Reverberate for Survivors of Kent State," NPR, May 3, 2010. Paragraph 7: Profile of Elaine Holstein, Jeff's mom, "Twenty Contentious Years Haven't Ended the Pain Inflicted by the Tragic Shootings at Kent State," *People*, April 30, 1990. Paragraph 8: Gallup poll results; "1970 Kent State Shootings Are an Enduring History Lesson," *USA Today*, May 4, 2010. Paragraph 9: The Hardhat Riot. "War Foes Here Attacked by Construction Workers," *NYT*, May 9, 1970; "Nixon Meets Heads of 2 City Unions," *NYT*, May 27, 1970. Paragraph 10: "Jackson State: A Tragedy Widely Forgotten," NPR, May 3, 2010.

Page 253: Paragraph 1: *Ken Burns' Vietnam*. Paragraph 2: Oral histories from students and professors, May 4 Collection. Paragraph 3: *Record-Courier*, May 10, 1970. Paragraph 4: "FBI 'Students' at KSU," *ABJ*, June 23, 1970. Paragraph 5: Scranton Commission Report, May 4 Collection. Paragraph 6: "Trustees Search for White's Successor," *DKS*, February 19, 1971. Paragraph 7: "Judge Acquits Guardsmen in Slayings at Kent State," *NYT*, November 9, 1974. Paragraph 8: Photo by Wide World Photos, a photo agency that provided images to the wire services and publications, 1974. Paragraph 9: *Ken Burns' Vietnam*; casualty figures from the National Archives. Paragraph 10: "Settlement Best Thing We Could Do: 8-Year Legal Battle Ends," *ABJ*, January 5, 1979.

EPILOGUE

Page 280: Source: Transcript of Nixon tape, University of Virginia's Miller Center. Uncovered by an archivist at the behest of Bob Woodward for his appearance as the keynote speaker at the 2019 May 4 Commemoration at Kent State.

SIXTEEN MONTHS LATER.
SEPTEMBER 13, 1971
4:36 PM
EPILOGUE
CHIEF-OF-STAFF H.R. HALDEMAN IS BRIEFING NIXON ON THE ATTICA PRISON RIOT, WHICH WAS CRUSHED EARLIER THAT DAY.
TEN HOSTAGES AND 33 INMATES WERE KILLED, MOST IN A HAIL OF GUNFIRE WHEN STATE TROOPERS STORMED THE PRISON.
THE CONVERSATION IS RECORDED ON A NIXON TAPE.

...THERE'S NO INTELLIGENCE OF ANY FURTHER BLACK UPRISINGS.
YOU KNOW WHAT I THINK?
THIS MIGHT HAVE A CERTAIN SALUTORY EFFECT. Y'KNOW, THEY TALK ALL THEY WANT ABOUT THE RADICALS...
...YOU KNOW WHAT STOPS THEM?

KILL A FEW!

REMEMBER KENT STATE?

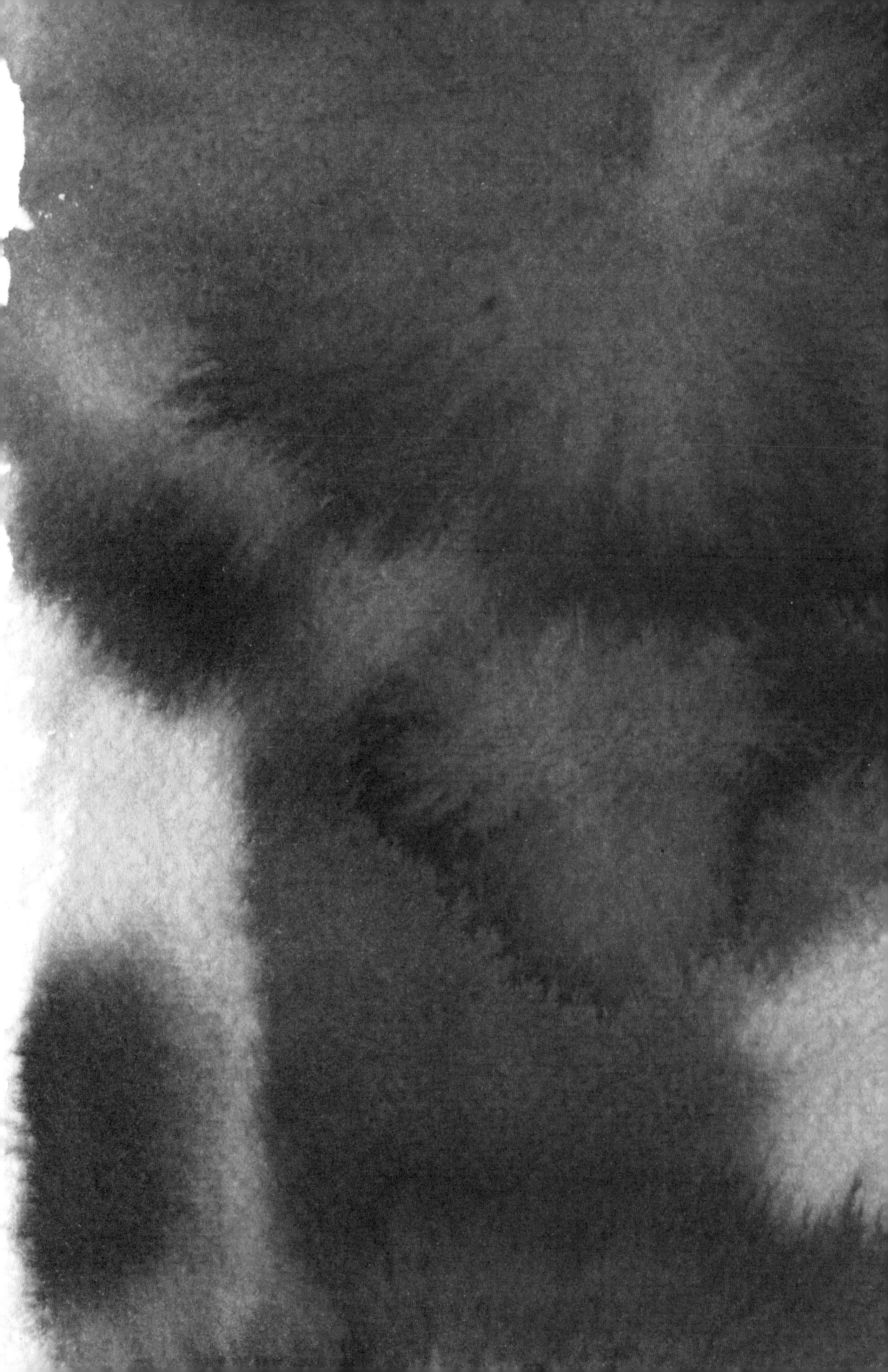